МАКСИМ ГОРЬКИЙ

СТАТЬИ И ПАМФЛЕТЫ

ИЗДАТЕЛЬСТВО ЛИТЕРАТУРЫ НА ИНОСТРАННЫХ ЯЗЫКАХ

МОСКВА 1950

MAXIM GORKY

ARTICLES AND PAMPHLETS

FOREIGN LANGUAGES PUBLISHING HOUSE

MOSCOW 1950

М. Горький

CONTENTS

5

IN AMERICA

THE CITY OF THE YELLOW DEVIL

. . . Over earth and ocean hangs a fog well mixed with smoke, and a fine slow rain is falling over the dark buildings of the city and the muddy waters of the roadstead.

The immigrants gather at the ship's side and stare silently about them with the curious eyes of hope and apprehension, fear and joy.

"Who's that?" a Polish girl asks softly, staring in wonder at the Statue of Liberty.

"The American god," someone replies.

The massive figure of the bronze woman is covered from head to foot with verdigris. The cold face stares blind ly through the fog, out to the wastes of ocean, as though the bronze is waiting for the sun to bring light to its lifeless eyes. There is very little ground under Liberty's feet, she appears to rise from the ocean, her pedestal—the frozen petrified waves. Her arm, raised aloft over the ocean and the masts of the ships, gives a proud majesty and beauty to her pose. The torch so tightly gripped in her hand seems about to burst into a bright flame, that would drive away the grey smoke and bathe all around in fierce and joyous light.

And around that insignificant strip of land on which she stands, huge iron vessels like prehistoric monsters glide over the waters, and tiny launches dart like hungry birds of prey. Sirens, resembling the voices of fabulous giants, roar, angry whistles shrill, anchor chains clang, and the ocean waves grimly lap the shore.

Everything is running, hurrying, vibrating tensely. The screws and paddles of the steamers rapidly thresh the water which is covered with a yellow foam seamed with wrinkles.

And everything—iron, stone, water and wood—seems to be protesting against a life without sunlight, without songs and happiness, in captivity to exhausting toil. Everything is groaning, howling, grating, in obedience to some mysterious force inimical to man. All over the bosom of the waters, ploughed and rent by iron, besmirched by greasy spots of oil, befouled with chips and shavings, straw and remains of food, a cold and evil force labours unseen. Grimly and monotonously it jolts this stupendous machine, in which ships and docks are only small parts, and man an insignificant screw, an invisible dot amid the unsightly, dirty tangle of iron and wood, the chaos of vessels, boats and some flat barques loaded with cars.

Overwhelmed, deafened by the noise, irritated by this dance of inanimate matter, a two-legged creature, all sooty and oily, with his hands thrust deep in his pockets, stares curiously at me. There is a layer of greasy dirt on the face, relieved not by the gleam of human eyes but by the ivory of white teeth.

* * *

Slowly the vessel makes her way among the crowd of shipping. The faces of the immigrants look strangely grey and dull, with something of a sheeplike sameness about the eyes. Gathered at the ship's side, they stare in silence at the fog.

In this fog something incomprehensibly vast, emitting a hollow murmur, is born; it grows, its heavy odorous breath is wafted to the people and its voice has a certain threatening avid note.

This is a city. This is New York. Twenty-storey houses, dark soundless skyscrapers, stand on the shore. Square, lacking in any desire to be beautiful, the stiff ponderous buildings tower gloomily and drearily. A haughty pride in its height, its ugliness is felt in each house. There are no flowers at the windows and no children to be seen. . . .

From this distance the city seems like a vast jaw, with uneven black teeth. It breathes clouds of black smoke into the sky and snuffles like a glutton suffering from his obesity.

Entering the city is like getting into a stomach of stone and iron, a stomach that has swallowed several million people and is consuming and digesting them.

The street is a slippery, greedy throat, in the depths of which float dark bits of the city's food—living people. Everywhere—overhead, underfoot, alongside, iron clangs, exulting in its victory. Awakened to life and animated by the power of Gold, it casts its web about man, strangles him, sucks his blood and brain, devours his muscles and nerves, and grows and grows, resting upon voiceless stone, and spreading the links of its chain ever more widely.

Locomotives like enormous worms wriggle along, dragging cars behind them; the klaxons of the automobiles quack like fat ducks, electricity whines drearily, the stifling air imbibes thousands of strident sounds as a sponge imbibes moisture. Crushed down upon this grimy city, soiled with the smoke of factories, it hangs motionless among the high, soot-covered walls.

* * *

In the squares and small public gardens where the dusty leaves of the trees droop lifelessly on the branches, dark monuments rise. The faces of the statues are covered with a thick layer of dirt, the eyes that once glowed with love for their country are filled with the dust of the city. These bronze people, lifeless and solitary amid the network of many-storeyed houses, look dwarfish in the dark shadow of the high walls, they have lost their way in the chaos of madness around them, pause and, half-blinded, watch mournfully, with aching hearts, the rapacious bustle of the people at their feet. Little black figures hurry fussily past the monuments, none of them ever casting a glance at the face of the hero. The ichthyosaurs of capital have effaced from the people's memory the significance of those who created freedom.

The bronze men seem engrossed by one and the same sad thought:

"Is this the life I meant to create?"

Around them the fevered life seethes like soup on a stove, and the little people scurry and whirl, vanishing in the bubbling vortex like grains of meal in broth, like matchwood in the sea. The city bellows and swallows them up one after the other in its insatiable maw.

Some of the heroes on the monuments have dropped their hands, others have raised them, stretching them out over the heads of the people in warning:

"Stop! This is not life, this is madness. . . ."

All of them are superfluous in the chaos of street life, all are out of place in the savage howl of rapacity, in the cramped duress of this gloomy fantasy made of stone, glass and iron.

One night they will all descend from their pedestals and pass, with the heavy tread of the wronged, through the streets, bearing the anguish of their loneliness away from this city, into the fields, where the moon is shining and there is fresh air and serene peace. When a man has toiled his whole life long for the good of his country, he has surely deserved this—that he should be left in peace after his death.

*   *   *

People hurry to and fro on the pavements, in every direction the streets take. They are sucked up by the deep pores in the stone walls. The exultant rumble of iron, the loud piercing whine of electricity, the clatter of work on some new network of metal, new walls of stone, drown out human voices as a storm at sea drowns the cries of the birds.

The people's faces wear an immobile calm; none of them, apparently, is aware of his misfortune in being the slave of life, nourishment for the city monster. In their pitiable arrogance they imagine themselves the masters of their fate, consciousness of their independence gleams occasionally in their eyes, but clearly they do not understand that this is only the independence of the axe in the carpenter's hand, the hammer in the smith's hand, the brick in the hand of that unseen bricklayer, who, with a sly chuckle, is building one vast but cramping prison for all. There are many virile faces among them, but in each face, one notices the teeth first of all. Inner freedom, the freedom of the spirit does not shine in these people's eyes. And their freedomless energy reminds one of the cold gleam of a knife that has not yet been blunted. It is the freedom of blind tools in the hands of the Yellow Devil—Gold.

This is the first time I have seen so monstrous a city, and never before have people seemed to me so insignificant, so enslaved. At the same time nowhere have I met people so tragicomically satisfied with themselves as are these in this voracious and filthy stomach of the glutton, who has grown imbecilic from greed and, with the wild bellowing of cattle, devours brains and nerves. . . .

* * *

It is painful and dreadful to talk of the people.

Shrieking and clattering, the car of the Elevated railway train rushes by between the houses in the narrow street, at the height of the third floor, amid the monotonous tangle of fire escapes and staircases. Windows are open and figures can be seen in nearly every one of them. Some people are working, sewing or counting, their heads bent over their desks, others are simply sitting at the windows or leaning across the sills, watching the railway cars that flash past every minute. The old, the young and the children are alike silent, monotonously unruffled. They have grown used to this effort for no purpose, grown used to thinking that this is the purpose. Their eyes hold no wrath at the domination of iron, no hatred of its triumph. The passage of the trains shakes the walls of the houses,—the women's bosoms, the men's heads, tremble; shakes the bodies of children, sprawled on the fire escapes, accustoming them to take this abominable life for granted, as inevitable. In brains that are constantly being shaken it is impossible, surely, for thoughts to weave their beautiful bold lace patterns, impossible for a living, daring dream to be born.

There is a passing glimpse of the dark face of an old woman in a dirty blouse open in front. The tortured, poisoned air, making way for the train, has rushed in terror to the windows, and the old woman's grizzled hair lifts and flaps like the wings of a grey bird. She has closed her dim, leaden eyes. And vanished.

In the obscurity of interiors glimmer iron bedsteads heaped with rags, dirty crockery and remains of food on tables. One longs to see flowers in the windows, one looks out for someone reading a book. The walls flow by as though molten, a turbid flood coming to meet one, and in its swift flow the voiceless people swarm, sadly.

A bald head gleams for an instant behind a dusty windowpane. The head rocks to and fro above a workman's bench. A slim, red-haired girl sits at a window, knitting a sock, her dark eyes intent on counting the stitches. The current of air has pressed her back from the window, but she does not raise her eyes from her work, nor smooth down the dress disarranged by the wind. Two little boys of about five are building a house of chips on a fire escape. It collapses with the shaking. The two children clutch at the frail chips with their little paws, to prevent them slipping through the bars of the fire escape into the street below, and they too do not look at the train which is the cause, the hindrance to their task. Faces, more faces, one after another, seen momentarily at the windows, as broken fragments of one whole—of something large, but smashed into the tiniest splinters, ground into gravel.

Driven by the mad race of the trains, the air flutters the hair and clothing of the people, surges in a warm stuffy wave in their faces, thrusts and pushes thousands of sound into their ears, flings fine biting dust into their eyes, blinds them, and deafens them with a long-drawn-out, unceasing howl. . . .

To the living man, who thinks, who creates in his own mind dreams, pictures, images, who begets desires, who yearns, wants, denies and waits,—to the living man this wild howling, screeching and roaring, this trembling of the stone walls, this timorous shivering of glass in window frames—would all be a hindrance. Wrathful, he would go out of his house and smash and destroy this abomination—the Elevated; he would silence the insolent shriek of iron, he is the master of life, life is for him, and all that hinders him from living should be destroyed.

The people in the houses of the City of the Yellow Devil calmly endure all that kills man.

* * *

Below, in the dirt and dust of the pavements under the iron network of the elevated railway, children are playing, voicelessly—voicelessly, though they laugh and shout like children all over the world but their voices are drowned, like raindrops in the ocean, by the racket overhead. The children are like flowers, tossed by some rough hand out of the window into the dirt of the street. Their bodies feed on the greasy exudations of the city, they are pale and sallow, their blood is poisoned, their nerves irritated by the malevolent screech of rusty metal, the mournful wail of enslaved lightning.

Will these children grow up healthy, bold, proud?— one asks oneself. Grinding, guffawing, angry screeching is the only reply.

The trains dash past East Side, where the poor live, the cesspool of the city. Here the deep gutters of streets lead people somewhere into the heart of the city where, one imagines, there must be a vast bottomless hole, a cauldron or a pan, into which all these people pour and are boiled down into gold. The gutters of the streets swarm with children.

I have seen a great deal of poverty, its bloodless, emaciated green face is well familiar to me. I have seen its eyes everywhere, dull from hunger, and burning with greed, cunning and vengeful or slavishly meek and always inhuman, but the horrors of East Side poverty are more dismal than anything I have ever known.

In these streets, as tightly packed with people as sacks of meal, children search greedily in the dustbins on the sidewalks for rotten vegetables and devour them, mildew and all, on the spot, in this bitter dust and heat.

A crust of mouldy bread arouses the most savage enmity among them; possessed by the desire to devour it, they fight like little dogs. Like flocks of voracious pigeons they swarm the pavements; at one o'clock, two in the morning and even later, they are still grubbing in the filth, pitiful microbes of poverty, a living reproach to the avarice of the wealthy slaves of the Yellow Devil.

At the corners of the mean streets stand a species of stoves or braziers, in which something is cooking; the steam, escaping through a thin pipe into the air, blows a little whistle at its tip. This thin piercing whistle dominates with its vibrating keenness all other street sounds, and drags on interminably like a cold dazzling white thread, twines itself about the throat, confuses the thoughts, maddens, impels one somewhere, and never for a moment silent, quivers in the odour of decay that pollutes the air, quivers derisively, malevolently pervading that life lived in dirt.

Dirt is an element, it has impregnated everything: the walls of the houses, the glass in the windows, the people's clothing, the pores of their bodies, their brains, desires, thoughts. . . .

In these streets the dark hollows of the doorways are putrid wounds in the stones of the wall. When, glancing into them, one sees the filthy steps of the stairs, littered with refuse, it seems that everything within must have decayed into putrefaction as in the loins of a corpse. And the people must be like worms. . . .

A tall woman with large dark eyes is standing in a doorway with a baby in her arms; her bodice is open, and the bluish breast hangs limply like a long bag. The baby cries, scratching at the mother's jaded, hungry form, nuzzles her, making sucking sounds, then after a moment's silence, bursts into louder wailing, beating and kicking the mother's breast. She stands as though turned to stone, staring with eyes as round as an owl's at some point in front of her. One feels that those eyes see nought but bread. Her lips are tightly compressed, she breathes through her nose, the nostrils quivering as she inhales the thick malodorous air of the street; this woman lives on memories of food devoured yesterday, dreams of the morsel she may chance to eat sometime in the future. The baby screams, his small, yellow body convulsed, but she does not hear his screams nor feel his feeble blows. . . .

An old man, hatless, tall, thin, grey, with a predatory face, is cautiously grubbing in a rubbish heap, wrinkling the red lids of his sore eyes as he picks out bits of coal. When anyone comes near him, he turns his torso clumsily, like a wolf, and mutters something.

A youth, very pale and thin, slouches against the lamppost and his grey eyes look along the street. From time to time he tosses his curly head. His hands are thrust deep in his trouser pockets, the fingers moving convulsively . . . .

Here in these streets, a man is noticed, his voice, angry, irritable and revengeful, is heard. Here a man has a face —hungry, excited, anguished. That these people feel is evident, that they think is noticeable. They swarm in the filthy gutters, rub up against one another like flotsam in a turbid stream; they are tossed and whirled by the force of hunger, they are animated by the compelling desire for something to eat.

While waiting for a meal and dreaming of the enjoyment of being satiated, they drink in the poison-laden air, and in the dark depths of their souls sharp thoughts, cunning emotions, and criminal desires are born.

They are like disease germs in the stomach of the city, and the time will come when they will infect it with those same noxious poisons it so generously nourishes them with now!

The youth leaning against the lamppost shakes his head from time to time. His hungry teeth are tightly clenched. I seem to understand what he is thinking of, what he wants—to possess enormous hands of frightful strength and wings on his back, that is what he wants, I believe. So that, soaring one day over the city, he may reach down with hands like steel levers and reduce the whole to a heap of rubbish and ashes, mixing bricks and pearls, gold and the flesh of slaves, glass and millionaires, dirt, idiots, temples, the trees poisoned by dirt, and these foolish many-storeyed skyscrapers, everything, the whole city into one heap, into a dough compounded of dirt and the blood of people,—into a loathsome chaos. This frightful wish is as natural in this youth's brain as an ulcer on the body of a sick man. Where there is much work for slaves, there can be no place for free, creative thought, there only the ideas of destruction, the poisonous flowers of vengeance, the turbulent protest of the brute beast can flourish. This is understandable—if you warp a man's soul you must not expect mercy from him.

Man has the right to vengeance—that right has been given to him by men.

* * *

The day fades in the dull soot-clouded sky. The huge houses grow gloomier and more ponderous. Here and there lights twinkle in their dark depths, shining like the yellow eyes of strange beasts who have to watch all night by the dead riches of these tombs.

People have finished the day's work and—never thinking of why it was done, whether it was necessary for them or not—hurry home to bed. Dark floods of human bodies pour over the sidewalks. All the heads are covered by the same round hats, and all the brains—as may be seen by the eyes—are already asleep. Work is done, there is nothing more to think about. They think only for their boss, what is there to think about themselves. If there is work there will be bread and the cheap enjoyments of life, beyond which nothing more is needed by man in the City of the Yellow Devil.

People go to their beds, to their women, to their men, and sweaty, slippery with sweat in those stuffy rooms at night, will kiss, so that new, fresh nourishment may be born for the city. . . .

They go. No laughter or cheerful talk is heard, smiles do not sparkle here.

The automobiles quack, the whips crack, the electric cables hum, the trains clatter. Music is being played somewhere no doubt.

The newsboys bawl the names of the papers. The ignoble sound of the hurdy-gurdy and a sudden yell merge in the tragicomic embrace of the murderer and the show-booth comedian. The little people move involuntarily like stones rolling downhill. . . .

More and more of the yellow lights flare up—now entire walls blaze with words of fire about beer, whiskey, soap, new razors, hats, cigars and theatres. The clang of iron, driven everywhere along the streets by the insatiable goading of Gold, never dies down. Now, when lights glow everywhere, this unintermittent howl gains in significance, acquires new meaning, a new and more oppressive power.

The dazzling effulgence of molten Gold pours from the walls of the houses, the windows of restaurants. Insolent, blatant, it triumphs everywhere, making the eyes smart, distorting faces with its cold glitter. This cunning radiance is possessed of an unquenchable desire to draw the insignificant grains of their earnings out of the people's pockets, and it converts its winking into fiery words that silently beckon workers to cheap pleasures and offer them handy knickknacks. . . .

There is a terrifying abundance of light in this city! At first it seems attractive, it excites and delights. Light is a free element, the proud child of the sun. When it

21

comes to a luxuriant flowering, its blossoms vibrate and live, more lovely than any flowers on earth. It cleanses life, it can destroy all that is outworn, dead and dirty.

But, in this city, when one looks at light, enclosed in transparent prisons of glass, one understands that here light, like everything else, is enslaved. It serves Gold, it is for Gold and is inimically aloof from people. . . .

Like everything—iron, stone, wood—light is in the conspiracy against man: dazzling him, it calls:

"Come here!"

And wheedles him:

"Hand over your cash!"

People respond to his summons, buy rubbish they do not need and gaze at entertainments that only dull their wits.

It is as if, somewhere in the heart of the city, a huge lump of Gold is spinning at a terrific pace with voluptuous squeals, powdering the streets with the finest particles, which people catch and seek and clutch at eagerly all day long. But evening falls at last, the lump of Gold begins to spin in the opposite direction, raising a cold blazing whirlwind, drawing people into it so that they will give back the gold dust they caught during the day. They always give back more than they got and next morning the lump of Gold has grown larger, it revolves at a swifter pace, and the exultant screech of iron, its slave, the clang of all the forces it has enslaved, sound louder.

Then even more voraciously, with even greater power than the previous day, it sucks the blood and brain of people so that by evening this same blood, this brain, is converted into cold yellow metal. The lump of Gold is the heart of the city. All the life of the city is in its throbbing, all the meaning of this life is in its growth.

It is for this that, day after day, people dig the earth, forge iron, build houses, breathe the smoke of factories, absorb through the pores of their bodies the dirt of sickly, poisoned air, it is for this that they sell their beautiful bodies.

The vile wizardry lulls their souls, makes them flexible tools in the hands of the Yellow Devil, the metal out of which He smelts unceasingly the Gold that is His flesh and blood.

*   *   *

Night comes in from the ocean waste and wafts a cool, salty breath over the city. The cold lights pierce it with a thousand arrows; it stalks on, benignantly cloaking with its dark vestments the ugliness of houses and the meanness of the narrow streets, and veiling the squalid rags of poverty. A savage wail of greedy madness rushes out to meet it, rending its silence; still it moves, slowly extinguishing the insolent glitter of the enslaved light and shading with its soft hand the purulent ulcers of the city.

But as it enters the maze of the streets it finds itself powerless to vanquish and scatter with its fresh breath the city's poisonous vapours. It rubs against the stone of the walls, warmed by the sun, it creeps over the rusty iron of the roofs, over the filth of the pavements, and, saturated with the poisonous dust, gorged with the city smells, it folds its wings and comes to rest limp and motionless on the housetops and in the gutters. Darkness is all that remains of it—its freshness and coolness are gone, swallowed up by stone, iron, wood, and the people's polluted lungs. It has no stillness any more, no poetry. . . .

The city falls asleep in the oppressive darkness, it growls like some huge animal. It gorged itself with too much food during the day, it feels hot and uncomfortable, and its slumbers are disturbed by heavy nightmares.

Flickering, the light goes out, its miserable job of provocateur and advertisement lackey done for the day. The houses suck people, one after another, into their stone bowels.

A gaunt man, tall and stooped, stands on a street corner and, turning his head slowly, looks with dull, colourless eyes to right and left of him. Where is one to go? All the streets are alike, and all the houses, their windows bleary and wall-eyed, stare at one another with the same lifeless apathy. . . .

A stifling oppressiveness clutches at the throat with a warm hand, making it difficult to breathe. Over the roofs of the houses hovers a hazy cloud—the day's vapours of this wretched, accursed city. Through this misty veil, in the remote infinity of the heavens, the peaceful stars gleam faintly.

The man takes off his hat, raises his head, and looks up at the sky. The immense height of the houses in this city pushes the sky further away from the earth than anywhere else in the world. The stars are tiny, lonely specks.

From afar, alarmingly, comes a brassy blare. The man's long legs jerk queerly and he turns into one of the streets, stepping slowly, his head bent and his arms swinging. It is late, and the streets grow more and more deserted. Lonely little people disappear like flies, and are swallowed up by the darkness. Policemen in grey hats stand motionless at street corners with clubs in their hands. They chew tobacco, their jaws moving slowly.

The man walks past them, past the telephone poles and the multitude of black doors in the walls of the houses —black doors, their square jaws yawning sleepily. Somewhere far away a streetcar clatters and wails. The night suffocates in the deep cages of the streets, the night is dead.

The man walks with measured stride, swaying his long, bent frame. There is something about him showing a mind at work, something undecided, yet decisive. . . .

I think he is a thief.

It is good to see a man who feels himself alive in the dark toils of the city.

The open windows let out the nauseating odour of human sweat.

Strange, dull sounds stir drowsily in the stifling, dreary darkness. . . .

Asleep and raving in its sleep is the lurid City of the Yellow Devil

REALM OF BOREDOM

WHEN night falls a phantom city of lights rears itself skyward on the ocean. A myriad of glowing sparks scintillate in the darkness, tracing with exquisite subtlety against the dark background of the sky stately turrets of wondrous castles, palaces and temples of coloured crystal. A golden cobweb quivers in the air, weaves itself into a translucent pattern of fire and hangs motionless admiring the beauty of its reflection in the water. Enchanting and incomprehensible is this fire, which burns but does not devour; inexpressibly beautiful is its magnificent, barely perceptible shimmer that creates a magic spectacle of a city of fire amid the bare expanses of sky and ocean. Over it hovers a ruddy glow, and the water gives back its contours, merging them in fantastic splashes of molten gold. . . .

This play of lights gives rise to curious thoughts: one feels that yonder in the halls of the palaces, amid the bright radiance of fiery exultation, the soft, proud accents of music such as was never heard before must sound. On the waves of its delicious harmonies, like winged stars, the noblest thoughts on earth are borne. In some sublime measure they touch one another and, blazing forth in momentary embrace, give birth to new flames, new thoughts,

One feels that there in that velvety darkness some great cradle, miraculously woven of golden threads, flowers and stars, rocks gently on the rippling breast of the ocean, and in it the sun reposes till morn.

*   *   *

The sun brings man closer to the facts of life. By daylight the enchanting city of fire is seen as nought but a collection of white flimsy buildings.

The blue haze of the ocean's breath mixes with the thick, grey smoke of the city; the delicate white structures are enveloped in a transparent veil, and like a mirage they quiver alluringly, beckoning and promising something splendid and soothing.

There in the background amid the clouds of smoke and dust crouch the rectangular buildings of the city that fills the air incessantly with its insatiable, hungrily-avid roar. This raucous noise that causes the air and the soul to shudder, this persistent shrieking of steel strings, the dreary lament of the forces of life ground down by the power of Gold, the cold, mocking whistle of the Yellow Devil—this sound drives one away from an earth crushed and befouled by the stinking body of the city. And so people go to the shore of the ocean where stand these handsome white buildings holding promise of peace and restfulness.

They are huddled close together on a long sand spit plunged like a sharp knife deep into the dark waters. The sand sparkles warmly in the sunshine and the diaphanous buildings look like exquisite white silk embroidery on its yellow velvet. It is as though Someone had come down to the sand spit and plunged into the waters, tossing his rich raiment on their bosom.

27

One is seized with the desire to go and touch the soft, caressing fabrics, to stretch oneself out on their luxurious folds and feast one's eyes on the vast expanses where white birds dart about swiftly and noiselessly, where ocean and sky slumber in the burning glare of the sun.

. . . .

This is Coney Island.

On Mondays the city's newspapers triumphantly inform the reader:

"Yesterday 300,000 people visited Coney Island. Twenty-three children were lost."

. . . It is a long journey by streetcar through the dusty, noisy streets of Brooklyn and Long Island before one sets eyes on the dazzling splendour of Coney Island. And, indeed, as soon as a man stands before the entrance to this city of fire he is blinded. It flings hundreds of thousands of cold white sparks into his eyes, and for a long time he cannot make out anything in the sparkling dust; everything about him is a stormy maelstrom of fiery froth, everything whirls, glitters and beckons. The man is stunned at once, his mind is blotted out by all this brilliance, all thought is driven out of his head and he becomes a particle of the crowd. Their minds reeling, people wander aimlessly amid the scintillating lights. An opaque white mist penetrates their brain, a feeling of eager anticipation lays a viscid shroud over the soul. Dazzled by the glitter, the crowd of people pours, a dark stream, into the motionless pool of light hemmed in on all sides by the dark frontiers of the night.

Tiny lamps shed a dry, cold light over everything: they are attached to all the poles and walls, to the window frames and cornices of buildings, they stretch in even rows along the tall chimney of the power station, they burn on all the roofs, they scratch at the eyes of the people with sharp needles of lifeless brilliance—the people blink and, smiling stupidly, drag themselves slowly over the ground like the heavy links in some tangled chain. . . .

It takes a great effort of will for a man to find himself in this crowd that is crushed by awe and devoid of delight or joy. And he who does find himself sees that these millions of lamps shed a dreary, denuding light that, while hinting at the possibility of beauty, lays bare the stupid, dismal ugliness all around. A phantom from afar, the magic city rises now a meaningless labyrinth of straight lines in wood, cheap, hastily-built structures put up to amuse children, the work of some fussy old pedagogue who is worried by the escapades of the children and desires to imbue them with humility and meekness even through their games. There is an ugly variety about the dozens of white buildings, and not one of them has even a hint of beauty. They are made of wood, covered with peeling white paint, and all seem to be suffering from the same skin disease. The tall towers and low colonnades stretch in two deadly even lines and huddle tastelessly together. Everything is stripped bare and robbed by the impartial glitter of the lights; it is everywhere, and there are no shadows. Every building stands like some gaping fool with its mouth hanging open, and within a cloud of smoke, the raucous howls of brass, the shrieking of organs, and the dark figures of people. People eating, drinking and smoking.

But Man is not heard. The air is filled with the even hissing of the arc lights, ragged fragments of music, the pious whining of wooden organ pipes and the thin,

29

incessant whistle of the peanut stands. All this merges in an irritating hum as of some invisible string, thick and taut, and when a human voice invades this incessant sound it seems like a frightened whisper. Everything glitters insolently, baring its dismal ugliness. . . .

The soul is gripped by a burning desire for a live, red, flowering flame that would deliver people from the bondage of this mottled boredom that deafens and blinds. . . . One would wish to set fire to all this prettiness, and to dance in wild merriment, to shout and sing in the tempestuous play of the colourful tongues of a living flame, to revel in a voluptuous feast of destruction of the lifeless magnificence of spiritual poverty. . . .

* * *

This city has indeed hundreds of thousands of people in its thrall. Over the whole of its vast area, closely packed with white cagelike structures, in all the halls of the buildings they swarm like clouds of black flies. Pregnant women placidly carry the weight of their bellies before them. Children walk along gaping in silence and staring with dazzled eyes around them so intently and gravely that one aches with pity for them, for that look that is nourishing their souls with the ugliness which they mistake for beauty. The clean-shaven faces of the men, looking strangely alike are stolid and heavy. Most of them have brought along their wives and children, and they regard themselves as the benefactors of their families for providing them not only with bread but with magnificent spectacles besides. They themselves like this glitter, but they are too serious to give vent to their feelings and hence they all compress their thin lips and narrow their eyes and frown with the air of persons whom nothing can impress. Yet behind this outward composure born of mature experience one feels a burning eagerness to taste all the pleasures the town has to offer. And so these respectable people, with deprecating smiles calculated to hide the glow of pleasure that lights up their eyes, climb onto the backs of the wooden horses and elephants of the electric merry-go-round, and, swinging their legs, wait in excited anticipation for the keen pleasure of being whirled over the rails, tossed upwards and dropped down again whistling through the air. This bumpy journey completed, they stretch the skin tightly over their faces again and move on to other pleasures. . . .

The entertainments are innumerable: on the top of an iron tower slowly swing two long white wings to the ends of which are attached cages with people in them. When one of the wings soars heavily skywards, the faces of the people in the cages grow painfully serious, and with identical expressions they stare in tense, round-eyed silence at the receding earth. And in the cages of the other wing, which is carefully descending at the same time, the faces of the people blossom out in smiles, and squeals of delight are heard. The sound reminds one of the joyous squeal of a puppy when he is dropped onto the floor after having been held in the air by the scruff of his neck.

Boats fly in the air around the tip of another tower, a third, revolving, sets in motion some metal cylinders, a fourth and a fifth—they all move, ablaze, and beckon to the people with the soundless shout of their cold lights. Everything swings, squeals, booms, making the people dizzy and complacently dull, exhausting their nerves with the tortuous maze of movement and glitter of lights. Light eyes grow lighter as though the brain were turning pale, drained of blood in the weird weaving of white sparking wood. And it seems that boredom, expiring under the burden of self-abomination, is whirling round and round in a slow agony, drawing into its melancholy dance tens of thousands of monotonously dark people, sweeping them, as the wind sweeps the rubbish on the streets, into will-less heaps, and scattering them again only to sweep them together once more. . . .

* * *

Pleasures await the people inside the buildings as well, but these are serious pleasures, they educate. Here the people are shown Hell with its austere regime, and the diverse torments that await men and women who violate the sanctity of the laws that have been made for them. . . .

Hell is made of papier-mâché painted a dull crimson, the whole steeped in a fireproof substance exuding the foul odour of some heavy fat. Hell is very badly made—it is capable of arousing the disgust even of the most unexacting spectator. It represents a cave chaotically strewn with boulders and filled with a dull red gloom. On one of the boulders sits Satan in scarlet tights, contorting his gaunt brown face into diverse grimaces, and rubbing his hands like a man who has just brought off a successful business deal. He is no doubt most uncomfortable seated on that pasteboard boulder which creaks and sways under him, but he appears oblivious of the fact, his attention being absorbed by the torments his devils are inflicting on the sinners at his feet.

Here is a young girl who has bought herself a new hat and is contentedly admiring herself in the mirror. A couple

32

of small and apparently very hungry devils steal up to her from behind and seize her by the arms; she cries out, but too late! The devils lay her in a long, smooth chute which descends steeply into a pit in the middle of the cave; grey vapour issues from the pit, tongues of red-paper flame rise up, and down the chute into this pit slides the girl along with the mirror and hat.

A young man drinks a glass of whiskey—the devils immediately dispatch him too into the hole under the stage.

It is stuffy in Hell, the devils are puny and feeble; they appear to be utterly worn out by their work, the monotony and the obvious uselessness of it clearly irritates them, and hence they waste no time with the sinners and toss them into the chute like logs of wood. Looking at them you want to shout:

"Enough of this nonsense! Why don't you go on strike, boys!"

A young girl steals a few coins from her neighbour's purse, only to be instantly disposed of by the devils, much to the satisfaction of Satan who swings his legs in delight and giggles nasally. The devils throw angry looks at the idler and malevolently hurl into the maw of the fiery pit everyone who—either on business or out of idle curiosity—happens to look into Hell. . . .

The public regards these horrors in grave silence. It is dark in the hall. A hefty young man with curly hair and wearing a thick jacket delivers a harangue in a deep voice of gloom.

Pointing to the stage he declares that if people do not want to fall victim to the bowlegged Satan in the red tights, they should know that it is wrong to kiss girls without being wedded to them, otherwise the girls may become prostitutes; it is wrong to kiss young men without the sanction of the church because little boys and girls may be born as a result; prostitutes must not steal money from their clients' pockets; people in general ought not drink wine and any other liquids that excite the passions; they must go to church instead of to beer saloons, it is better for the soul and cheaper. . . .

He says all this in a dreary, monotonous voice and it is evident that he himself does not believe in the kind of life he has been instructed to advocate.

One is sorely tempted to say to the proprietors of this edifying entertainment for sinners:

"Gentlemen! If you want morals to have the effect, if only of castor oil, on the human soul, you must pay your moralists more!"

At the conclusion of this awesome performance a disgustingly handsome angel appears from a corner of the cave. He is strung up by a wire and moves through the air across the entire cave with a wooden trumpet covered with gilt paper between his teeth. On sighting him Satan darts like an eel into the pit after the sinners, there is a crackling noise, the pasteboard boulders roll one atop the other, the devils scamper off happily to relax from their labours—and the curtain falls. The crowd rises and leaves the hall. A few make so bold as to laugh, but the majority are grave. Perhaps they are thinking: "If Hell is so horrible, maybe it's better not to sin."

They move on. In the next building they are shown "The Hereafter." This is a large institution, also of papier-mâché, representing pits in which the badly-dressed souls of the dead roam about aimlessly. You may wink at them, but you must not pinch them—that is quite clear. It must be extremely dull for them in the gloom of the subterranean labyrinth amid the rough walls that are dampened by a cold stream of moist air. Some of the souls have bad coughs, others silently chew tobacco, ejecting streams of yellow spittle onto the ground; one soul, leaning against the wall in a corner, is smoking a cigar. . . .

As you pass them they look at you with their colourless eyes, and, tightly compressing their lips, hide their chilly hands in the grey folds of their unearthly rags. They are hungry, these poor souls, and many of them are clearly afflicted with rheumatism. The public stares silently at them and, inhaling the moist air, nourishes its soul on dreary boredom that extinguishes thought like a filthy wet rag thrown onto feebly smouldering embers. . . .

In another building you can see "The Flood" which, as everyone knows, was sent to punish people for their sins. . . .

Indeed all the sights in this city have a single aim: to show people how and wherewith they will be punished for their sins after death, to teach them to live on earth meekly and to obey laws. . . .

"Thou shalt not!" is their one commandment.

For the overwhelming majority of the people are working folk.

* * *

But one must make money, and so in the quiet corners of the glittering city, as everywhere on this earth, lust mocks at hypocrisy and lies. Of course, it is concealed and, naturally, it is dull, for it too is "for the people." It has been organized as a profitable business, an instrument for extracting a man's pay from his pocket, and permeated as it is with a passion for gold, it is triply odious and repulsive in this quagmire of scintillating dullness. . . .

The people feed on it. . . .

. . . They flow in a dense stream between two rows of brightly-lighted buildings and the buildings swallow them up in their hungry maws. The buildings on the right terrorize them with the horrors of eternal torment, proclaiming:

"Do not sin! It is dangerous!"

In a spacious dance hall to the left women circle slowly on the floor and everything about the establishment urges:

"Sin! It is pleasant. . . ."

Blinded by the glitter of lights, tempted by the cheap but dazzling luxury, intoxicated by the din, the people swing around in the slow dance of gnawing boredom and eagerly, blindly, go to the left—to sin—and to the right— into the houses that preach piety.

This listless flow of the throng stupefies it in equal measure and is equally profitable to the traders in morals and the merchants of vice.

Life is ordered so that people shall work six days and on the seventh sin—and pay for their sins—and confess— and pay for the confession; and that's all.

* * *

The arc lights hiss like so many hundreds of thousands of angry snakes, and the dark fly swarms of people buzz with a dreary impotence as they slowly swirl, caught in the gleaming, fine cobweb of the buildings. Without haste, without a smile on their smooth-shaven faces, they indolently enter every door, linger in front of the animal cages, chew tobacco and spit.

In a huge cage a man, firing a revolver and mercilessly slashing with a fine whip, chases Bengal tigers. The handsome beasts, maddened with fear, blinded by the lights, deafened by the music and the shooting, race wildly to and fro among the iron rods, roaring and growling, their green eyes flashing; their lips quiver, exposing angry fangs, and now one, now another paw slashes viciously at the air. But the man fires into their eyes and the loud reports of the blank shells and the searing pain of the lash drives the powerful, sinuous body of the beast into a corner of the cage. Seized by a paroxysm of wrathful indignation, the bitter resentment of the strong, choking with the anguish of humiliation, the captive beast freezes momentarily in his corner and, the snakelike tail twitching nervously, stares before him with frenzied eyes. . . .

The elastic body contracts into a hard bundle of muscle and quivers, ready to leap into the air and sink its claws into the flesh of the man with the whiplash, to tear him to pieces, to destroy him. . . .

The hind legs twitch like springs, the neck stretches out, in the green pupils leap blood-red sparks of joy.

The colourless, coldly expectant gaze of the monotonously yellowed faces that merge into a dull coppery blotch beyond the bars of the cage pierces the pupils of the beast with hundreds of blunt jabs.

Terrifying in its lifeless immobility, the face of the multitude waits—the crowd too wants to see blood and is waiting for it, waiting not out of a desire for vengeance, but out of curiosity as a wild beast tamed long since might wait.

The tiger draws its head into its shoulders, widens its eyes, in anguish, and with a soft, rippling movement draws back its body as if its hide, feverish with the thirst for revenge, was doused suddenly with an icy shower.

The man fires, cracks his whip, shouts like a madman— he shouts to hide his deadly terror in the face of the tiger and his slavish anxiety to please the herd, that calmly watches his capers, tensely awaiting the fatal leap of the beast. It waits, a primitive instinct has awakened in it; it thirsts for battle, longs for that sweet convulsion that will pass through its being when two bodies will clinch, blood spurt and rent steaming human flesh fly to the floor of the cage, and a roar and a cry will reverberate in the air. . . .

But the brain of the herd has already been permeated with the poison of diverse interdictions and fears; though it longs for blood, the crowd is afraid, it both wants it and does not want it, and in this dark contest with itself it finds keen delight—it lives. . . .

The man has terrorized all the animals, the tigers retreat on padded feet to the back of the cage, and he, perspiring and relieved that today he has survived, smiles with pallid lips whose trembling he endeavours to conceal, and bows to the copper face of the crowd as if paying obeisance to an idol.

The multitude bellows and claps its hands and breaks up into dark clots, to continue crawling over the sticky mire of boredom around it. . . .

Having relished to the full the spectacle of man's contest with the beasts, the herd goes on in search of some other amusement. Here is the circus. In the centre of the ring a man tosses two children into the air with his long legs. The children flash above him like two white doves with broken wings; every now and then they miss from the man's feet, drop on to the ground and, casting a fearful glance at the upturned blood-suffused face of their father or employer, they are up again spinning in the air. A crowd has gathered around the ring. They all stare. And when one of the children misses the artist's foot, a tremor of animation flits over all these faces just as light ripples sweep before the wind over the somnolent water of a muddy puddle.

It would be a welcome relief to see a drunk with a beaming face come rolling along, jostling, singing, shouting, happy because he is drunk and wishing all good people the same from the bottom of his heart. . . .

Music strikes up, ripping the air to ribbons. The band is bad and the musicians tired, the notes blared forth lack cohesion as if they limped and were unable to keep in step; they race along in a broken line, jostling, overtaking and upsetting one another. For some reason the imagination pictures each note as a sheet of tin to which human likeness has been imparted—a mouth, eyes and an opening for the nose cut out, and long white ears attached. The man swinging a baton over the heads of the bandsmen, who do not pay any attention to him, seizes these bits of metal by the handlelike ears and invisibly hurls them aloft. They clash with one another, the air whistles in the mouth slits, and this produces a music from which even the circus horses, inured to everything, shy away in fright, twitching their ears nervously as if to shake out the piercing, tinny sounds. . . .

Curious fantasies are born of this music of beggars for the amusement of slaves. One wants to wrest the biggest of the brass horns from the hands of its player and to blow into it with all one's might, to blow a blast long and loud and so terrifying that all should flee from captivity impelled by the horror of that wild sound. . . .

Near the orchestra is a cage with bears. One of them, fat, brown with tiny, crafty eyes, stands in the centre of the cage and shakes his head in measured rhythm. He seems to be thinking:

"I can accept this as rational only if I am shown that it has all been arranged deliberately in order to blind people and to deafen and deform them. In that case, of course, the end justifies the means. . . . But if people sincerely believe that all this is amusing, I have no more faith in their mental powers! . . ."

Two other bears sit opposite each other as if playing chess. A fourth, with a serious mien, paws at some straw in a corner of the cage, his black claws catching in the bars. There is a look of calm resignation on his face. Evidently he expects nothing of this life and has decided to go to sleep. . . .

The animals evoke keen interest—the watery eyes of the people follow their every movement as if searching for something long-forgotten in the powerful movements of the graceful bodies of lions and panthers. Standing before the cages, people silently poke sticks through the bars and jab the animals in the stomach or the sides, curious to see what will happen.

Those of the beasts that have not yet learned to know the character of humans grow indignant, strike at the bars with their paws and roar, opening wide jaws trembling with rage. This pleases the crowd. Protected by iron from the blows of the animals, sure of their safety, people calmly look into the bloodshot eyes and smile with satisfaction. But most of the beasts disregard the humans. Given a jab with a stick or spat at, they get up slowly and without as much as glancing at the tormentor withdraw to a far corner of the cage. There in the gloom lie the powerful, graceful bodies of lions, tigers, panthers and leopards and through the darkness round eyes blaze with the green fire of contempt for men. . . .

And the people, after another look at them, walk away saying:

"That's a dull animal. . . ."

* * *

In front of the band which plays with desperate zeal at the half-open entrance to some dark yawning maw wherein the backs of the chairs jut like rows of teeth—in front of the musicians stands a pole on which, tied with a thin chain, are two monkeys, a female and infant. The infant clings close to its mother's breast, its long skinny arms, with the tiny fingers, crossed over her back; the mother holds it tight with one arm while the other is stretched out warily with the fingers crooked ready to scratch and strike. The mother's eyes are tensely dilated, they express an impotent despair, an anguished anticipation of unavoidable injury, a weary anger and resentment. The infant, its cheek pressed against the mother's breast, looks with cold horror out of the corner of its eye at the people—it has evidently known fear from the very first day of its life and fear has petrified within it for the rest of its days. The mother, baring her small white teeth, and not for a second removing the arm that holds the small body close to hers, with the other ceaselessly wards off the sticks and umbrellas poked at her by the witnesses of her suffering.

There are so many of them, these white-skinned savages, men and women, in bowlers and hats with feathers, and they all find it frightfully amusing to see how agilely the mother monkey defends her child from the blows aimed at its little body. . . .

The monkey moves swiftly on a round surface the size of a plate, risking any moment to fall under the feet of the spectators, and she indefatigably repels all who seek to lay hands on her babe. Now and again, failing to parry a blow, she emits a piteous wail. Her arm swings around like a whip, but there are so many spectators, and each one of them is so anxious to strike, to pull the monkey's tail, or jerk the chain around her neck, that she cannot manage them all. And her eyes flutter piteously, and lines of pain and misery appear around her mouth.

The infant's arms press against her breast, it clings so tightly to her that its fingers are almost hidden in the thin fur on the mother's skin. Its eyes stare fixedly at the yellow blobs of faces, the dim eyes of the people who derive a faint pleasure from its horror of them. . . .

Now and again one of the musicians trains the foolish brass mouth of his trumpet at the monkey, drenching her with raucous sound—she cringes, bares her teeth and turns her sharp eyes on the musician. . . .

The crowd laughs and nods to the musician in approval. He is pleased, and a moment later he repeats his performance.

There are women among the spectators; some of them doubtless are mothers. Yet not one of them utters a word in protest against this vicious entertainment. They all enjoy it. . . .

Some eyes seem ready to burst with the strain of watching the torments of the mother monkey and the wild horror of the child.

Next to the band is the cage of the elephant, an elderly gentleman with shabby, shiny skin on his head. He has thrust his trunk through the bars of his cage and is swaying it reflectively as he watches the public. And being a kind and sensible animal, he is thinking:

"Of course, this scum that has been swept this way by the filthy broom of boredom is capable of mocking even its own prophets—as I have heard aged elephants say. Yet I cannot help feeling sorry for the monkey. . . . I have heard, too, that men, like the jackals and hyenas, sometimes, tear each other to pieces but alas that does not make it any easier for the monkey!"

. . . One looks at that pair of eyes in which trembles the misery of the mother, helpless to protect her child, and at the eyes of the infant frozen with a deep, cold horror of humans, one looks at people who find pleasure in tormenting a living creature, and turning to the monkey, one murmurs:

"Animal! Forgive them! In time they will grow better. . . ."

It is ridiculous and foolish, of course. And useless. Is there a mother who could forgive the torturers of her child; there are no such mothers I think, not even among dogs. . . .

Pigs, perhaps. . . .

* * *

Well, well. . . .

And so—when night comes—an enchanted phantom city of lights blazes forth on the shore of the ocean. It glows for a long time—without burning—against the dark background of the nocturnal sky, its beauty reflected in the shining expanses of the ocean.

In the brilliant cobweb of translucent buildings tens of thousands of grey people with colourless eyes crawl tediously, like lice in a beggar's rags.

Avid and base, they are shown the disgusting nakedness of their lies and the naivete of their cunning, their hypocrisy and the insatiable power of their greed. The cold gleam of the dead light lays bare the intellectual poverty, which with a triumphant glitter has laid its stamp on everything around these people. . . .

But the people have been thoroughly blinded and in silent delight they quaff the evil potion that poisons their souls.

Boredom moves slowly in a sluggish dance, expiring in the agony of its own impotence.

One thing alone is good in that city of lights—in it you can steep your soul in lifelong hatred of the power of stupidity. . . .

THE MOB

...THE window of my room faces a square; all day long people pour into it from five streets very much like potatoes rolling out of sacks. They mill around and then scurry on, and again the streets suck them into their gullets. The square is round and filthy, like a pan long used for frying meat but never yet scoured. Four streetcar lines lead into this crowded circle, and almost every minute cars jammed with people come rolling in, screeching on the turns. They throw out the hasty, troubled clang of iron as they rush along; above them and under their wheels sounds the harrowing drone of electricity. The dusty air is charged with the sickly tremor of their windowpanes and the shrill squeak of their wheels against the rails. The infernal music of the city wails incessantly—it is a savage battle of raucous sounds that stab and choke one another, evoking strange and sombre fantasies.

...A mob of frenzied monsters armed with huge tongs and knives and saws and everything else that can be made of iron, writhes like a mass of worms, eddies in dark insanity over the body of a woman whom it has clutched with its greedy hands and thrown to the ground, into the dirt and dust—and it tears at her breasts, cuts her flesh, drinks her blood, rapes her, and fights over her blindly, hungrily, tirelessly.

Who this woman is cannot be seen; she is burried under a huge dirt-yellow mass of people who have fastened themselves on her from every side, twined their bony bodies around her, who cling wherever there is room for their greedy lips, and now suck the lifeblood from every pore of her body. . . . In the throe of a voracious and indefatigable craving, they drive one another away from their prey, strike, trample, crush and destroy one another. Each one wants as much as he can get, and they all tremble in a feverish paroxysm of fear lest they be left with nothing. They gnash their teeth, the iron clangs in their hands; moans of pain, howls of greed, cries of disappointment, the roar of hungry rage—all this merges in a funereal wail over the corpse of the murdered prey, which lies slashed and despoiled by thousands of rapes, and sullied by all the multicoloured filth of the earth.

And merging with this savage wail is the miserable anguish of the defeated, who have been cast aside and slobber repulsively in hungry longing for the joy of a full stomach; weak and cowardly, they cannot fight for it.

That is the picture drawn by the music of the city.

* * *

It is Sunday. People do not work.

Because of this many faces wear downcast, perplexed, almost worried, looks. Yesterday had a simple and definite meaning—they worked from morning till evening.

They woke up at the usual hour and went to the factory or office or out into the street. They stood or sat in customary and therefore comfortable places. They counted money, sold goods, dug earth, chopped wood, cut stone, drilled and forged—they worked with their hands all day. They went to bed feeling a familiar weariness—and today they have awakened to find idleness staring them questioningly in the eye, demanding that its void be filled. . . .

They were taught to work but not to live, and so the day of rest is a hard day for them. Tools quite capable of creating machines, cathedrals, great ships and pretty little knickknacks of gold, they do not feel themselves capable of filling in the day by anything except their everyday mechanical work. Cogs and wheels—in the factories, offices and shops they are calm and feel they are human beings; there they join with cogs and wheels like themselves to make up one harmonious organism which busily creates values from the living fluid of its nerves—but not for them.

Six days of the week life is simple. It is a huge machine, and they all are its cogs; each knows his place in it and each assumes that he is familiar with and understands its blind, grimy face. But on the seventh day—the day of rest and idleness—life looms before them in a strange dismantled guise. Its face breaks up—it loses its face. . . .

They roam the streets, they sit in the saloons and in the park, they were in church, they stand on street corners. There is movement, as usual, but one feels that in a minute, or perhaps in an hour, it will stop in suspens —
something is lacking in life, and something new is striving

47

to enter it. No one is quite conscious of this feeling, no one can express it in words, but everyone is painfully aware of something unusual and disturbing. All the small, intelligible meanings have suddenly fallen out of life, like teeth out of gums.

People stroll along the streets; they board streetcars, they chat; outwardly they are composed—there are fifty-two Sundays in a year, and they have long since developed the habit of spending them all in the same manner. But everyone feels that he is different from what he was yesterday, and that his comrade is not the same, either—somewhere inside there is a gnawing, throbbing emptiness, and from within it something obscure, troubling—terrifying, perhaps—may all of a sudden emerge. . . .

Each senses a covert doubt stir within himself, and instinctively he tries to avoid facing it. . . .

Impulsively they huddle close to one another, merge into groups; they stand silently on street corners, staring at what goes on about them; more and more living segments come up to them, and the striving of the parts to make a whole creates a mob.

* * *

. . . Unhurriedly the men fall in with one another. A common feeling, a troubled hollowness within the breast, draws them into a heap—like a magnet iron filings. Almost without glancing at one another they stand shoulder to shoulder, drawing up closer and closer—and in a corner of the square a thick black body with myriad heads takes form. Mutely expectant, sullen and tense, it is almost motionless. The body appears, and immediately after the spirit becomes manifest; a wide and dull face is blocked out, and hundreds of blank eyes acquire a common expression and a common stare—a watchful, suspicious stare which unconsciously searches for that of which the instinct fearfully apprises.

Thus is born that terrifying beast which bears the stolid name of Mob.

* * *

. . . When someone passes by along the street who does not look like an ordinary person, either because he is differently dressed or because he walks faster than the rest, the Mob watches him, turning its hundreds of heads towards him and probing him with an all-encompassing gaze.

Why does not he dress like everybody else? Suspicious. And what could be making him walk so fast along this street on a day when everyone walks slowly? Strange. . . .

Two young men walk by laughing loudly. The Mob tenses itself. What is there to laugh about in a life where everything is so unintelligible when there is no work to do? Laughter rouses in the beast a faint irritation, inimical to gayety. Several heads turn sullenly and, grumbling, follow with their eyes the gay pair. . . .

But the Mob itself breaks out laughing when it sees a newsman on the square trying to dodge streetcars that are closing in on him from three sides, threatening to crush him. The panic of a man threatened by death is something it understands, and anything it understands in the mysterious bustle of life gives it joy. . . .

There, riding by in his car, is a man known throughout the city, throughout the country even—the Boss. The Mob looks at him with a deep interest, it fuses the stare of its numerous eyes in one ray, lighting the shrivelled, bony, sallow face of the Boss with the dull gleam of its respect. It is thus that old bears who have been tamed when cubs look at their master. The Mob understands the Boss—he is a power. He is a great man—thousands toil that he may live, thousands! The Mob sees a perfectly clear meaning in the Boss—the Boss provides work. But there in a streetcar sits a grey-headed man; he has a grim face and stern eyes. The Mob knows who he is, too; he is often described in the newspapers as a maniac who wants to destroy the state, to take away all the factories, railroads, ships—to take away everything. . . . The papers call this a mad and ridiculous project. The Mob stares at the old man with reproach, with cold condemnation, with scornful curiosity. A madman is always interesting.

The Mob only senses, only sees. It cannot convert its impressions into thoughts; its spirit is numb and its heart blind.

. . . People walk along, one after another, and this is strange, uncomprehensible, inexplicable—where are they going, and why? There is a tremendous number of them, and they differ far more than the pieces of metal, wood and stone, than the coins, fabrics and all the tools with which yesterday the beast worked. This irritates the Mob. It vaguely feels that there is another life, different from the one it leads, with other ways and habits, a life full of a strange attraction. . . .

A suspicion of danger slowly feeds on this feeling of

irritation, its fine needles prick the blind heart of the beast. The eyes of the beast darken, its thick, formless body grows visibly tense, and, gripped by an unconscious excitement, it trembles all over. . . .

People flash by, streetcars, automobiles. . . . In the store windows, shiny baubles tease the eye. Their use is obscure, but they attract attention and provoke a desire to possess them. . . .

The Mob is perturbed. . . .

It vaguely feels itself alone in this life, lonely and disclaimed by all these smartly dressed people. It notices how clean are their necks, how slender and white their hands, how smooth and glossy their calm, well-fed faces. It can just picture the food these people gorge themselves with every day. Wonderful tasting food it must be, to give the skin such a sleek look and make the bellies fill out to such globous magnificence. . . .

The Mob feels envy stir within itself, insistently tickling its stomach. . . .

Lovely, supple-bodied women ride by in light, costly carriages. They recline provocatively on their cushions, their legs stretched out to show their little feet; their faces are like stars, and their beautiful eyes bid the people smile.

"See how lovely we are!" the women mutely call out.

The Mob attentively scrutinizes these women and compares them with its wives. Very bony or over-stout, the wives are always greedy and frequently sick. More than anything else their teeth trouble them and their stomachs get upset. And they are always wrangling among themselves.

The Mob sensually strips the women in the carriages of their clothes, feels their breasts and legs. And picturing the nude, round, firm, sparkling bodies of the women, the Mob cannot withhold its admiration and voices it in lusty words which smell of hot, oily sweat, words that are pithy and strong, like the slap of a heavy, dirty hand. . . .

The Mob wants a woman. Its eyes glitter, greedily hugging the slim, firm bodies of the beauties that flash by.

Their children, too, are a lovely sight. Their laughter and cries ring in the air. Neatly dressed, healthy children, with straight, slender legs. Rosy-cheeked, high-spirited. . . .

The children of the Mob are sickly and sallow-faced, and their legs, for some reason or other, are crooked and bowed. That is very common—children with crooked legs. The mothers must be at fault; they probably do something they shouldn't when giving birth to them. . . .

These comparisons breed envy in the Mob's dark heart.

To its irritation is added hostility, which always flowers out luxuriantly on the fertile soil of envy. The huge black body clumsily moves its limbs, hundreds of eyes meet all they find strange and inexplicable with an intent and prickly stare.

The Mob feels that it has an enemy, a crafty and powerful enemy who is scattered everywhere and therefore elusive. He is somewhere close and yet he is nowhere. He took for himself all the savoury dishes, the beautiful women, the rosy children, the carriages, the bright fabrics of silk, and he gives all this away to those he chooses

—but not to the Mob. The Mob he despises, disclaims, and sees not, just as it him. . . .

The Mob searches, sniffs; it watches everything. But all is as usual. And though there is much in the life of the streets which is new and strange, it flows on, flits past the Mob, without touching the taut strings of its hostility and its obscure desire to grab someone and crush him.

In the middle of the square stands a policeman in a grey helmet. His clean-shaven face shines like copper. This man is unconquerably strong—he holds a short thick club loaded with lead.

The Mob looks at the club out of the corner of its eye. It knows clubs, it has seen hundreds of thousands of them, and they are all just wood or metal.

But in this short and blunt club lies concealed a fiendish force one cannot counter.

The Mob is blindly, dimly hostile to everything. It is agitated and ready for something terrible. Impulsively it measures with its eyes the short blunt club. . . .

In the dark litter of the unconscious, fear ever smoulders. . . .

*   *   *

Life roars ceaselessly, tireless in its movement. Where does it get this energy on a day when the Mob is not at work?

With a greater and greater clarity the Mob realizes how lonely it is, senses some deception, and, its irritation mounting, vigilantly watches for something to lay its hands on.

53

It now becomes sensitive to and receptive of impressions—nothing new escapes its glance unperceived. Its jibes are keen-edged and full of malice, and the man in the grey hat with the overwide brim must needs quicken his steps under the pricks of its mocking stare and the lashing sting of its remarks. A woman, as she crosses the square, lifts her skirts a trifle, but when she sees the way the Mob stares at her legs, her fingers go suddenly limp, as if someone had struck her hand, and she lets the skirts fall. . . .

From somewhere a drunkard reels out into the square. His head sunk to his breast, he walks, muttering something; his sodden body sways flabbily, and any second he may crash to the pavement or the rails. . . .

One hand is thrust in his pocket. In the other he holds a crumpled, dust-coated hat; he waves it above his head, and he sees nothing.

On the square, engulfed in a wild vortex of metallic sound, he comes round a little, stops, and looks about him with moist, bleary eyes. Streetcars and carriages are speeding towards him from all sides—some long, moving thread on which dark beads are strung. A clanging of bells comes from the streetcars in angry warning, there is a clicking of horseshoes, everything booms, clatters, and thrusts itself upon him.

The Mob senses the possibility of something amusing. Again it fuses hundreds of its stares in one ray and watches expectantly. . . .

The streetcar motorman clangs the bell; leaning over the railing he yells at the drunkard, his face red from the strain. The drunkard amiably waves his hat at him and steps on the rails just in front of the streetcar.

His whole body thrown back, his eyes closed, the motor-man violently jerks the handle around. The car shivers and crashes to a stop. . . .

The drunkard ambles along—he has put his hat on and let his head sink to his chest again.

But from behind the first streetcar a second slowly slides out and knocks the drunkard's legs out from under him; he falls heavily onto the fender, then drops softly to the rails, and the fender pushes and carries along his crumpled body over the ground. . . .

The drunkard's arms and legs can be seen flapping against the ground. Blood curls out in a thin red line, like a beckoning smile. . . .

Women scream out shrilly in the car, but all the sounds are eclipsed by the deep, triumphant howl of the Mob—it is as if a massive bedspread, damp and heavy, is suddenly flung over them. The troubled clang of bells, the hoof beats, the whine of electricity—all is smothered by a spasm of terror of the Mob, the black wave of the Mob, that surges forward, roaring, like a beast, strikes against the cars, dashes its dark spray all over them, and begins its work.

Shivering in startled little gasps the window glass in the streetcar is shattered into bits. Nothing can be seen but the enormous body of the Mob, thrashing and quivering, and nothing can be heard except its howl, its exultant cry, with which it joyfully proclaims itself a power and announces that it, also, has at last found something to do.

Hundreds of big hands cut through the air; scores of eyes glitter with the greedy sparkle of a strange, sharp hunger.

It pommels someone, the black Mob; it tears at him, it wreaks its vengeance. . . .

From the storm of its merged cries, more and more insistently, comes a hissed word that glitters like a long-bladed, flexible knife:

"Lynch!"

The word has the magic power of unifying all the Mob's vague desires, of fusing its cries in one dense roar:

"Lynch!"

Some of the Mob's segments swing themselves up onto the roofs of the streetcars, and from there, too, coiling through the air and swishing like a whip, sounds a smooth and winding:

"Lynch!"

* * *

In the centre of the Mob a compact ball has formed; it has engulfed something, sucked it in, and is in motion, drifting out into the open. The Mob's thick body compliantly yields to the pressure from the centre, and, splitting, it casts from out of its bowels this bulky black mass—its head, its jaws.

In its teeth there sways a tattered, bloody figure— he was the streetcar motorman, as one can see from the stripes on the remnants of his uniform.

Now he is just a piece of chewed meat—fresh meat, stained to tempting and savoury brightness with blood.

The black jaws of the Mob carry him along, still crunching, and its arms, like the tentacles of an octopus, twist about this body without a face.

The Mob bellows:

"Lynch!"

And it lines up behind its head, shaping into a long, thick body that is ready to devour a great quantity of fresh meat.

But suddenly a clean-shaven man with a copper face appears before it. He has pulled his grey helmet down over his eyes, and he towers like a grey rock in the Mob's way, his club raised mutely in the air.

The head of the Mob swerves to the right, then to the left, to escape the club, to pass it by.

The policeman stands stock-still; the club in his hand does not waver, and his hard eyes are calm and unwinking.

The policeman's confidence in his strength throws a chill into the burning face of the Mob.

If one man can stand up before it, with no regard for its heavy, powerful, lava-like will, if he can be so calm— then he must be unconquerable! . . .

The Mob screams something into his face, it waves its tentacles as if it would twine them around the policeman's broad shoulders, but in its very cry, angry though it is, there is a plaintive note. And when the copper face of the policeman darkens grimly, when he raises higher the hand with the short, blunt club—the Mob's roaring voice breaks strangely, and its trunk slowly and gradually pulls apart; but the head still grumbles, still swerves this way and that; it wants to crawl on.

Unhurriedly two more men with clubs move near. The Mob's tentacles grow suddenly weak and let go of the body in their grip; the body falls on its knees, prostrating itself at the feet of the representative of the law, and he raises above it the short and blunt symbol of his authority. . . .

The head of the Mob, too, slowly breaks up into pieces. It no longer has any trunk; tired and cowed, the men creep across the square, their dark figures scattering over its filthy surface like the black beads of an enormous necklace.

Into the gutterlike streets the people drift, grim and silent. Broken people, disbanded people. . . .

MY INTERVIEWS

A KING WHO KNOWS HIS WORTH

A RETAINER with a long sabre, his breast resplendent with an array of decorations, conducted me to His Majesty's sanctum and took his stand by my side at the entrance, keeping his eyes steadily fixed on my hands.

The King was not there, and I attentively examined the laboratory where the great man compounded those schemes which set the whole world amazed. His Majesty's study was a chamber about two hundred feet long and at least a hundred feet wide.

The ceiling was of glass. Near the wall on the left models of warships floated in a sunken tank. The wall was lined with shelves on which tiny figures of soldiers clad in diverse uniforms were symmetrically arranged. Along the entire right wall stood a row of easels on which were perched unfinished paintings, and the floor in front of them was inlaid with great strips of ebony and ivory, arranged like the keys of a piano.

Everything else in the chamber was on the same grand scale.

"Listen, my friend," I said, turning to the attendant.

But he rattled his sabre, and rejoined:

"I am the Master of Ceremonies. . . ."

"Glad to hear it," I said, "but tell me. . . ."

He interrupted me with the demand:

"When His Majesty enters and greets you, what will you say?"

"How do you do?" I told him.

"That will be impertinent!" he warned me impressively, and he began to instruct me what I was to say in reply to the King.

His Majesty entered with the heavy tread of a being who was confident that his palace was solidly built. The fact that His Majesty does not bend his legs, keeps his arms rigidly to his sides and does not stir a limb, adds greatly to the grandeur of his deportment. His eyes are likewise immovable, as the eyes of an inflexible being accustomed to gazing into the future should be.

I bowed, my escort saluted, His Majesty graciously wriggled his moustaches.

"What can I do for you?" he inquired in a solemn voice.

"I have come, Your Majesty," I replied, as instructed, "to sip a few immortal drops from the ocean of your wisdom."

"I trust I shall be none the duller for that," the monarch retorted wittily.

"That, Your Majesty, is impossible," I replied, respectfully playing up to his subtle humour.

"Well then, let us converse!" he said. "When talking to a monarch one should stand, but you may sit down . . . if it will not make you uncomfortable. . . ."

I was quickly getting used to the novel situation, and so I took a seat. His Majesty hunched his shoulders in silence and let them fall again. I observed that when the King spoke his tongue moved, but all the rest of him preserved its majestic immobility. He took two evenly spaced steps to one side and, standing like a monument in the middle of the chamber, continued:

"And so, before you, you see a king, to wit, me. Not everyone can boast that he has seen a king! What do you want to know?"

"How do you like your job?" I inquired.

"Being a king is not a job, it's a vocation!" he said sententiously. "God and King are two beings whose nature is beyond the grasp of the mind."

The being raised an arm until it formed one line with his body and, pointing a finger at the glass ceiling, went on:

"That ceiling is made of glass in order that God may always see what the King is doing. Then God can understand the King. He alone can control him. . . . The King and God are creators. One, two!—and God created the world. One, two, three!—and my grandfather created Germany! And I am perfecting it. I and a loyal subject of my ancestors, a man by the name of Goethe, have done more for the Germans than anyone else, I daresay. Perhaps I have even done a little more than Goethe. At any rate, there is no question that I am more versatile than he. His Faust, after all, was simply a man of dubious morality. I have shown the world a mailed Faust. That was something everyone understood and at once, which is more than can be said for the second part of Goethe's book. Yes. . . ."

"Do you devote much of your time to art, Your Majesty?" I asked.

"All my life!" he replied. "All my life. Ruling a nation is the most difficult of all arts. To master it to perfection one must know everything. And I know everything! Poetry is a king's natural element. You have to see me at a parade to realize how deeply in love I am with everything beautiful and harmonious. True poetry, let me tell you, is the poetry of discipline. It can be understood only at parades and in verses. A regiment of soldiers—there's a poem if you like! A word in a line of verse and a soldier in a file is one and the same thing. . . . A sonnet is a platoon of words lined up to assault your heart. Fix bayonets, charge!—and a sequence of lovely harmonies pierces your heart. Fire!—and your brain is perforated by a dozen well-aimed words. . . . Verses and soldiers are one and the same thing, I tell you. The King is the first soldier in the land, he is its divine word, and he is its first poet. . . . That's why I march so finely and why verses come to me so easily. . . . See here. M-ar-ch!"

His left leg shot upward, and, following it, his right arm flew to the level of his shoulder.

"'Shun!" the King commanded, and leg and arm at once returned to their places. He continued:

"That's what is called free discipline of the limbs. It acts independently of the consciousness. The jerk of the leg itself lifts the arm—presto! The brain has nothing to do with it. It's almost miraculous. That's why the best soldier is the one whose brain doesn't function at all. It is not the mind that sets the soldier in motion, it's the sound of command. . . . M-ar-ch!—and he will go to heaven or hell, or anywhere else. Fix bayonets, charge!—and he'll run his father through—if his father is a Socialist—or his mother, or his brother—it's all one to him! He'll go on until he hears the command: Halt! It's perfectly magnificent, this action of the body without the mind! . . ."

He sighed and went on in the same level and firm voice:

"Perhaps I will create an ideal state . . . if not I, then one of my descendants will. All that is needed is that everybody in the country shall come to appreciate the beauty of discipline. When man stops thinking altogether, kings will be great and nations will be happy. Money!—the King will command, and all his loyal subjects will line up in a row. One!—and, without a word said, forty million hands will drop into forty million pockets. Two!—forty million hands will each tender the King ten marks. Three!—the forty million will salute their King and silently go back to their work. Isn't that beautiful? You see for yourself, people don't need brains to be happy; the King does the thinking for them. The King is capable of attending to every side of life. . . . That is what I am striving for. So far I am the only one who has such profound views on the functions of a king. . . . Not all kings behave as their dignity demands. Kinsmen in blood, they are not always brothers in spirit. They must unite and become a single force. That can be very easily done, and this is just the right moment to do it. More attention should be given to Socialism: there is something in it that's good for kings. The red spectre of Socialism strikes terror into the hearts of all decent people everywhere. It wants to devour the soul of civilized society—its property. The kings must unite all and sundry to fight this monster, and lead them, like the chieftains of old. Fear of Socialism must be fostered. And when society has gone crazy with fear, kings will come into their own. The days have gone by when kings conferred constitutions—the time has come to take them back!"

He paused for breath, and then went on. I listened gasping—from sheer relish of his wisdom.

"That is my program for every king in our day! And when my Navy is strong enough to permit me to propose this program to all the kings of Europe, I am sure they will accept it. . . . Meanwhile, I devote myself to peaceful cultural pursuits, to perfecting my good people. I have mastered all the arts and I have set them to keep watch over the idea of the divine origin of the power of kings. You have seen my Siegesallee? In it the Muse of Sculpture demonstrates to the Germans how many Hapsburgs and Hohenzollerns there have been on earth. A man has only to march twice back and forth along that avenue—left, right! left, right!—and he will know that all my ancestors were great men. This awakens in him a sense of pride for the kings of his country and, without himself noticing it, makes him a sincere admirer of monarchical rule. In time I shall erect statues of my ancestors in all the streets of my cities. Men will see how many kings there have been in the past and will then realize that they cannot get along without them in the future either. Sculpture is useful to man, but I was the first to demonstrate it so forcefully!"

"Your Majesty," I asked, "why were most of your ancestors bandy-legged?"

"They were all made in one and the same tombstone shop. But that does not prevent anybody from perceiving the grandeur of their spirit. . . . But have you heard my music? No? I will show you how I do it."

He majestically folded his erect body into the shape of a bayonet, sat down on a chair, stretched out a leg, and said to the retainer who had brought me there:

"Count, help me off with my boots! So. . . . And the socks. . . . Thank you . . . although monarchs are not obliged to thank their subjects for their services . . . that is done out of courtesy!"

Having tucked up his trousers to the knee, he bent his neck an angle of forty-five degrees and attentively examined his legs.

"I shall give orders to have them cast in bronze while I am still alive," he said. "Let several dozen casts be made for future statues. It is quite true, a king's legs should be straight. Bowlegs might suggest the idea that the king is imperfect."

He went up to the right wall, took up a brush and, making a half-turn to the left, continued:

"I engage in music and painting simultaneously. Look, these are keys fitted into the floor. The instrument is under the floor. The notes are recorded by a mechanical device, which is also concealed beneath the floor. I paint a picture—one!" He passed the brush over the canvas on one of the easels.

"And stamp with my feet on the keys—two!" A very powerful sound was emitted.

"And there you are!—It is very simple and economizes time, of which a king has always very little to spare. God ought to double the earthly life of leaders of nations. We are all so sincerely devoted to the work of promoting the happiness of our subjects that we are not at all in a hurry to exchange it for the joys of life eternal. . . . But I keep getting away from the subject. The thoughts of kings flow perpetually, like the waters of rivers. A king has to think for all his subjects, and no one else has the right to do so . . . unless he is ordered to by authority. . . . And now I shall acquaint you with a new piece. . . . I stamped it out only yesterday. . . ."

He took a sheet of music and, passing his finger along the lines, said:

"This is a file of notes in the middle register. . . . See in what strict order they are arranged. Tra-ta-tam. Tra-ta-tam. On the next line they are scaling a slope, as though about to take a fort by storm! They move fast, spread out in skirmishing order. . . . Ra-ta-ta-ta-ta! That's very effective. It reminds you of a colic in the stomach—you will know why later. Then they again arrange themselves in rigid line at the command of this note—Boom! Something like a signal shot . . . or a sudden gripe in the stomach. . . . Here they have broken up into separate groups . . . dozens of beats! The cracking of bones! . . . This note goes on continuously and unbrokenly, like the agony of a dislocated joint. And, lastly, all the notes concentrate their onslaught on one point. R-r-ram! r-rata-tam! Boom! Here the notes are in utter disorder, but that is how it should be. This is the finale, a scene of general jubilation. . . ."

"And what's the thing called?" I asked, deeply interested in his description.

"This piece," said the King, "this piece is called 'Birth of a King.' It is my first essay in the propagation of absolutism through the medium of music. . . . Not bad, eh?"

He was evidently satisfied with himself. His moustaches waggled convulsively.

"Among my subjects there have been some pretty good musicians before me, but I decided to go in for it myself, so that all might dance only to my tune."

His moustaches twitched, he was obviously intending to smile, then, with a half-turn to the right, he went on:

"Now look at this. . . . What do you think it is?"

On a huge canvas, a headless monster was painted in lurid red. It had a multitude of arms, and in each hand it clutched shafts of lightning. On one shaft was written in black letters, "Anarchism," on another, "Atheism," a third bore the inscription, "Destruction of Private Property," a fourth, "Atrocity." The monster strode through towns and villages, scattering his thunderbolts and starting conflagrations everywhere. Tiny black human figures were fleeing before the monster in horror and amazement, while in his wake surged a jubilant throng of red men, beings without eyes and covered with fiery-red hair from head to foot, like gorillas. The artist had not stinted red paint. The dimensions of the picture staggered the eye.

"Horrible?" the King asked.

"Horrible!" I agreed.

"That's just what is wanted," he said, and his eyes made a full swing from right to left. "You get my idea, of course? Yes, this is Socialism. You see, it has no head, it sows vices, disseminates anarchism and turns men into animals. Yes, this is Socialism clear enough. That's high-pressure work, if you like! While the lower half of my body is affirming the power of the king, the upper part is busy fighting the chief enemy of his power. Never has art performed its duty so zealously as under my reign!"

"But do Your Majesty's subjects appreciate your arduous labours?" I asked.

"Do they appreciate me?" he said, re-echoing the question, and I thought I detected a note of weariness in his voice.—"They should. I have built them dozens of battleships, I have lined whole streets with sculptures, I make music and pictures, I conduct the liturgy. . . . But . . . sometimes a sinful thought enters my head. . . . I get the suspicion that it is the fools among my subjects who love me, while the clever ones are all Socialists. There are Liberals too. But, as always, the Liberals want too much for themselves and leave far too little for the King, although they don't give the people anything either. In a word, they are nothing but a nuisance. Only the absolute power of the king can save the people from Socialism. But no one, it seems, understands that. . . ."

He bent himself at right angles in two places and sat down. His eyes rolled meditatively in their orbits from left to right, and his whole figure was suffused with melancholy. Seeing that he was tired, I put my last question :

"What else have you to say, Your Majesty, on the subject of the divine origin of kingly power?"

"Anything you like!" he responded swiftly. "First of all, it's unshakable, and it is the one and only truth, because it's miraculous! When millions of people have for thousands of years recognized the unlimited power of one man, only idiots can deny it . . . that's clear. I am a king, true, but I am human, and when I see people obeying my will, I've got to admit it's a miracle . . . isn't that so? Surely, I cannot assume that these millions are all idiots! I want to spare their self-esteem and to think that it's they who are the clever ones. I should be a bad king if I had such a low opinion of my subjects. And since God alone performs miracles, it is clear that I have been chosen by him, as a demonstration of his power and of my own virtues. What can be said against that? This is where the truth lies, and it is as adamant as a diamond, because the majority believe it. . . ."

A moist flicker of satisfaction gleamed in his eyes, but it was gone immediately, and His Majesty sighed, like the engines of a warship letting off steam.

"I must not take up any more of Your Majesty's time," I said, rising from my chair.

"Very well!" graciously replied the leader of a great people. "Farewell. I wish you . . . what is the pleasantest thing I can wish you? Well, I wish you get the chance to see a king again in your lifetime!"

He majestically drooped his under lip and graciously lifted his moustaches. I interpreted this as a bow, and set off for the Zoo to rest my eyes on intelligent animals. . . .

Somehow, after you have talked with some men, you feel such a passionate craving to pet a dog, or smile to a monkey, or respectfully raise your hat to an elephant. . . .

ONE OF THE KINGS OF THE REPUBLIC

. . . THE kings of steel and oil, and all other kings of the United States have always troubled my imagination. I could not imagine that people with so much money could be like ordinary mortals.

It seemed to me that every one of them must have at least three stomachs and about a hundred and fifty teeth. I was convinced that a millionaire ate all day long without pause from six o'clock in the morning until midnight; that he consumed the most expensive foods: geese, turkeys, suckling pigs, radishes with butter, puddings, cakes and all sorts of other delicacies. By evening his jaws grew so stiff that he ordered his Negroes to chew the food for him and he merely gulped it down. Finally, when he was utterly exhausted, gasping and dripping with sweat, they carried him off to bed. And the next morning he woke at six o'clock to resume the arduous routine.

But even with this strenuous effort, he did not consume even fifty per cent of the interest on his capital.

It stood to reason that this was a hard life. But what was to be done? What was the use of being a millionaire if you could not eat more than an ordinary person did?

It seemed to me that his underclothing must be made of brocade, that the heels of his boots were attached with gold nails, and that instead of a hat he wore some diamond headgear. His jacket must be made of the most expensive velvet, it was at least fifty feet long and trimmed with no less than three hundred gold buttons. On holidays he put on eight jackets and six pairs of pants one on top of the other. This, of course, would be both awkward and uncomfortable. . . . But so wealthy a man could not dress like everyone else. . . .

The millionaire's pocket I imagined to be like a hole into which he could easily put away a church, the Senate building and sundry necessities. . . . But while believing that this gentleman's stomach must have a capacity equal to that of the hold of a good seagoing vessel, I could never picture to myself the length of the legs and trousers of such a being. I believed, however, that the quilt under which he slept must be no less than a mile square. And if he chewed tobacco, it was naturally of the highest quality and one or two pounds at a time. If he took snuff, he must use at least a pound in one pinch. One had money in order to spend it. . . .

His fingers were remarkably sensitive and possessed the miraculous power of growing longer at will: for example, if from New York he espied a dollar sprouting somewhere in Siberia, he stretched his hand across the Bering Strait and plucked the favourite plant without stirring from his seat.

Oddly enough, with all this I could not imagine what the head of the monster was like. Moreover, I felt that a head was entirely superfluous with such a mass of muscle and bone moved by the sole desire to squeeze gold out of everything. In general my conception of the millionaire was somewhat vague. In a word, what I saw primarily was a pair of long flexible arms. They had seized the globe in their embrace and drawn it close to the dark, cavernous mouth which sucked, gnawed and chewed at our planet, beslavering it as if it were a hot baked potato. . . .

You may well imagine my surprise when on meeting a millionaire I found him to be a most ordinary person.

Seated before me in a deep armchair was a long, wizened old man whose brown, wrinkled hands of normal size were folded calmly on his stomach. His flabby cheeks were carefully shaven, and the drooping lower lip exposed well-made dentures, with teeth of gold. His upper lip— shaven, bloodless and thin—was glued to his chewing apparatus and barely moved when the old man spoke. There were no eyebrows over his colourless eyes, and his tanned skull was completely hairless. One felt that the face could do with a trifle more skin; reddish, immobile and smooth, it resembled the face of a newborn babe. It was difficult to determine whether this being had just come into the world or was about to depart from it. . . .

His dress too was that of an ordinary mortal. All the gold there was on him was in his ring, watch and teeth. Altogether it probably weighed less than half a pound. In general, the man had the appearance of an old servant in one of Europe's aristocratic homes. . . .

The room in which he received me was remarkable neither for luxury nor beauty. The furniture was massive, this was practically all that could be said of it.

The idea suggested by this furniture was that elephants perhaps sometimes visited this home.

"Are you . . . the millionaire?" I asked, unable to believe my own eyes.

"Oh, yes!" he replied with a convincing nod.

I pretended to take him at his word, but decided to call his bluff there and then.

"How much meat can you consume at breakfast?" I asked.

"I eat no meat!" he declared. "A slice of orange, an egg, a small cup of tea, and that's all. . . ."

His innocent baby eyes gleamed dully like two large drops of murky water, and I could not detect the slightest hint of falsehood in them.

"Very well!" said I, perplexed. "But, pray be frank, tell me candidly, how many times a day do you eat?"

"Twice a day!" he said calmly. "Breakfast and dinner—that is quite enough for me. For dinner I have a plate of soup, some white meat and a sweet. Fruit. A cup of coffee. A cigar. . . ."

My astonishment was growing as rapidly as a pumpkin. He looked at me with the eyes of a saint. I paused for breath, and then went on:

"But if this is true, then what do you do with all your money?"

He shrugged his shoulders slightly, and his eyes rolled in their sockets, as he replied:

"I use it to make more money. . . ."

"What for?"

"In order to make still more money. . . ."

"What for?" I persisted.

He leaned forward, resting his elbows on the arms of the chair, and with a slight shade of curiosity asked:

"Are you mad?"

"Are you?" I retorted.

The old man bent his head and through the gold of his teeth, drawled:

"An amusing fellow. . . . I don't think I've ever met anyone like this before. . . ."

Then he raised his head and stretching his mouth almost as far as his ears, he proceeded to scrutinize me in silence. Judging by his calm demeanour, he evidently considered himself quite normal. I noticed a pin with a small diamond in his tie. Had this stone been the size of a heel I might have known where I was.

"And what do you do with yourself?" I asked.

"I make money," he said shortly with a shrug of the shoulders.

"A counterfeiter?" I exclaimed with joy, feeling that I was on the verge of solving the mystery. But at this point he began to hiccup. His whole body shook as if he were being tickled by some invisible hand. His eyes blinked rapidly.

"This is funny!" he said, calming down and presenting me with a moist, satisfied look. "Now ask me something else, please!" he invited and for some reason puffed his cheeks.

I reflected for a moment and then asked firmly:

"And how do you make money?"

"Ah! That's more like it!" he said with a nod. "It is quite simple. I have railways. The farmers produce goods. I deliver them to the markets. You just figure how much money to leave the farmer so that he won't starve to death and be able to keep on working, and you pocket the rest as freight charge. Quite simple."

"And are the farmers satisfied?"

"Not all of them, I presume!" he said with childlike simplicity. "But people are never satisfied, they say. You will always find cranks who grumble. . . ."

"Does not the government interfere with you?" I ventured with diffidence.

"The government?" he echoed and rubbed his forehead thoughtfully with his fingers. Then as if recalling something, he went on with a nod: "Ah. . . . You mean those fellows . . . in Washington? No, they don't bother me. They're fine lads. . . . Some of them belong to my club. But you don't see much of them. . . . That's why you're liable to forget about them sometimes. No, they don't interfere," he repeated, and directing a curious glance at me, queried:

"Do you mean to say there are governments that prevent people from making money?"

I felt embarrassed at my own naïvete and his wisdom.

"No," I said quietly. "I did not mean that. . . . You see, I thought the government ought sometimes to forbid downright robbery. . . ."

"Now, now!" he objected. "That is idealism. It is not done here. The government has no right to interfere in private affairs. . . ."

I felt increasingly humble before this calm childlike wisdom.

"But is it a private matter when one man ruins many?" I queried politely.

"Ruin?" he echoed, opening his eyes wide. "Ruin means when labour costs are high. Or when there is a strike. But we have immigrants. They always bring down wages and willingly take the place of the strikers. When there will be enough immigrants in the country, who will work for low wages and buy a lot of goods, then everything will be fine."

He grew slightly animated and looked less like a cross between an old man and an infant. His thin brown fingers stirred and his dry voice crackled in my ears as he went on:

"The government? That is indeed an interesting question. A good government is important. It sees to it that there should be as many people in the country as I need, to buy all that I want to sell; that there should be just enough workers to avoid any shortage of them for my purposes. But no more! Then there will be no socialists. And no strikes. The government must not levy high taxes. I myself will take all that the people have to give. That is what I call a good government."

"He betrays stupidity—an unquestionable sign that he is aware of his own greatness," I reflected. "He really must be a king. . . ."

"What I need," he went on in a firm, confident tone, "is order in the country. The government hires for a small salary all sorts of philosophers who spend at least eight hours every Sunday teaching the people to respect the laws. If the philosophers cannot manage, then call in the troops. It is not the method, but the result that counts. The consumer and the worker must be made to respect the law. That is all!" he concluded, twiddling his fingers.

"No, he is not stupid, he can hardly be a king!" I reflected, and then asked: "Are you satisfied with the present government?"

He did not reply at once.

"It does less than it could. I say: immigrants should for the time being be admitted to the country. But we have political liberties which they enjoy, and this must be paid for. Let each one of them bring in at least 500 dollars. A man who has 500 dollars is ten times better than

78

one who has only 50. . . . Bad people—tramps, paupers, the sick and other idlers are of no use anywhere."

"But," I ventured, "this will reduce the influx of immigrants."

The old man nodded in agreement.

"In time I shall propose that the doors of our country be closed to them completely. . . . But in the meantime, let each one bring in a little gold. . . . It is good for the country. Furthermore, it is necessary to lengthen the probation period for naturalization. In time it will have to be abolished altogether. Let those who wish to work for the Americans do so, but it is not at all necessary to grant them the rights of American citizens. We have made a sufficient number of Americans as it is. Each one of them is quite capable of adding to the country's population. All this is the government's concern. But it should be organized on a different basis. The members of the government must all be shareholders in industrial enterprises, then they will more easily and quickly understand the interests of the country. At present I have to buy over senators to convince them that I must have . . . some trifle or another. Then that will no longer be necessary. . . ."

He sighed, jerked his leg and added:

"Only from the summit of a mountain of gold does one get a correct view of life."

"And what do you think about religion?" I asked now that he had made his political views quite clear.

"Ah!" he exclaimed, slapping his knee and moving his eyebrows energetically. "I think very well of it! Religion is essential for the people. I sincerely believe this. As a matter of fact I myself preach in church on Sundays . . . indeed, I do!"

"And what do you say?" I queried.

"Everything that a devout Christian can say in church!" he replied with conviction. "I preach in a humble parish, of course, the poor always need a kind word and paternal instruction. . . . I say to them. . . ."

For a moment his face assumed an infantile expression, then he pressed his lips tightly together and his glance travelled towards the ceiling where cupids were shamefacedly hiding the nude body of a fleshy woman with the pink skin of a Yorkshire sow. The colours of the ceiling were reflected in the depths of his lustreless eyes, making them sparkle. And he began quietly:

"Brothers and sisters in Christ! Do not let yourselves be tempted by the cunning demon of envy, shun all things worldly. Life on this earth is short: a man is a good worker only until the age of forty, after forty he can no longer be employed in the factories. Life is not secure. One false movement of your hand at work and the machine will break your bones; a sunstroke and it is all over with you! Disease and misfortune haunt you at every step! The poor man is like a blind man on the roof of a tall house—whichever way he turns he will fall and meet his doom, as apostle James, the brother of Judas, tells us. Brethren! You must not treasure earthly life—it is the work of the devil, the despoiler of human souls. Your kingdom, beloved children of Christ, like the kingdom of your father, is not of this world; it is in heaven. And if you are patient, if you go through this earthly life quietly, patiently, without murmur and complaint, he will receive you into the abode of paradise and reward you with eternal bliss for your labours on this earth. This life is only a purgatory for your souls, and the more you suffer here the greater the bliss awaiting you there, as apostle Judas himself tells us."

He pointed towards the ceiling, and after reflecting for a while, continued in a cold, hard voice:

"Yes, dear brothers and sisters! This life is empty and trivial, if we do not sacrifice it for the love of our neighbour whoever he may be. Surrender not your hearts to the power of the demons of envy! What is there to envy? Earthly blessings are mere illusions, they are the play-things of the devil. We shall all die, rich and poor, kings and coal miners, bankers and street cleaners. It may be that in the cool gardens of paradise miners will become kings, and a king will work with a broom to sweep the garden paths of fallen leaves and the paper wrappers from the candies that you will eat every day. Brothers! What is there to wish for on this earth, in this dark forest of sin where the soul blunders like a babe? Follow the ways of love and meekness to paradise, endure in patient silence everything that falls to your lot. Love your fellow men, even those that humiliate you. . . ."

He closed his eyes again, and rocking in his chair, went on:

"Turn a deaf ear to those who excite in your hearts the sinful feeling of envy by contrasting the poverty of some with the wealth of others. These people are the en-voys of the devil, the Lord forbids you to envy your neigh-bour. The rich too are poor, they are poor in love. Love the rich man for he is the elect of the Lord! exclaimed Judas, brother of the Lord, pontiff of the church. Do not harken to the gospel of equality and other inventions of the devil. What is equality here, on this earth? You must only aspire to equal one another in purity of soul before your God. Bear your cross patiently, and obedience will lighten your burden. God is with you, my children, and you need nothing else!"

The old man fell silent, his mouth stretched wide, his gold teeth flashing, and looked triumphantly at me.

"You make good use of religion," I remarked.

"Yes, indeed! I know its worth," he said. "Religion, I repeat, is necessary for the poor. I like it. It says that everything on the earth belongs to the devil. Man, if you want to save your soul, do not wish for nor touch anything here on earth. You shall have all the joys of life after death—everything in heaven is for you! When people believe in this, it is far easier to deal with them. Yes, Religion is a lubricant. And the more we use it to oil the machine of life, the less friction will there be among the parts, and the easier the job of the operator of the machine. . . ."

"He really is a king," I decided.

"And do you consider yourself a Christian?" I respectfully asked this recent descendant of a swineherd.

"I certainly do!" he exclaimed with full conviction. "But," and, pointing upwards, he said with an imposing air, "at the same time I am an American and, as such, a strict moralist. . . ."

His face assumed a dramatic expression: he pursed his lips and his ears moved closer to his nose.

"What exactly do you mean?" I inquired lowering my voice.

"Let this be between us!" he warned me in a whisper. "It is impossible for an American to recognize Christ!"

"Impossible?" I whispered after a slight pause.

"Decidedly," he confirmed in a whisper.

"But why?" I queried after a moment's silence.

"He was born out of wedlock!" The old man winked at me and his glance travelled around the room. "Do you understand? A man born out of wedlock cannot even be an official in America to say nothing of a god. He is not received anywhere in decent society. Not a single girl will agree to marry him. Oh, we are very strict! And if we were to recognize Christ, we would also have to accept all the illegitimately born as respectable people . . . even if they were born of a Negro and a white woman. Think how horrible that would be! Eh?"

It must indeed have seemed very horrible, for the eyes of the old man turned green and grew round as an owl's. Pulling up his lower lip with an effort, he pressed it against his teeth. He evidently believed that this grimace made his face more impressive and stern.

"And you flatly refuse to recognize the Negro as a human being?" I queried, oppressed by the morality of a democratic country.

"You are a naïve fellow!" he exclaimed with pity. "Why, they are black! And they smell. We lynch a Negro as soon as we find out that he has taken a white woman as his wife. We put a rope round his neck and hang him on the nearest tree . . . no time wasted! We are very strict, when it comes to morals. . . ."

He now inspired me with the respect that one cannot help feeling for a decomposing corpse. But I had undertaken a job and was determined to pursue it to the very end. I went on asking questions, eager to speed this process of torturing truth, liberty, reason and all that is noble and splendid, all I believe in.

"What is your attitude towards the socialists?"

"They are the real servants of the devil!" he retorted quickly, slapping his knee. "Socialists are the sand in the machine of life, sand that penetrates into everything, preventing the mechanism from working smoothly. With a good government there should be no socialists. Yet they are born in America. This means that the people in Washington don't quite understand their business. They must deprive the socialists of citizenship rights. That would be something. I say a government must be more closely connected with life. And it would be if all its members were millionaires. That's the point!"

"You are a very consistent man!" I said.

"Ah, yes!" he agreed with a nod of approval. The childlike expression had vanished from his face and deep wrinkles appeared on his cheeks.

I wanted to ask him a few questions about art.

"What is your attitude . . ." I began, but he raised his finger and began to speak:

"Atheism in the head and anarchism in the stomach, that's what a socialist is. His soul has been equipped by the devil with wings of madness and fury. . . . In order to fight the socialist we need more religion and more soldiers. Religion against atheism, soldiers against anarchy. First fill the head of the socialist with the lead of church sermons. And if this does not cure him, then let the soldiers pump lead into his stomach!"

He nodded with conviction and said firmly:

"Great is the power of the devil!"

"It is indeed!" I readily agreed.

This was the first time I had had an opportunity to observe the powerful influence of that Yellow Devil—

Gold—in such a striking form. The dry, rheumatic, gout-ridden bones of the old man, his feeble, emaciated body encased in its sack of old skin, the whole little pile of decrepit rubbish, was now animated by the cold and cruel will of the Yellow Father of lies and spiritual corruption. The eyes of the old man gleamed like two new coins, and he seemed to have become stronger and drier. His resemblance to a lackey was even more striking than before, but now I knew who his master was.

"What do you think of art?" I asked.

He glanced at me, and passing his hand over his face wiped away the expression of harsh anger. Once again there was something childlike in this face.

"What did you say?" he asked.

"What do you think of art?"

"Ah!" he responded calmly. "I don't think of it, I simply buy it. . . ."

"I am aware of that. But perhaps you have your own views on art and what you expect of it?"

"Oh! Of course, I know what I want from art. . . . Art must be amusing—that is what I want. It must make me laugh. There is not much to laugh about in my business. The brain sometimes requires a sedative . . . and sometimes the body needs a stimulant. Artistic decorations for the ceiling or walls should stimulate the appetite. . . . Advertisements should be painted in the best and most attractive colours. The advertisement must lure you from afar, from a mile away, and lead you at once where it wishes. Then it pays for itself. Statues or vases are always best made of bronze rather than of marble or porcelain: servants are liable to break porcelain sooner than bronze. Cock fights and rat hunts are fine. I have seen them in London . . . very fine indeed! Boxing is also good, but it should not be allowed to end in killing. . . . Music should be patriotic. A march is always good, but American marches are the best. America is the best country in the world; that is why American music is the best on earth. Good music is always to be found among good people. The Americans are the best people on earth. They have the most money. No one has as much money as we have. That is why the whole world will soon be coming to us. . . ."

As I listened to the smug chatter of this sick child, I thought with gratitude of the savages of Tasmania. It is said that they too are cannibals, but their esthetic sense is nevertheless developed.

"Do you go to the theatre?" I asked the old slave of the Yellow Devil, in order to interrupt his boasting of the country which he had polluted with his life.

"The theatre? Oh, yes! I know, that's art too!" he said with a confident air.

"And what do you like in the theatre?"

"It's nice when there are many young ladies wearing low-necked gowns and you can look at them from above!" he replied, after a moment's thought.

"But what do you like most of all in the theatre?" I asked, growing desperate.

"Oh!" he exclaimed, stretching his lips nearly all the way to his ears. "The actresses, of course, like everybody else. . . . If the actresses are young and beautiful, they are always good. But it is hard to tell at once which of them is really young. They put up such a good front. I understand, that is their profession. But sometimes you think—ah! there's a fine girl! Then you learn that she is fifty years old and has had at least two hundred lovers. That is unpleasant, of course. The circus girls are better than the actresses. They are almost always younger and more supple. . . ."

He was apparently an authority on the subject. Even I, a hardened sinner, who has wallowed in so much vice in my time, had something to learn from him.

"And how do you like poetry?" I asked.

"Poetry?" he echoed, looking down at his shoes and frowning. He thought for a moment, raised his head and showing all his teeth at once, went on: "Poems? Ah, yes! I like poems. Life will be very jolly, if everybody begins to publish ads in verse."

"Who is your favourite poet?" I hurried on to the next question.

The old man looked at me in confusion, and asked slowly:

"What did you say?"

I repeated my question.

"Hm you are a very amusing fellow!" said he, shaking his head dubiously. "Why should I like any poet? And why should any particular poet be liked?"

"I beg your pardon!" said I, mopping my perspiring forehead. "I meant to ask what is your favourite book, that is, apart from your checkbook. . . ."

"Ah! That is quite a different matter!" he agreed. "The two books I like best are the Bible and the Ledger. They are equally stimulating for the mind. As soon as you take them up you feel that they possess a strength that gives you everything you need."

"He's making sport of me!" I thought and looked squarely into his face. No. The eyes dispelled every doubt as

87

to the sincerity of this infant. There he was seated in the chair, looking like a withered nut in its shell, and it was quite obvious that he fully believed in the truth of his words.

"Yes!" he went on, scrutinizing his nails. "They are excellent books! One was written by the prophets, and I myself created the other book. You will find very few words in my book. It contains figures. They show what a man can do if he is willing to work honestly and industriously. The government would do well to publish my book after my death. Let people know what they must do to rise to my exalted station."

And he gestured to the right and left of him with the triumphant air of a victor.

I felt that it was time to end the interview. Not every head can stand being trampled upon.

"Perhaps you would like to say something about science?" I asked quietly.

"Science?" He lifted a finger and raised his eyes ceilingwards. Then he produced his watch, looked at the time, snapped the lid and winding the chain around his finger, swung the watch in the air. After all this he sighed and proceeded to speak:

"Science . . . yes, I know! Books! If they speak well of America they are useful books. But you will rarely find the truth in books. These . . . poets, who make the books, earn very little, I believe. In a country where everyone is occupied with his business no one has time to read books. . . . Yes, the poets are furious because their books are not bought. The government ought to pay the writers of books well. A well-fed man is always kind and cheerful. If books about America are necessary at all, then good poets should be hired, and then all the books America needs will be made. . . . That is all."

"Your definition of science is rather narrow," I observed.

He closed his eyes and was lost in thought. Then he opened them again and continued confidently:

"Well, yes, teachers, philosophers . . . that is also science. Professors, midwives, dentists, I know. Lawyers, doctors, engineers. All right. They are necessary. Good sciences . . . ought not to teach anything bad. . . . But my daughter's teacher once told me that there are social sciences. . . . That is what I do not understand. I believe that this is harmful. Good science cannot be created by a socialist. Socialists must not have anything to do with science at all. Edison, he is creating science that is useful or amusing. The phonograph, the cinematograph— that is useful. But many books of science—that is too much. People should not read books which might put . . . all sorts of doubts into their heads. Everything on this earth is as it should be . . . and there is no need whatever to get mixed up with books."

I rose.

"Oh! You are going?" he asked.

"Yes!" I said. "But perhaps, now that I am leaving, you will tell me what, after all, is the sense in being a millionaire?"

He began to hiccup and jerk his legs instead of answering. Perhaps this was his manner of laughing?

"It is a habit!" he cried, when he had caught his breath.

"What is a habit?" I queried.

"To be a millionaire . . . it's a habit!"

After reflecting for a while I asked my last question:

"Then you think that tramps, opium addicts and millionaires are beings of the same order?"

This remark must have offended him. His eyes grew round and his spleen turned them green.

"I think you are ill-bred," he snapped.

"Good-bye!" said I.

He saw me politely to the porch and remained standing on the top of the steps, staring down at his shoes. In front of his house was a lawn covered with thick, evenly-cut grass. I was walking over the lawn exulting in the thought that I should never see this man again when I heard a voice behind me.

"Hallo!"

I turned back. He was still standing on the porch and staring at me.

"Have you more kings than you need over there in Europe?" he asked slowly.

"If you ask me we don't need any of them!" I replied.

He turned aside and spat.

"I was thinking of hiring a couple of good kings for myself," he said. "What do you say to that?"

"But what for?"

"It would be amusing, you know. I would order them to box right here. . . ."

He pointed to the lawn in front of his house and added in the tone of a query:

"From one to half past one every day, eh? It would be pleasant to indulge in art for a half hour after lunch . . . very good."

He was in earnest, and I could feel that he would do everything to satisfy this wish.

"But why must you have kings for the purpose?" I asked.

"Because nobody here has thought of that yet!" was his explanation.

"Yes, but kings are accustomed to have others do their fighting for them!" I said and started off.

"Hallo!" he called me again.

I paused once more. He was still standing in the same place, his hands in his pockets. There was a sort of a dreamy expression in his face.

"What is it?" I asked.

He moved his lips as if he were chewing, and said slowly:

"What do you think, how much will it cost—two kings to box half an hour every day for three months, eh?"

A PRIEST OF MORALITY

. . . HE came to me late at night and, glancing suspiciously around the room, asked in a low voice:

"Could I talk to you alone for half an hour?"

In his tone, and in the whole of his thin, rather stooping figure, there was something mysterious and secretive. He sat down gingerly on a chair, as if afraid the furniture wouldn't bear the weight of his long, sharp bones.

"Could you lower the blind?" he asked softly.

"Certainly," said I, and hastened to comply.

Nodding gratefully, he winked towards the window and remarked more softly still:

"They're forever on the watch."

"Who?"

"Why, the reporters."

I took a good look at him. Dressed very presentably, rather smartly, in fact, he nevertheless gave the impression of being a poor man. His bald, angular skull gleamed modestly and unassumingly. A clean-shaven, very thin face; grey eyes, smiling apologetically and half-shaded by light lashes. When he raised the lashes and looked up into my face, I had a feeling of being confronted with a vague, not very deep emptiness. He sat with his feet drawn back under the chair, his right hand on his knee, and the left, with the derby hat in it, dangling to the floor. His long fingers trembled slightly, and there was a heavy droop to the corners of his tightly-compressed lips—a sign that this man had paid dear for his clothes.

"Let me introduce myself," he began, with a sigh and sidelong glance at the window. "I'm a professional sinner, so to speak. . . ."

I pretended not to have heard, and asked matter-of-factly:

"Pardon?"

"I'm a professional sinner," he repeated word for word, and added: "My speciality is offences against public morality. . . ."

There was nothing but humility in the tone in which the sentence was spoken; I didn't catch a shade of penitence in his words or face.

"You . . . wouldn't like a drink of water, would you?" I suggested.

"No, thank you," he declined, and his eyes with their apologetic smile came to rest upon me. "You don't quite understand me, I think?"

"Why not?" I countered, resorting to jauntiness as cover for my ignorance, in the accepted manner of European journalists. But he didn't seem to believe me. Swinging his derby in the air and smiling modestly, he started talking:

"Let me tell you something about my job, so that you will know who I am. . . ."

Here he sighed and dropped his head. And again I was surprised to hear only weariness in the sigh.

"You remember," he began, swinging the hat gently, "there was a story in the papers about a man . . . that is, about a drunk? The row at the theatre?"

"The gentleman in the front row, who got up during the most heart-rending scene, put on his hat and started shouting for a cab?" I asked.

"Yes," he confirmed, and added obligingly: "That was me. The item headlined 'Child-Beating Beast' was about me too, and so was another—'Husband Sells Wife'. . . . The man who molested a lady in the street with indecent suggestions—that was me too. . . . In general, they write about me at least once a week, and always when it's a case of proving how depraved public morals are. . . ."

He said all this quietly, very distinctly, but without any air of boasting. I couldn't make head or tail of him, but didn't want to give myself away. Like all writers, I always make a show of knowing life and men like the palm of my hand.

"Hm!" said I, trying to sound like a philosopher. "And do you enjoy spending your time that way?"

"Well, in my younger days, it used to amuse me, I own," he replied. "But now I'm forty-five, married, two daughters. . . . And so it's very uncomfortable to be held up in the papers two and three times a week as a fount of moral turpitude. And reporters watching all the time to see that you do your work punctually and scrupulously. . . ."

I coughed to conceal my bewilderment. Then asked commiseratingly:

"It's a disease with you, is it?"

He shook his head in denial, fanned himself with his hat, and answered:

"No, it's my profession. I told you, my speciality is making minor disturbances in the streets and public

94

places. . . . Other people at our Bureau handle bigger and more responsible jobs—such as outraging religious feelings, seductions of women and girls, thefts—though of no more than a thousand dollars. . . ." He sighed, looked around and added: "And other offences against morality. . . . And I only make minor disturbances. . . ."

He was talking the way a tradesman talks of his trade. It was beginning to annoy me, and I inquired sarcastically:

"And it doesn't satisfy you?"

"No," he answered simply.

His simplicity was disarming, and excited my keen curiosity. After a pause, I asked:

"Have you been in prison?"

"Three times. Ordinarily, though, I keep within the limits of a fine. It's the Bureau that pays the fines, of course," he explained.

"The Bureau?" I echoed mechanically.

"Oh, yes. You'll agree I couldn't pay the fines myself," he said with a smile. "Fifty dollars a week is very little for a family of four. . . ."

"Let me think about it," I said, getting up.

"Certainly," he agreed.

I began walking past him up and down the room, searching my memory for all the different kinds of mental disorders. I was anxious to diagnose his ailment, but I couldn't. One thing was clear—it wasn't megalomania. He watched me with a polite smile on his thin, emaciated face, and waited patiently.

"And so there's a Bureau?" I asked, coming to a halt opposite him.

"Yes," he said.

"And it employs a lot of people?"

"In this town, a hundred and twenty-five men and seventy-five women. . . ."

"In this town? Then . . . in other towns there are Bureaus too?"

"Why, of course, all over the country," he said, smiling patronizingly.

I began to feel sorry for myself.

"But . . . how do they . . ." I asked hesitantly, "what do they do, these Bureaus?"

"Offend against the laws of morality," he answered modestly, got up from his chair, shifted to the armchair, took a stretch and began reading my face with frank curiosity. He evidently thought me a savage, and wasn't troubling any more to be on his best behaviour.

"Damn it!" I thought. "Mustn't let on that I don't know what it's all about. . . ." And, rubbing my hands, I said brightly:

"Why, that's interesting! Most interesting! . . . Only . . . what are they for?"

"What?" he smiled.

"These Bureaus for offending against the laws of morality?"

He laughed, the adult's good-natured laugh at a child's foolishness. I looked at him and found myself thinking that, true enough, ignorance is the source of all the disagreeable things in life.

"What do you think, a man wants to live, eh?" he demanded.

"Well, of course."

"And live so that he'll enjoy it?"

"Yes indeed!"

He got up, walked over to me and slapped my shoulder.

"And how can you have a good time without breaking the laws of morality, hey?"

He fell back, gave me a wink, sprawled in the armchair again like a boiled fish on a platter, brought out a cigar and lit up without asking my permission. Then he went on:

"Who wants to eat strawberries with carbolic acid?"

And he dropped the burning match on the floor.

It's always that way—as soon as a man realizes that he has an advantage over another, he begins to act towards him like a pig.

"I have some difficulty in understanding you," I confessed, looking into his face.

He grinned and said:

"I had a higher opinion of your abilities. . . ."

Minding his manners less and less, he flicked the cigar ash onto the floor, half-closed his eyes, and, watching the wreaths of cigar smoke through his lashes, informed me, with the air of an authority on the subject:

"You don't know much about morality, that's what. . . ."

"I've come up against it occasionally," I protested humbly.

He took the cigar out of his mouth, stared at the end of it and observed philosophically:

"Knocking your head against a wall doesn't mean that you've studied the wall."

"Yes, I agree with you there. But somehow I always seem to rebound from morality, the way an indiarubber ball does from a wall. . . ."

"It's a fault of upbringing," he pronounced sententiously.

"Quite possible," I agreed. "The most desperate moralist I ever saw was my grandfather. He knew all the paths that led to heaven and was always driving everybody who came his way to follow them. The truth had been revealed to him alone, and he was most sedulous in knocking it, with anything that came to hand, into the heads of his family. He knew exactly what God wants of man, and taught even cats and dogs how to behave in order to attain perpetual bliss. All the same, he was greedy, spiteful, was an unconscionable liar and usurer, and with the coward's cruelty—an attribute of all and every moralist—would beat his household in convenient leisure moments as best he could and chose. . . . I tried to influence the old fellow, thought to make him more tractable: one time I threw him out of the window; another day, I hit him with a mirror. The window and mirror got smashed, but it didn't work any improvement in the old man. He lived and died a moralist. And I've had a sort of aversion to morality ever since. . . . Perhaps you'll tell me something to reconcile me with it?" I suggested.

He pulled out his watch, took a look at it and said:

"I've no time to give you lectures. . . . Still, now that I've come, I might as well. Once you start a thing, you've got to finish it. Maybe you'll be able to do something for me. . . . I'll be brief. . . ."

He half-closed his eyes again and launched forth impressively:

"You've got to have morality—must remember that! Why have you got to have it? Because it protects your home, your rights and your property—in other words, it protects the interests of 'thy neighbour.' 'Thy neighbour'—that's always you, nobody else, see? If you've got a pretty wife, you tell everybody around you: 'Thou shalt not covet thy neighbour's wife.' If a man's got money, oxen, slaves, asses, and isn't an idiot himself—he will be a moralist. Morality serves your ends if you've got everything you need and want to keep it just for yourself; it doesn't serve your ends if you've got nothing you can spare except for the hair on your head."

He stroked his bald crown and continued:

"Morality is the guardian of your interests, you try to put it into the souls of the people around you. In the streets you post policemen and detectives, and inside a man you thrust a host of principles that are to become rooted in his brain and crush, strangle, destroy in him all ideas that operate against you, all desires that could endanger your rights. Morality is always strictest where economic antagonisms are most apparent. The more money I have, the stricter a moralist I am. That's why in America, where there are so many rich men, they profess a 100 hp morality. Get me?"

"Yes," I said, "but where does the Bureau come in?"

"Wait!" he retorted, raising his hand solemnly. "And so the purpose of morality is to impress on everyone that they mustn't interfere with you. Now if you've got a lot of money, you have a lot of desires and full opportunity to satisfy them—right? But most of your desires can't be satisfied without infringing the principles of morality. . . . So what are you to do? You can't preach to others what you repudiate yourself: it's awkward, and then people mightn't believe you. After all, not all of them are fools. . . . For instance, you sit in a restaurant drinking champagne and kissing a very pretty lady, although she isn't your wife. . . . According to the standards that you consider obligatory for the general public, that is immoral. But for yourself, this kind of pastime is indispensable: it's a delightful habit of yours, you get so much pleasure out of it. And so you're faced with the problem of how to reconcile the preaching of abstinence from pleasurable vices with your own partiality for them? Another example: you tell everybody, 'Thou shalt not steal.' Because you wouldn't like it at all, would you, if people started stealing your property. But at the same time, though you have money, you feel an uncontrollable urge to steal a little more. Then again, you hold very strictly to the principle 'Thou shalt not kill.' Because you value life, it is a pleasant, enjoyable affair. One day the workers in your coal mines demand higher pay. You have troops called out—you can't help it—and, bang!—a few dozen workers are killed. Or you have no market for your goods. You point out the fact to your government and persuade it to open a new market for you. The government obligingly sends a little army to some place in Asia or Africa and carries out your wish, after shooting down a few hundred or thousand natives. . . . All this doesn't chime very well with your preaching of brotherly love, abstinence and chastity. But in shooting down workers or natives, you can vindicate yourself by pleading the interests of the state, which cannot exist if people don't bow to your interests. The state, that's you—if you're a man of substance, of course. It's much harder for you in the little things—loose living, stealing, and so on. In general, the rich man's position is a tragic one. It's absolutely vital for him that everybody should love him, abstain from forming designs upon his property or interfering with his habits, and behave with due regard for the chastity of his wife, his sister, his daughters. For himself, on the other hand, there is no need whatever to love people, to abstain from stealing, to respect the chastity of women, and so on—in fact, just the opposite is the case! All that would only cramp his activity and undoubtedly interfere with his success. As a rule, his whole life is nothing but stealing; he robs thousands of people, the whole country—that's essential for the increase of capital, that is, for the country's progress—understand? He seduces women by the dozen— it's a very delightful pastime for a man of leisure. And whom is he to love? For him, all people fall into two groups—one group he robs, the other competes with him in doing it."

Pleased with his knowledge of the subject, my speaker smiled and, tossing the cigar-end into a corner, continued:

"And so, morality is useful to the rich man and bad for people at large, but at the same time it is superfluous for him and obligatory for everybody else. That's why the moralists try to drill the principles of morality into the inside of people's heads, but themselves always wear them on the outside, like ties or gloves. The next question is, how to persuade people that they must submit to the laws of morality? Nobody cares to be the one honest man among thieves. But if you can't persuade them—hypnotize them! That always works. . . ."

He nodded emphatically and, with a wink at me, repeated:

"You can't persuade them—then hypnotize them!"

Then he put his hand on my knee, peered into my face, and lowering his voice, went on:

"The rest is between ourselves, agreed?"

I nodded.

"The Bureau I work for hypnotizes public opinion. It's one of America's most original institutions, I'll have you know!" he added proudly.

I nodded my head again.

"You know," he said, "that our country lives with the one idea of making money. Everybody wants to be rich here, and one man is for another just something that a few grains of gold can always be squeezed out of. And the whole of life is a process of extracting gold from human flesh and blood. The people in this country—and everywhere else, I've heard—are just ore from which yellow metal is refined; progress is the concentration of the physical energy of the masses, that is, the crystallization of human flesh, bone and nerve into gold. Life's very simply arranged. . . ."

"Is that your own view?" I queried.

"That? Why, of course not," he said with pride. "It's simply somebody's fancy. . . . I don't remember how it got into my head. . . . I only use it when I'm talking to people who . . . aren't quite normal. . . . Well, to continue. The people here have no time to indulge in vices—they have no leisure left for that. The hours of hard work so exhaust a man that he has neither the strength nor the desire left to sin in his leisure hours. People have no time to think, they have no energy to desire anything, they live only in their work and in order to work, and that makes their lives highly moral. Only that once in a while, on some holiday, a few fellows will string up a couple of Niggers; but then, that doesn't transgress against morality, because a Nigger isn't a white man, and besides, there are lots of these Niggers around. Everybody behaves more or less respectably, and against the drab background of this stolid life, confined within the narrow compass of the old Puritan morality, any breach of its principles stands out like a smudge of soot. That's a good thing, but it's bad too. The upper classes of society can take pride in the conduct of the lower, but at the same time this sort of conduct cramps the style of the rich. They've got money—that means they have the right to live as they please, without bothering about morality. The rich are greedy, the glutted—sensual, the idle—dissolute. Weeds thrive on rich soil, profligacy—on a soil of satiety. What's to be done then? Repudiate morality? That's impossible, because it would be stupid. If your interests require people to be moral, then manage to keep your vices out of sight. . . . That's all. Nothing particularly new in it. . . ."

He glanced over his shoulder and dropped his voice still lower.

"And so, some Society people in New York hit on a wonderfully happy idea. They decided to institute in this country a secret society for overt violation of the laws of morality. A sizable capital was built up by contributions, and Bureaus for hypnotizing public opinion were opened—under cover, of course—in different towns. They hired various people like your humble servant, and gave them the job of committing offences against morality. Each Bureau is headed by a dependable and experienced man, who directs its operations and distributes the assignments. . . . As a rule, it's some newspaper editor. . . ."

"I don't understand the purpose of the Bureaus!" I said unhappily.

"It's quite simple!" he returned. All of a sudden, his face took on an expression of uneasiness and nervous expectancy. He got up and, putting his hands behind his back, began walking slowly about the room.

"Quite simple," he repeated. "I've told you that the lower classes don't sin much—they haven't the time. On the other hand, it's essential to have morality sinned against!—after all, you can't leave it to be a barren old maid. There's got to be a perpetual clamour about morality, that deafens the public and keeps it from hearing the truth. If you throw a lot of small chips into a river, quite a big log can float past among them unperceived. Or if you have incautiously extracted the wallet from your neighbour's pocket, but promptly sidetrack attention to an urchin who has stolen a handful of nuts, it may save you from unpleasantness. Only shout 'Stop thief!' as loud as you can. What our Bureau does is to create a host of minor disturbances by way of covering up big offences."

He gave a sigh, stopped in the middle of the room and said nothing for a few moments.

"For example, the rumour gets about town that a certain prominent and respected citizen beats his wife. The Bureau promptly gets me and a few other agents to beat our wives. We duly beat them. The wives know all about it, of course, and scream for all they are worth. All the papers write up the story, and the commotion they raise blots out the rumours about the prominent citizen's treatment of his wife. Why worry your head about rumours, when here are solid facts? Or maybe talk will start about Senators being bribed. At once the Bureau arranges several cases of bribery of police officials, and exposes their corruption to the public. Again the rumours are submerged by facts. Somebody in high Society insults a woman. Right away, it is arranged that in restaurants, in the streets, a number of women shall be insulted. The Society gentleman's offence disappears from sight entirely in a string of similar offences. And it's that way always, in everything. A big theft has a multitude of petty larcenies piled on top of it, and all big crimes generally are snowed under with trifles. That is what the Bureau does."

He walked over to the window, peered out cautiously into the street, and sat down again, continuing in the same undertone:

"The Bureau shields the upper class of American society from the judgment of the people; and at the same time, by evoking a perpetual outcry about breaches of morality, fills the people's heads with petty scandals staged to cover up the vices of the rich. The people are in a state of chronic hypnosis, they have no time to think for themselves, and only listen to what the papers tell them. The papers belong to the millionaires, the Bureau is sponsored by them too. . . . Get the point? It's a very smart idea. . . ."

He stopped and fell to thinking, head bent low

"Thank you," I said. "You've told me a great deal that is interesting."

He raised his head and gave me a gloomy look.

"Y-yes, it's interesting, of course," he brought out slowly and reflectively. "But it's beginning to tire me. I'm a family man, three years ago I built a house of my own. . . . I'd like to have a bit of a rest. It's very wearing, this job of mine. Maintaining respect for the laws of morality is no easy matter, believe me. Look: liquor is bad for me, but I have to get drunk; I love my wife and like quiet home life—and here I have to gad about restaurants, make rows . . . and forever see myself in the papers . . . . Under a false name, of course, but still. . . . Some day my own name will come out, and then . . . then I'll have to get out of the town. . . . I need advice. . . . I've come to ask your opinion about something . . . a very perplexing business!"

"Go ahead!" I told him.

"You see," he began, "it's like this. Down in the Southern states, the upper classes have taken lately to keeping Negro mistresses . . . two and three at a time. People have started talking. The wives don't like it. Some of the papers have received letters from women exposing their husbands. There may be a big scandal. The Bureau has at once gone about producing 'counterfacts,' as we call them. Thirteen agents, and I'm one of them, are to get themselves Negro mistresses. Two or even three at the same time. . . ."

He jumped up nervously and, putting his hand to his breast pocket, declared:

"I can't do it! I love my wife . . . and she wouldn't let me, anyway! And at least if there only had to be one!"

"Why don't you refuse?" I suggested.

He gave me a pitying look.

"And who's going to pay me fifty dollars a week? And a bonus if the thing goes well? No, no, you can keep that sort of advice for yourself. . . . An American doesn't refuse money even the day after he's dead. Think up something else."

"I find it hard," I said.

"Hard? Why should you find it hard? You Europeans are very lax on the moral side. . . . Your moral iniquity is notorious."

He said it with a firm conviction of its being true.

"Look here," he went on, bending forward towards

me, "you probably have some European friends? I'm sure you must have!"

"What do you want them for?" I asked.

"What do I want them for?" He stepped back a pace and struck an attitude. "I tell you, I simply cannot take on this job with the Negro girls. Judge for yourself: my wife won't allow it, and I love her. No, I positively can't. . . ."

He shook his head vigorously, passed his hand over its bald surface, and continued ingratiatingly:

"Maybe you could recommend some European for the job? They don't recognize morality, so it doesn't matter to them. Some poor immigrant, eh? I'd pay him ten dollars a week—that's fair, isn't it? I'll go about with the Negresses myself . . . in fact, I'll do everything myself— he'll only have to see to it that children result. . . . It's got to be settled tonight. . . . Just think what a scandal might flare up if this business in the South wasn't buried in time under a lot of fakes! If morality is to triumph, there's no time to lose . . . ."

. . . When he had rushed out of the room, I went over to the window and held my hand, bruised against his skull, to the glass pane to cool it.

He was standing below and making signs to me.

"What do you want?" I asked, opening the window.

"I forgot my hat," he said modestly.

I picked up the derby from the floor and tossed it into the street. And as I closed the window, I heard him making this business proposition:

"And if I offer fifteen dollars a week? It's good money!"

THE LORDS OF LIFE

"Come with me to the fountains of truth!" the Devil said, laughing, and he brought me to the cemetery.

As we slowly wound our way along narrow paths among the old tombstones and cast-iron slabs he spoke in the tired voice of an old professor weary of the barren preaching of his wisdom.

"Beneath your feet," he said to me, "lie the makers of the laws that you are governed by. With the sole of your boot you trample upon the ashes of the carpenters and blacksmiths who wrought a cage for the beast you have inside you."

He laughed as he said this, and the laugh was full of a scourging contempt for people; the grass on the graves and the mould on the tombstones were flooded with the cold, dismal light of his greenish eyes. The rich soil of the dead stuck to my feet in heavy clods, and it was difficult to walk along the footpaths, among the tombstones which marked the graves of worldly wisdom.

"Man, why don't you bend low in gratitude before the dust of those who moulded your soul?" the Devil said in a voice which was like the draught of a damp autumnal wind. It sent a shiver down my spine, and my heart was chilled and wrung with a dreary disquiet. The melancholy trees above the graves swayed gently, brushing my face with their cold, moist branches.

"Pay homage to the counterfeiters! It is they who wrought the cloud banks of petty grey thoughts that are the small coin of your intellect. It is they who formed your habits, your prejudices, and all you live by. Give them your thanks—the dead have left you a tremendous legacy!"

Yellow leaves slowly floated down on my head and dropped at my feet. The graveyard soil gave out a greedy smacking sound as it gorged on fresh food: the dead leaves of autumn.

"Here lies a tailor who clothed the souls of men in heavy grey robes of prejudice. Would you care to take a look at him?"

I nodded in acquiescence. The Devil kicked the old rust-eaten slab on one of the graves, he kicked it and he said:

"Hey, you, bookwright! Get up. . . ."

The slab rose, there was a heavy sigh of disturbed slush, and a shallow grave, like a worm-eaten purse, was revealed. From out of its wet murk came a querulous voice:

"Who ever heard of waking the dead after twelve?"

"You see?" the Devil said with a grin. "The makers of the laws of life are true to themselves even after they rot away."

"Oh, it's you, Master!" the skeleton said, seating himself on the edge of the grave and greeting the Devil with an independent nod of his hollow skull.

"Yes, it's me!" the Devil replied. "I brought one of my friends to see you. . . . He has grown stupid among the men you taught wisdom, and now has come to its primary source to be cured of his infection. . . ."

I looked at the sage with proper deference. No flesh was left on his skull, but the look of smug self-content had not faded from his face. Each bone shone dully with the consciousness of its belonging to a system of bones of absolute perfection, to a unique system. . . .

"Tell us what you did on earth," the Devil suggested.

Haughtily and pompously the dead man smoothed down with the bones of his arms the dark shreds of shroud and flesh that hung like a pauper's rags on his ribs. Then he proudly raised the bones of his right arm shoulder level, and, pointing with the bare joint of his finger into the darkness of the graveyard, he began to speak calmly and impassively:

"I wrote ten big books which impressed on the people's minds the great idea of the superiority of the white race over the coloured. . . ."

"Translated into the language of truth," the Devil rejoined, "it would sound like this: I, a sterile old maid, have all my life used the dull needle of my mind to knit foolscaps from the frayed wool of threadbare ideas for those who like to keep their skulls in quiet and warmth. . . ."

"Aren't you afraid of offending him?" I quietly asked the Devil.

"Oh!" he exclaimed. "Men of wisdom lend but a poor ear to truth even when they're alive."

"Only the white race," the sage went on, "could have created so advanced a civilization and worked out such strict moral principles, thanks to the colour of its skin and the chemical composition of its blood, as I proved. . . ."

"He proved it!" the Devil echoed with a nod of assent. "There is no barbarian more settled in his belief that cruelty is his right than a European. . . ."

"Christianity and humanism are the products of the white race," the dead man continued.

"Of a race of angels who should rule the world," the Devil broke in. "That is why they so zealously dye it their favourite colour—red, the colour of blood. . . ."

"They have created great literature, introduced miraculous technical achievements," the dead man enumerated, twitching his finger bones. . . .

"Some thirty good books and countless guns for the extermination of men . . ." the Devil explained with a laugh. "Where else is life so broken up and man brought so low as among the whites?"

"Could it be that the Devil is not always right?" I ventured.

"The art of the Europeans has reached an immeasurable height," the skeleton muttered in a dull, rasping voice.

"Say rather that the Devil would like to be mistaken!" my companion exclaimed. "It's terribly boring to always be right. But men live only so as to give food to my scorn. . . . The seeds of vulgarity and falsehood yield the richest harvests in the world. Here is one of the sowers before you now. Like all of them—he did not bring forth anything new, he only revived the corpses of old prejudices by clothing them in the garb of new words. . . . What has been done on earth? Palaces have been built for the few, churches and factories for the many. Souls are slaughtered in the churches and bodies in the factories, so that the palaces may stand intact. . . . Men are sent deep down into the earth for coal and gold—and in payment for this degrading work they get a piece of bread seasoned with lead and steel."

"Are you a socialist?" I asked the Devil.

"I want harmony!" he replied. "It makes me sick when man, by nature an entity, is shattered into matchwood, made a tool for the greedy hand of another. I don't want slaves—slavery is repulsive to my spirit. . . . That is why I was banished from heaven. Where idols exist, spiritual slavery is inevitable and the mould of falsehood will ever spread. . . . Let the earth live—all of it! Let it burn all day even though nothing but ashes are left of it by night. Once in their lives all people ought to fall in love. . . . Love, like a wondrous dream, comes only once, but in this one moment there is all the meaning of existence. . . ."

The skeleton stood leaning against a black rock, and the wind moaned softly in the empty cage of his ribs.

"He must be cold and uncomfortable," I said to the Devil.

"I enjoy looking at a scientist who has freed himself of everything superfluous. His skeleton is the skeleton of his idea. . . . I can see how original it was. . . . Next to this one lie the remains of another sower of truth. . . . Let's wake him, too. In their lifetime they all like peace and quiet, and they labour to devise codes of thought, sentiments and life—they distort newborn ideas and make cosy little coffins for them. But after death—they want to be remembered. . . . Comprachikos—get up! I've brought you a man who needs a coffin for his thoughts."

And once again a bare and empty skull, toothless, yellow, yet glistening with self-satisfaction, emerged from the earth. He must have been lying below ground for a long time—his bones were bare of flesh. He stood by his tombstone, and his ribs were silhouetted against the black stone like the stripes on the uniform of an officer of the court.

"Where does he keep his ideas?" I inquired.

"In his bones, my friend, in his bones! Their ideas are like rheumatism or gout—they penetrate deep into the ribs."

"How is my book selling, Master?" the skeleton asked in a flat voice.

"It's still lying on the shelves, Professor!" the Devil replied.

"Why, have people forgotten how to read?" the professor brought out after a moment's reflection.

"No, they still read nonsense quite willingly—but boring nonsense sometimes has to wait a long while before it claims their attention. . . . The professor here," said the Devil turning to me, "spent his whole life measuring women's skulls to prove that a woman is not a human being. He measured hundreds of skulls, he counted teeth, he measured ears, he weighed dead brain matter. Working with dead brains was the professor's favourite occupation. All his books] evidence this. Have you] read them?"

"I don't walk into a temple through a pub," I rejoined, "and I don't know how to study human beings by reading about them—people in books are always fractions, and I'm weak in arithmetic. But I do think that a human being who has no beard and goes around in a skirt is no better and no worse than one who has a beard and a moustache and wears pants. . . ."

"Yes," said the Devil, "vulgarity and stupidity invade the brain regardless of what you wear and the abundance of hair on your head. But, still, that problem of women has been quaintly put." At this the Devil laughed, as was his wont, which is one reason why it's so pleasant to chat with him. He who can laugh in a graveyard loves life and loves men—assuredly. . . .

"Some, who require a woman only as a wife and slave, maintain that she is not a human being at all," he went on. "Others would like to exploit her working energy without refusing to use her as a woman, and these claim that she is no less suited for work than a man and can work on an equal basis with him, that is, for him. But, of course, they neither of them would admit a girl they had raped into their society—they are convinced that after they touch her she remains forever sullied. . . . Yes, the feminine problem is frightfully amusing! I like it when men tell naïve lies—at such moments they resemble children, and one has hope that in time they will grow up. . . ."

I could see by the Devil's face that he had no intention of saying anything flattering about the men of the future. But since I myself can say much that is not flattering about the men of today, and, as I had no desire to have the Devil compete with me in this pleasant and easy pastime, I interrupted him:

"There's a saying that where the Devil hasn't time to go himself he sends a woman. Is that true?"

He shrugged his shoulders and said, "It does happen. . . . If there's no man around who is clever and mean enough. . . ."

"It strikes me somehow that you've lost your love of evil," I challenged.

"There is no such thing as evil any more!" he replied with a sigh. "Only vulgarity! Evil was once a power that had beauty. And now—even when men are killed it is grossly done: first their hands are tied. There are no more villains left—only henchmen. And a henchman is nothing but a slave, a hand and an axe set in motion by the power of fright, by the twinges of fear. . . . Men kill those they are afraid of. . . ."

Two skeletons stood side by side at their graves, and the leaves of autumn slowly drifted down on their bones. The wind dolefully played on the strings of their ribs and howled in the voids of their skulls. Humid and strong-scented darkness looked out from the deep sockets of their eyes. They were both shivering. I felt sorry for them.

"Let them go back to their places!" I entreated.

"So you are a humanist even in the graveyard!" he exclaimed. "Well, humanism is far more in place among the dead: here it can offend no one. In prisons and mines, in the factories, on city squares and streets, wherever there are living people, humanism is ridiculous and is even apt to kindle wrath. Here there is no one to mock at it—the dead are always serious. And I am certain that they enjoy hearing about humanism—after all, it is their stillborn child. . . . No, they weren't idiots, those who wanted to place this splendid side scene on the stage of life to cover the black horror of man persecuted, and the cold cruelty of a small group which owes its strength to the stupidity of all men. . . ."

And the Devil broke into a laugh, the harsh laugh of ominous truth.

Stars quivered in the dark sky. The black stones stood motionless above the graves of the past. A rotting smell broke through the earth, and the wind carried the breath of the dead into the drowsy city streets that were enveloped by the stillness of the night.

"There are quite a few humanists lying here," the Devil went on, taking in the graves about him with a sweeping gesture. "Some of them were actually sincere—there are plenty of droll contradictions in life, and maybe this one isn't the funniest. . . . And next to them, peacefully and amicably, there lie men of another type, the teachers of life who attempted to lay a solid foundation under the old edifice of lies that was so painstakingly and laboriously erected by thousands upon thousands of the dead. . . ."

From afar came the sound of singing. . . . Two or three gleeful cries floated, quivering, over the cemetery. Some reveler, most likely, tramping lightheartedly in the dark to his grave.

"Under this heavy stone there proudly rots the body of a sage who taught that society is an organism similar to a monkey or a pig—I've forgotten which now. It's just the right thing for people who like to consider themselves the brain of the organism. Nearly all politicians and most of the gangster ringleaders are adherents of this theory . If I'm the brain, why, then I can move the hands at will and I'd always be able to overcome the instinctive resistance of the muscles to my regal power—oh, yes! And here rests the dust of one who urged men to go back to the time when they walked on all fours and devoured worms. Those were the happiest days of existence, he insisted. To walk around on your two feet wearing a well-fitting frock coat and advise people to grow hairy again like their ancestors—isn't that what you'd call original? To read poetry, listen to music, go to museums, be transferred hundreds of miles in a day, and to teach people to go back to a primitive life in the forests and to crawl on all fours—not half bad, really! Now this one here tried to pacify people and justified the kind of life they led by claiming that criminals were not like other people, that they were men of sick will, a kind of peculiar antisocial type. He maintained that since they were natural enemies of the laws and morals of society, there was no reason to stand on ceremony with them, and he affirmed that death was the only cure for those addicted to crime. Bright idea that! Make one individual responsible for the crimes of all by recognizing him for a natural receptacle of vice and an organic bearer of evil—not foolish at all. You can always find someone who will try to justify the ugly, soul-distorting structure of life. The wise won't even blow their noses without a good reason. Ah, yes, the graveyards abound in ideas for a bettering of conditions of life in the towns. . . ."

The Devil took a look round him. A white church, like the finger of a giant skeleton, mutely rose from the copious field of the dead and pointed up at the dark sky, a still meadow of stars. A thick wall of stones above the fountains of wisdom, dressed in robes of mould, surrounded this chimney, which sent across the wastes of the universe the stinging smoke of the complaints and prayers of men. The wind, drugged with the oily smell of decay, softly swayed the branches of the trees, snipping off the dead leaves which noiselessly fell onto the dwellings of the makers of life. . . .

"Now we'll organize a small parade of the dead, a rehearsal for the Day of Judgment!" the Devil said as he marched ahead of me down a path that wound like a snake among the mounds and stones. "The Judgment Day will come, you know! It will come here, on earth, and it will be humanity's happiest day! It will come when men wil realize the immensity of the crimes committed by the teachers and lawmakers of life who tore the human being up into worthless pieces of senseless flesh and bone. All that now goes under the name of man is but a part of him. A wholehearted man has not yet been created. He will rise up from the ashes of experience lived through by the world, and, absorbing the world's experience like the sea absorbs the rays of the sun, he will flame out over the earth like another sun. I shall see it! I am creating this man, and he shall be!"

The old man was beginning to brag a little and to lapse into a lyrical mood which was rather unusual for a devil. I forgave him. What can be done? Life warps even the Devil, eating away with its poisonous acids his well-forged soul. Then again, all men have round heads, but their thoughts are angular, and everyone, when he looks in the mirror, sees a handsome face.

Pausing in his steps in the midst of some graves, the Devil bellowed in the voice of a monarch:

"Who among you is a wise and honest man?"

There was a moment of silence, then—suddenly—the ground rocked under my feet, and, it was as if drifts of dirty snow had covered the hills, as if thousands of lightnings had ploughed it through inside, or as if some giant monster had stirred convulsively within its depths. Everything about us flushed a dirty yellow; everywhere, like the blades of dry grass in the wind, the skeletons waved and shook, filling the surrounding quiet with the grating of bones and the dry rub of joints against one another and against the tombstones. Jostling each other, the skeletons crept out on the stones; skulls popped out everywhere like dandelions; a thick net of ribs surrounded me like a narrow cage; the skeletons' shins were tense and quivering under the weight of their gruesomely gaping hipbones; everything round us seethed, a mute ferment of activity. . . .

The cold laugh of the Devil drowned out all the impersonal sounds.

"Look. They've all crawled out, every last one of them," he said. "Even the town halfwits. The earth felt sick and it vomited, throwing up from its bowels the dead wisdom of men. . . ."

The soggy noise grew steadily—it was as if some invisible hand were greedily rummaging in a heap of wet litter, swept by the garbage man into a corner of the yard.

"Look at the number of wise and honest men that lived in the world!" the Devil exclaimed, spreading his wings wide above the thousands of broken fragments that pressed close to him on all sides.

"Which of you has done people the most good?" he asked in a loud voice.

There was a noise like mushrooms sizzling when they are fried in sour cream on a large pan.

"Let me through, please!" someone cried in a peevish voice.

"I'm your man, Boss, I'm your man! It was I who proved that the individual is a zero in the sum of society."

"I went even further than he," a voice called out pro-testingly from afar, "I taught that all of society is a sum of zeros, and that because of this the masses must do what the group wills."

"And the group is led by the individual—that is, by me!" someone roared in a pompous bass.

"Why you?" several voices rejoined in alarm.

"My uncle was a king!"

"Ah, then it was Your Majesty's uncle whose head was cut off so prematurely?"

"Kings always lose their heads when they should," the bones of a descendant of bones who had once sat on the throne proudly returned.

"Oho!" someone brought out in a delighted whisper. "There's a king among us! It isn't every graveyard that can boast of that. . . ."

Significant murmurs and the grating of bones were beginning to merge into a tangle of sound that steadily became heavier and more dense.

"Look here, is it true that the bones of royalty are blue in colour?" a stunted skeleton with a crooked spine breathlessly inquired.

"Let me tell you. . ." a skeleton who sat astride a monument impressively began.

"The best corn plaster is one invented by me!" some-one behind him cried.

"I am the architect. . . ."

But a short squat skeleton, pushing everyone away with the stumpy bones of his hands, shouted, his voice muffling the rustle of other dead voices:

"Brothers in Christ! Am not I your spiritual physi-cian? Did not I use the plaster of gentle solace to remove the callosities from your souls, that were caused by the misery in your lives?

"There are no sufferings!" someone declared in a nettled tone, "Everything exists in imagination only."

" . . . the architect who deviced low-structured doors. . . ."

"And I invented flypaper!"

" . . . so that people as they entered a house would inevitably bow their heads before its owner . . ." the irksome voice persisted.

"Does not priority belong to me, brethren? It was I who gave those who craved forgetfulness the sustenance of my meditations on the vanity of all things worldly!"

"All that is—shall be!" someone's rasping voice droned.

A one-legged skeleton, who sat on a grey stone, raised his leg, stretched it out, and yelled for some reason or other:

"No doubt of that!"

The graveyard turned into a market where everyone lauded his goods. A turbid river of stifled cries, a flood of foul bluster and crass vanity rushed into the dark and silent waste of night. It was as if a cloud of gnats were circling over a putrid swamp, and droning, wailing, buzzing, while it instilled the air with its noxious fumes, with all the poisonous vapours of the graves. Everyone was crowding about the Devil, their teeth clenched and their dark eye sockets fixed unmovingly on his face as though he were a dealer in old junk. Dead thoughts revived one after another, spinning in the air like the dreary leaves of fall.

The Devil watched this bubbling ferment with his green eyes, their cold stare flooding the heaps of bones with a shimmering phosphoric light.

121

The skeleton who sat at his feet raised his arm bones above his skull and, swinging them rhythmically in the air, said:

"Every woman should belong to one man. . . ."

Another sound stole into his whisper, and the words he said were strangely entangled with another's speech.

"Only the dead have a knowledge of truth! . . ."

More words came:

"The father, said I, is like a spider. . . ."

"Our life on the earth is a chaos of delusions, a mire of stark ignorance!"

"I was thrice married, and all three times lawfully. . . ."

"All his life he ceaselessly weaves the web of the family's welfare. . . ."

". . . and to one woman each time. . . ."

A skeleton, whose yellow, porous bones creaked shrilly, suddenly appeared. He raised his half-decayed face to the level of the Devil's eyes and said:

"I died of syphilis, yes! But still I had respect for the morals of society! When I found my wife to be untrue to me I myself brought her case up before a court of law and the justice of society and had her tried for her infamous conduct. . . ."

But he was pushed away, jostled on all sides by the bones of other skeletons, and a multitude of voices broke out again in a low howling drone like that of the wind in a chimney.

"I invented the electric chair! It takes away life quite painlessly. . . ."

"After death, I said to the people in solace, eternal bliss awaits you. . . ."

"The father gives the children life and food . . . a man is only complete when he becomes a father, till then he is but a member of a family. . . ."

A skeleton with a skull shaped like an egg and with shreds of flesh on his face called out above the heads of the others:

"I proved that art must be made to conform with the whole complex of the views and opinions, habits and needs of society. . . ."

Another skeleton, who sat astride a monument that was supposed to represent a broken tree, retorted:

"Freedom can only exist in the form of anarchy!"

"Art is a pleasant cure for a soul tired of life and of work. . . ."

"It was I who alleged that life is work," a voice called from afar.

"A book must be as pretty as the little pill-boxes you get in a pharmacy. . . ."

"All people must work and some of them must oversee the work. . . . All those whose virtues and merits make them deserving are entitled to the fruit of their labour. . . ."

"Art must be altruistic and harmonious. . . . When I get tired I want it to sing to me of leisure. . . ."

"And I prefer free art," the Devil said, "which serves no other deity but the goddess of beauty. I love it when, like a chaste youth, who dreams of immortal beauty and craves to delight in it, it tears the bright garments off the body of life . . . and life stands before it, an old libertine, her worn skin covered with wrinkles and sores. A mad wrath, a longing for beauty, a hatred for the stagnant mire of life—that is what I seek in art. . . . A good poet's friends are the Devil and the woman. . . ."

A loud moan of copper broke from the bell tower and drifted over the city of the dead, swaying liltingly and imperceptibly in the dark, like a large bird with transparent wings. . . . A sleepy watchman must have lazily pulled the bell rope with a lax, unsteady hand. The brazen sound melted in the air and died. But before its last thrill had faded, the bell of night, roused and alert, rang out sharp and clear. The sultry air vibrated softly, and through the gloomy drone of quivering copper there stole the rustle of bones, and the crackle of dry voices.

Again I heard the dull tirades of boring stupidity, the sticky words of dead vulgarity, the insolent voices of triumphant hypocrisy, the vexed grumble of self-conceit. All the thoughts that people live in in the towns came to life, but not one of which they could be proud. All the rusty chains that fetter the soul of life jangled and clanged, but the light that illumines the darkness of men's souls flared never once.

"Where are the heroes?" I asked of the Devil.

"They are modest, and their graves are forgotten. They were oppressed in life, and in the graveyard, too, the dead bones crush them!" he replied, waving his wings to dispel the oily smell of decay that closed in on us like a dark cloud in which the grey, dull voices of the dead dug like worms.

The shoemaker said that he was the first among the people of his profession who deserved the gratitude of his descendants since it was he who invented narrow-toed boots. A scientist who had described a thousand different varieties of spiders in his book averred that he was the greatest of all scientists. An inventor of artificial milk whimpered angrily, pushing back the man who had invented a rapid-fire gun and who stubbornly kept explaining to everyone around him the usefulness of his invention to the world. Thousands of thin, moist ropes tightened on the brain, driving into it like the fangs of a snake. And all the dead, no matter what their subject, spoke like severe moralists, like the gaolers of life who are enraptured by the work they are doing.

"Enough!" roared the Devil, "I'm tired of this. . . . I'm sick of everything I see in the graveyards of the dead and in the towns, the graveyards of the living. . . . You, there, guards of truth! Go to your graves! . . ."

His voice was the steel voice of a sovereign who was disgusted with the power that was his.

At this the ash-grey and yellow mass hissed, stirred, and foamed like the dust on the road when hit by a whirlwind. The earth opened thousands of its dark jaws, and, with a lazy, smacking sound, like that made by a sow that has had its fill, it swallowed once more the food it had thrown up and began to digest it anew. . . . All at once everything vanished, the stones veered and fell back into their places to stand there as firmly and unmovingly as ever. But an oppressive smell that clutched at the throat like a heavy, moist hand still lingered.

The Devil seated himself on one of the graves, and, resting his elbows on his knees, he squeezed his head with the long fingers of his black hands. His eyes were fixed immovably on the mass of stones and graves in the surrounding dark. . . . The stars shone brilliantly above him; up in the sky that had grown visibly lighter the bold chimes of the bell drifted quietly, rousing the night from its sleep.

"Did you see that?" the Devil said to me. "On the perilous, slimy, poisonous soil of mouldy stupidity, artless hypocrisy, and sticky vulgarity a dark, confining structure of the laws of life has been erected, a cage into which you were all driven by the dead like sheep. . . . Mental sluggishness and cowardice bind your prison cage like flexible bands. The true lords of your life are the dead; and even though you may be governed by living people they, too, are inspired by the dead. The graves are the sources of worldly wisdom. I say to you: your common sense is a flower that blooms on soil fed by the juices of dead bodies. The corpse soon rots away in the grave, yet he desires to live forever in the souls of the living. The fine, dry dust of dead ideas easily penetrates into the brain of the living; that is why your preachers of wisdom are always preachers of the death of the spirit!"

The Devil raised his hand, and his green eyes rested on my face like two cold stars.

"What is being propagated most actively here on earth? What is it men seek to establish as an immutable law? It is the fractioning of life; the lawfulness of different conditions of life for the people and the necessity for a oneness of their souls; a bricklike monotony of souls to make it convenient to lay them out in the geometrical figures desirable to the few who govern. This sermon hypocritically calls for the conciliation of the bitterness of the enslaved with the cruel duplicity of the enslavers; it was called forth by a base desire to make away with the free spirit of protest. It is nothing but an infamous plan to build a vault of the stones of falsehood for man's free spirit. . . ."

Dawn set in. The stars faded quietly in the sky, pale in expectation of the sun. But the eyes of the Devil burned brighter as he went on speaking.

"What should men be taught so they will learn to make their lives whole and beautiful?—A oneness of conditions for all and a differentiation of souls. Then life will become a bush of flowers, the roots of which will draw strength from the respect of all for the freedom of each man. It will be a fire fed by the glowing coals of mutual friendship and the common strife to rise higher. . . . Only ideas will fight then, men will stay comrades always. Do you think it's impossible?—I say it will be because it has not yet been!"

"Day is dawning!" the Devil went on, looking east. "But will the sun bring joy when night sleeps in man's very heart? The people have no time to enjoy the sun, most of them want only bread—some of them are busy giving out as little as possible of it; others move through the bustle of life in a lonely search for freedom, but it eludes them in their ceaseless struggle for bread. Miserable, despairing, embittered by their loneliness, they attempt to conciliate the irreconcilable. Thus do the best of men drown in the slime of vulgar lies—first, innocently, without noticing their faithlessness to themselves; then consciously, with a deliberate betrayal of their earlier beliefs and ideas. . . ."

He rose and spread his powerful wings.

"I think I'll go, too, along the road of my expectations towards a future of splendid possibilities. . . ."

And, followed by the dreary chiming of the bell—a dying clang of copper, he flew west. . . .

* * *

I told this dream to an American who seemed more like a human being than the rest. He became pensive for a moment, and then exclaimed with a smile:

"I get it! The Devil was an agent of a firm that deals in incinerators! Of course! All that he said was meant to show the need to cremate the dead. . . . But he was a very competent agent, let me tell you! He was so eager to accommodate his firm that he even appeared in people's dreams. . . ."

LA BELLE FRANCE

... I WALKED the streets of Paris a long time before I found her. No one I asked could tell me exactly where she lived.

One old man—he was probably joking, but for some reason he sighed as he said with a shrug of the shoulders:

"Who knows? There was a time when she lived all over Europe."

"In the street of the bankers!" a workingman said gruffly.

"Turn to the right!" others said.

It was noisy all around, and rather uncomfortable. There were guns and soldiers on all the squares, and workers in all the streets. As was now the custom in all countries, the soldiers kept firing their rifles along the streets, cavalry charged down upon people with drawn sabres, and workers hurled stones at the soldiers. The stifling air of the hoary city quivered nervously to the sound of angry abuse, and re-echoed to peremptory words of command. Here and there, the streets were stained with blood; men with battered skulls, clenching their fists in impotent rage, staggered homeward, and those who were unable to walk dropped in the roadway, and the police mercifully dragged them away from under the feet of horses and soldiers. Onlookers stood on the pavement, exchanging observations on the details of a scene that had become an habitual sight in the Christian city. . . .

At last, someone said:

"France? On the right, near the Bridge of Alexander III."

The police station in which she lived was a fairly ancient building which offered nothing to the eye in the way either of luxuriance or beauty. Near the door through which I entered stood two soldiers clad in pants made of the Red Flag of Liberty. There were the remains of an inscription over the entrance, of which one could only make out: "Lib . . . Equ . . . Fra . . . ty." This brought to mind the gang of bankers who had disgraced the land of Béranger and George Sand. The atmosphere was laden with the stench of mould, decay and corruption.

My heart beat violently. Like all revolutionaries, I too in my youth had loved this woman, who herself knew how to love sincerely and generously, and to make revolutions beautifully. . . .

Smiling politely, an individual dressed all in black and whose manners suggested a pimp of the expensive kind turned marquis, conducted me to a small dark cell, where I had the opportunity to admire the elegance of the *style moderne* of present-day France.

The walls were papered with diverse-coloured Russian loan bonds, and the floor was covered with the skins of colonial natives on which the words, "Declaration of the Rights of Man," were artistically chased. The furniture, made of the bones of men who had died on the barricades of Paris fighting for the liberty of France, was upholstered with a dark material on which was embroidered the treaty of alliance with the Russian Tsar. On the walls hung the coats of arms of European states, traced in iron incrusted in living human flesh: the mailed fist of Germany, the noose and knout of Russia, the beggar's pouch of Italy, and the arms of Spain—the black cassock of a Catholic priest and his two bony hands greedily clutching the neck of a Spaniard. There was also the emblem of France—the portly stomach of a bourgeois, with a masticated Phrygian cap inside it. . . .

The painting on the ceiling represented the open mouth of the German Kaiser, with his sixty-four teeth and formidable moustaches. . . . The windows were heavily draped. It was dark, as the drawing rooms always are of ladies of the Balzac period of life who have still not given up the hope of captivating men. A stifling mingled odour of false delicacy and spiritual corruption made one's head swim and impeded one's breathing.

She entered and through her drooping eyelashes swiftly scrutinized me with the glance of a connoisseur of men.

"You speak French?" she inquired, responding to my bow with the gesture of an actress who had long ceased to play queenly roles.

"No, madam, I speak only the truth," I replied.

"Who needs that?" she said, shrugging her shoulders. "Who listens to that? No one likes the truth—even in pretty verses. . . ."

She went up to the window, peeped through the curtains and immediately came away.

"So they are still at it, out there in the streets?" she said petulantly. "What children! What do they want? I simply can't understand. They have a republic and a Cabinet of Ministers such as you won't find anywhere else.

One of the Ministers was even a Socialist—isn't that enough to make a people happy?"

She capriciously tossed her head, and added:

"Isn't that so? However, you have come to talk. . . ."

She came over, sat down by my side, and, glancing into my eyes with a false caress, asked:

"What shall we talk about? Love? Poetry? Oh, my Alfred de Musset! . . . And my Leconte de Lisle! . . . Rostand! . . ." Her eyes rolled up to her brows, but encountering the teeth of the German over her head, she at once lowered them.

I did not hinder her as she prattled on about poets, and silently waited for the moment when she would begin talking about the bankers. I looked at this woman, whose image every gallant knight in the world had once worn in his heart. Her face was the unhealthy face of a woman who had loved much; its vivid hues had faded, worn away by thousands of kisses. The skilfully made-up eyes flitted restlessly from object to object, the lashes drooped wearily, covering the swollen lids. The wrinkles on her temples and neck were mute witnesses of stormy passions of the heart, and the puffy gorge and chin—of its fatty degeneration. She had grown flabby and stout, and it was clear that to this woman the poetry of the stomach was dearer than the lofty poetry of the soul, that the crude call of the bowels spoke louder to her than the voice of truth and liberty, which had once reverberated from her lips through the whole world. Of her former grace and suppleness there remained only the habitual jauntiness of a market-wife, a huckstress in the world market. And the charm of a great heroine battling for the happiness of mankind had given way to the loathsome coquetry of an old dame, the heroine of countless amorous adventures.

She was dressed in a heavy dark frock, adorned with lace which reminded me of the verdigris on the Statue of Liberty in New York and of tatters of sympathies torn to shreds by betrayal of the Spirit of Truth.

Her voice sounded tired, and it seemed to me she was talking only in order to forget something important, something honest, which at times still pricked with the sharp needle of memory her cold and dilapidated heart, in which there was no longer any room for disinterested feelings.

I looked at her in silence, suppressing with difficulty the shriek of poignant anguish which rose in my throat at the sight of this pitiful death agony of the spirit.

"Can this be France?" I asked myself. "Can this be the heroine of the world whom my imagination had always pictured clad in the flame of glittering thoughts, of the great ideas of equality, fraternity and liberty?"

"You are not a cheerful companion," she said, and smiled wearily.

"Madam," I replied, "no honest Russian today feels cheerful as a guest of France."

"But why?" she asked with a feigned smile and lifting her lashes in surprise. "In my Paris, everybody is cheerful . . . everybody and always!"

"I observed that just now in the streets . . . that is the sort of cheerfulness you see in my country, Russia. The bloody game of soldiers and people is the favourite sport of the Tsar of Russia—your friend. . . ."

"What a gloomy person you are!" she exclaimed with a grimace. "When the people demand that a king give them all he has, he should not give them even what he can. . . . That is what kings have always held—why should they think differently now? You should look at life more simply. You are not an old man—why, then, this dejection? When a man is capable of loving, life is splendid. Of course, Nicholas II is—how shall I put it?—he very easily succumbs to the influence of evil men, but, really, you know, he is not a bad sort. . . . After all, he has given you liberty, hasn't he? . . ."

"We took it from him at the cost of thousands of lives. . . . And even now that it has been wrenched from his hands, he keeps demanding more and more blood in payment. He wants to take back the favour which he granted only under pressure. . . . And you, you have now given him money to enable him to take it back. . . ."

"Oh, no!" she objected. "He will not take it back, believe me! . . . He, why, he's a gentleman and a man of his word. I know that. . . ."

"You realize that you have given money for murder?" I asked.

She drew her head back into the shadow, so that her face could not be seen. Then she said quietly:

"I could not help giving it. He, Nicholas, is the only one that can help me when that mouth there decides to bite off my head."

She pointed with a smile to the ceiling, where the teeth of the German glistened decoratively.

"To tell the truth, that voracious maw rather perverts me. But what's to be done. And, after all, perversion is not altogether repellant. . . ."

"Does it not repel you to lean on an arm that is always steeped to the shoulder in the blood of the people?"

"But if there is no other arm? It's difficult, you know, to find the arm of a king that is not stained in the blood of the people. They are like that today—what will they be like tomorrow? I am a woman, I need a friend. A republic and an Asiatic despot walking hand-in-hand in friendship is not a pretty sight, of course—although it is rather original, don't you think? But you don't understand politics, like all poets . . . and revolutionaries. . . . In politics, there is no room for beauty. . . . Only for the stomach, and the mind, which obediently works for the stomach. . . ."

"And doesn't it appear to you that with the gold you gave that tsar you gave away the fair glory of France?"

She stared at me with wide-open eyes, smiled and licked her painted lips with the tip of her sharp tongue.

"You are just a poet! That's an old song, my friend! We live in stern times, when one may write verses, certainly, but when to be a poet in everything is, to say the least of it, unpractical!"

And she smiled superciliously.

"My Shylocks have done a good piece of business, it seems to me. They have stripped your tsar of an interest worth one-third of his skin!"

"But to pay that interest the tsar will have to strip the whole skin off the people."

"Of course—that is, probably. But how else?" she asked with a shrug. "Government makes politics, the people pay for it with their labour and their blood—so it has always been. What is more, I am a republic and I can't prevent my bankers from doing what they like. Only Socialists are incapable of understanding that this is normal. And it's all so simple. Why vex yourself by revolting against common sense? My Shylocks have given a lot, and will have to give more in order to get at least something back. . . . Actually, they are in a dangerous position . . . if it should not be the tsar that wins, but. . . ."

She feared to mention the word that had made her glory. . . .

"They may find themselves beggars. . . . And even if he wins . . . I don't think they will get their interest so soon. . . . And they are my children, are they not? Rich men are the firmest stones in the edifice of state. . . . They are its foundation. Poets are an adornment, little decorations on the façade . . . and one can get along without them. . . . They add nothing to the strength of the structure. . . . The people are only the ground on which the house stands, revolutionaries are simply mad-men . . . and, to continue the simile, one may say that the army is a pack of hounds which protect the property and tranquillity of the tenants of the house. . . ."

"And in it live the Shylocks?"

"They and all others who find the premises comfortable. But let us leave that! When politics are not profitable, they are tedious."

I rose and silently bowed.

"Are you leaving?" she asked, indifferently.

"This is no place for me!" I said and quit the procuress of tsar and bankers.

I had not seen her whom I had come to see, I had seen only a cowardly cynical cocotte, who gives herself to thieves and hangmen for money, insincerely and coldblood-edly.

I walked the streets of Paris, the great city which that day hired soldiers—the hounds of that greedy old hag—

were holding captive with their bayonets and guns. I saw Frenchmen peering from behind street corners, faithful watchdogs of truth and liberty, silently measuring the strength of their enemy, ready to wipe the shameful stain from the face of the republic with their blood. . . . I felt that in their hearts the spirit of old France was being reborn, was growing and gaining strength, the spirit of the great mother of Voltaire and Hugo, the spirit of the France that sowed the flowers of liberty wherever reached the cries of her children—her poets and warriors.

I walked the streets of Paris and my heart sang a hymn to the France with whom I had talked in the dark cell.

Who in the dawn of his days has not loved thee with all his heart?

In the years of youth, when the soul of man kneels in worship before the Goddesses of Beauty and Liberty, the heart saw their bright shrine in none but thee, O great France!

France! To all honest and courageous men that dear word sounded like the precious name of a passionately beloved bride. How numerous were the great days in thy past! Thy battles were bright festivals for the peoples, and from thy sufferings they drew supreme lessons.

What beauty and strength there was in thy search for justice, how freely didst thou shed thy honest blood battling for the triumph of liberty! Can it be that thy blood has withered forever?

France! Thou wast the belfry of the world, from whose summit three strokes of the bell of justice once resounded through the earth, three cries that awakened the peoples from their secular slumber—Liberty, Equality, Fraternity!

Thy son, Voltaire, a man with the face of a devil, all his life fought banality like a titan. Potent was the venom of his sapient derision! Even the priests, who devoured thousands of books without damage to their stomachs, were killed by the poison of one page of Voltaire; even kings, the protectors of lies, he compelled to respect the truth. Great was the strength and audacity of his slaps at the face of falsehood. France, thou shouldst regret that he is now no more—he would have smacked thee soundly! Do not be offended. The smack of a son as great as he would be an honour to a mother as venal as thou. . . .

Thy son, Hugo, was one of the finest gems in the crown of thy glory. Tribune and poet, he sent his thunders through the world like a hurricane, stirring to life all that is splendid in the soul of man. Everywhere his books called forth heroes, called them forth no less than thou, France, in all the time thou didst march in the forefront of the peoples with the standard of Liberty in thy hand, a gay smile on thy lovely face, and hope in the triumph of truth and goodness in thy honest eyes. He taught all men to love life, beauty, truth, and France. Well it is for thee that he is dead now—alive, he would not have forgiven the villainy even of France, whom he loved like a youth even when his hair had grown white with years.

Flaubert, that high-priest of beauty, that nineteenth-century Hellene, who taught writers of all countries to respect the power of the pen and to comprehend its beauty, that magician of words, who was as objective as the sun which casts an equally vivid light on the mud of the streets and on a piece of precious lace—even Flaubert, for whom truth lay in beauty and beauty in truth, would not have forgiven thee thy greed and would have turned from thee in contempt!

All thy finest children are against thee. They lower their honest eyes in shame of thee, so that they may not see thy obese face, thou mistress of bankers. Thou hast become a loathsome huckstress. They who learned from thee to die for honour and liberty, will understand thee no more and will turn from thee with pain in their hearts.

France! Lust for gold has disgraced thee, intercourse with bankers has perverted thy honest soul, quenched its fire with filth and banality.

And thou, mother of Liberty, thou, Joan of Arc, hast given strength to brute beasts that they may seek again to crush the people.

Great France, who wast once the cultural leader of the world, dost thou realize the utter abomination of thy deeds?

Thy venal hand has for a time barred the road of liberty and culture to a whole nation And even if that time be only one day, thy crime will be none the less. But not for one day hast thou impeded the march towards liberty. By virtue of thy gold the blood of the Russian people will flow again.

May that blood stain the decrepit cheeks of thy false face with the crimson blush of eternal shame!

My beloved!

I too spit a gout of blood and gall in thy eyes!

New York,
May 1906

PUBLIC WRITINGS

OPEN LETTER TO MESSIEURS J. RICHARD, JULES CLARETIE, RENÉ VIVIANI AND OTHER FRENCH JOURNALISTS

DEAR SIRS,

I have acquainted myself with the fountains of eloquence that gushed from your inkwells, prompted by my article on the loan granted by the government and financiers of France to Nicholas Romanov for the institution in Russia of bloody reprisals, courts-martial and every imaginable atrocity. I have acquainted myself with the objections you level at me and—I don't congratulate you!

Alliance with the so-called Russian government is doing you good: you have begun to treat logic, the truth and the noble French language in exactly the way Cossacks treat women. One reason, you see, why tyranny is so atrocious is that it perverts even the unconcerned and indifferent onlooker, which is what has happened to you.

I never reply to personal attacks, and the ruder they are, the sooner they are forgotten. But, sirs, you accuse me of ingratitude—and that I cannot let pass.

You say: "we came out in Gorky's defence when he was in prison, yet he. . . ."

I take the liberty of giving you a piece of good advice: if, whether from inadvertence or for some other reason, you once allowed free play to your humane sentiments, don't brag about it! It isn't nice. . . .

"I was good to you, you should repay me with gratitude"—that is what is to be gathered from your words. But I don't feel grateful, and I consider your kindness a misunderstanding.

I am not the martyr or sufferer you would so zealously make me out to be. I am just a man who confidently does his small job and finds complete satisfaction in his work, and if for this I have sometimes been put in jail for brief periods—well, I just rested there from natural fatigue, without experiencing any particular discomfort, let alone suffering.

From the standpoint of common sense, you, sirs, ought to wish that I be put in prison more often and for longer periods, and when you protest against it, I find your conduct—forgive me!—just funny.

For we are enemies, and implacable enemies, I am certain. An honest writer is always an enemy of society, and even more an enemy of those who defend and justify greed and envy, those basic pillars of the modern social organization.

You also say: "We love Gorky, yet he. . . ."

Sirs, let me tell you quite sincerely: to me, a Socialist, the love of a bourgeois is profoundly offensive!

I trust that these lines will define our mutual relations accurately and for all time.

M. Gorky

FROM THE "FOREIGN CHRONICLE"

Not only China, the whole of Asia is beginning to become aware of the "White peril." Look how swiftly the movement of the Indians for national liberation and against Britain's harsh tutelage is spreading.

Anglo-Indian relations are very clearly portrayed in the journal, *Indian Sociologist,* published in Paris by the nationalist Krishnavarma, a man whom the Indians are fond of comparing with Mazzini, and for whom they presage the future of Garibaldi. A recent issue of the journal reproduces a speech by Lord Hardinge, Viceroy of India.

"I believe," Hardinge said, "that the Indian people are law-abiding at heart. In the nine days Their Majesties spent in our midst the enthusiasm mounted from day to day and reached a magnificent and splendid climax. I have been in many capitals, but never have I witnessed such delight as was manifested in Calcutta. I feel that the royal visit has infused a new spirit of hope and faith in the people of Calcutta and of all Bengal, and that it will bear rich fruit. It has already dispelled the cloud of suspicion that has darkened the horizon in these past years."

But following on this optimistic speech, Krishnavarma prints a message from his correspondent in Calcutta, where the speech was made:

"The greatest precautions were taken during the Viceroy's visit to Dacca last week. (Dacca is 150 miles north-east of Calcutta.) For two hours before the Viceroy passed through no one was allowed to leave his home without a printed permit."

A "spirit of faith" that has to be fortified by police measures is a bad spirit—that's known even in Russia!

"Britain!" exclaims Krishnavarma, "for more than two hundred years you have been playing the role of ancient Rome, devouring people. Rest assured that the fate of ancient Rome awaits you."

More and more frequently are voices being raised in India emphatically propagating the idea that the time has come when the Indians must take the work of social and political construction into their own hands, and that the British regime on the banks of the Ganges has outlived its day.

The character of this regime is indicated by the persecution instituted by the Government of India against the nationalist Savarkar. As we know, he was tried in secret, news of the trial was not allowed to be published, and he was sentenced to 48 years' imprisonment—until 1960; he is allowed to write to his wife only once a year.

All these extravagances are so discreditable to the traditional idea of British liberty and the British spirit of tolerance that one is involuntarily reminded of a Russian "case"—the story of N. G. Chernyshevsky.*

At the time of the coronation of King George, Maharajah Gaekwar of Baroda conducted himself rather independently. This was enough for the British Conserv-

* N. G. Chernyshevsky, the great Russian savant, writer, critic and revolutionary democrat, was accused by the tsarist government of composing revolutionary proclamations summoning the peasants to revolt. He spent more than twenty years in prison and as a convict in exile.

ative press to accuse him of particularism, demagogy and similar horrors.

The influential *Daily Express* wrote that the Government of India had long suspected the State of Baroda of being an asylum for rebels and seditious elements, and that Gaekwar himself during his unofficial visits to Europe had often had close contacts with the revolutionary Krishnavarma. The *Daily Telegraph* went even further and demanded Gaekwar's deposal. The scared maharajah was forced to cable the *Times* that he had not met Krishnavarma since the time the latter had left England in 1907.

Such are the "political" relations between the Indians and the British. The visit of the venerable Socialist, Kier Hardie, only added oil to the flames by exposing the terrible condition of the Indians and the tyranny of British rule. It goes without saying that, apart from the Socialists, there are quite a number of people in England who think India must be granted autonomy. Their voices are growing ever louder and more insistent, and there is a hope that the Government of India is intelligent enough to cede when it sees that it is essential in the interests of the state.

But in the meantime, while the Indians are organizing for the struggle for liberty, they are being exterminated in ever increasing numbers by the conditions created by British capitalism. Since in the silk and carpet mills and on the tobacco plantations of India it is mainly females that are employed, they are being killed off by capitalism in vast numbers and literally in the "flower of life." This process is brought out with startling clarity by the census of the Indian population just completed by the government.

It is statistically established that in childhood and old age the number of females is almost normal, i.e., almost equal to that of males, but in the middle-age categories it falls very low. Of the 43,000,000 persons below the age of five in Eastern India, girls outnumber boys by 690,000, but there are 18,500,000 boys and only 15,200,000 girls between the ages of 10 and 12!

In the Punjab, one of the biggest of the provinces, on March 10, 1910—the day the census was taken—there were 13,314,917 males and only 10,872,765 females. From this it follows that every fifth male must remain unmarried. This is truly the destruction of a people!

Mr. Gait, chairman of the statistical commission, arrives at the conclusion that the sex ratio at birth does not differ very much from that in Europe, but subsequent conditions are highly unfavourable for females who live by physical labour, and this constitutes a grave social danger to the country.

A similar phenomenon is to be observed in America, also called forth by capitalism: in Maine, Indiana, Ohio and other states, the reservation Indians, i.e., those tied to definite territories, are rapidly dying out, and betray no tendency to absorb American culture; the non-reservation Indians, forced to migrate to the stern north—to Saskatchewan, Prince of Wales Island and Alaska—are similarly dying out.

But the United States government has long ago given up the problem, having lost all hope of "introducing the savages to the blessings of culture." It is now preoccupied with the "colour problem."

In 1850, of a total of 23,000,000 citizens in the United States, about 4,000,000 were Negroes; in 1910, when

the population was 92,000,000, only 10,000,000 were Negroes. It should be borne in mind that in these sixty years
more than ten million Negroes were brought to America
or came there voluntarily after the war between North and
South. Dr. Stelzle, who has made a study of the "colour
problem," writes that only the Negro was brought to
America against his will; for 250 years coloured people
were systematically imported into America, the most
physically fit being selected for the purpose.

Now these "most physically fit" are being killed off
by tuberculosis, caused by outrageous and inhuman conditions of labour and overwork—and, in addition, by the
contempt of the "whites." The "Negroes," Stelzle says,
"are forced to live in the worst sections of our big cities,
often without drainage, plumbing or the most rudimentary
sanitary conditions, without which I, a white, would refuse to live. We ourselves introduce into the Negro sections the most disgusting forms of vice, physical perversion and moral turpitude. We cynically declare that the
Negro is good for nothing, forgetting that in the primary
schools some fifty per cent of the teachers are Negroes."

"Enough of racial and national intolerance!" exclaims
this American, overcome by shame.

Yes, it is high time to cry, "Enough!"—both to the
"yellows" and the "blacks" the white peril is becoming
too obvious. They see only the reverse side of the culture
we have paid so much for, while its profound inner meaning
is concealed from them. They have a legitimate right not
only to doubt the creative power of culture, whose purpose
is supposed to be to unite mankind, but also to reject it
as being an oppressive burden on them.

(1912)

"THE STATES OF WESTERN EUROPE BEFORE THE WAR"

(Typical Program for Pamphlets)

THE basic idea of these pamphlets is dictated by the logic of history in the following form: . . . The conditions which made the catastrophe (war) unavoidable and inevitable were produced by modern international capitalism—both types: industrial and financial. The basic and concealed purpose of war is to seize and divide up the continents of Asia and Africa. This urge is prompted by the greed of finance capital, which, developing out of industrial capital, compels it to produce the dearest and most profitable articles needed for the technique of war:— explosives, shells, weapons, etc.—as well as engineering and railroad equipment for the boundless expanses of Asia and Africa. Colonial policy envisages not so much new markets, as the necessity for creating them. . . . Capitalism should be indicted as the exciting cause of the present world catastrophe, and it should be pointed out that the anarchic activity of capital cannot but contain within it the germs of similar catastrophes.

FAT MEN'S MUSIC

NIGHT. Yet night is hardly the word for this marvelous sky of Southern Italy, for this air, transfused with a bluish luminence and the fragrant warmth of a kindly soil. The light seems to emanate, not from the sun reflected by the gold of the moon, but from this indefatigably fertile soil, industriously and skilfully tilled by the hand of man. Light streams silently from the silver-chased leaves of the olive trees, and from the stone walls on the hill slopes. These walls are there to prevent landslides; they shape the hillsides into flat terraces, on which grain, beans, potatoes and cabbages are grown, and vineyards and orange and lemon groves have been laid out. How much persistent and intelligent labour has been expended here! The orange and yellow fruits also gleam through the transparent silvery haze, lending the earth a strange resemblance to the star-blossomed sky. One might think that the earth had been lovingly decorated by its cultivators for a great holiday, that, having spent this night in rest, they will tomorrow rise with the sun to "rejoice and be glad."

The silence is absolute. So motionless is everything on earth, that it seems to have been engraven on it by the hand of a superb artist, or cast in bronze and bluish silver. The perfection of calm and beauty sets one jubilantly thinking of the inexhaustible power of labour, the creator of all the marvels of our world; it inspires one with confidence that in time this invincible power will compel the soil of the Far North, too, to work for man twelve months in the year, will tame it, as animals are tamed. One thinks joyfully and—"permit me the word," as the French say—prayerfully of man, the great wonder-worker, of the splendid future he is preparing for his children.

In one's memory rise the figures and faces of men of science: . . . one recalls what D. N. Pryanishnikov said of the potassium deposits in the upper reaches of the Kama; before one's eyes rise those whom one has oneself seen: that great man, I. P. Pavlov; Rutherford in his laboratory in Montreal, in 1906; one after another rise scores of Russian science-makers, and one recalls their books. And there unfolds a picture of the amazing fertility, the ever-increasing activity of the scientific workers of the world. We are living in an era when the gap between the wildest fantasies and absolutely practical realities is diminishing with incredible speed.

* * *

Not so long ago one of our regional natural historians, Comrade Andrei Bakharev, of Kozlov, reminded me in a letter of two miracle workers—Luther Burbank, the American self-taught horticulturist, and our genius, Ivan Vladimirovich Michurin. I will take the liberty of publishing a part of Comrade Bakharev's letter, and hope he will not be annoyed with me for doing so.

"Luther Burbank, as we know, discovered a number of secrets of interspecific hybridization of fruit plants, thanks to which he produced varieties of plants which, for their fecundity, adaptability, flavour, and immunity to pest and disease, are not only amazing but simply prodigious, thereby enriching the whole continent of North America. One need only recall his edible 'cactuses' which have lost their prickles, and the nuts whose stony shell Burbank has transformed into an envelope as thin as a leaf, to get an idea of the calibre of this horticultural giant.

"Here, in the U.S.S.R., near the town of Kozlov, Tambov Province, where the soil is ancient alluvium and overgrown with wild willow, poplar and maple, you will find the tiny but even more amazing nursery of Ivan Vladimirovich Michurin, hybridizer and plant originator.

"Luther Burbank produced for the benificent climate of subtropical California; Michurin for the stern climate of the central belt of Russia.

"Luther Burbank created many varieties of fruit plants whose products go to satisfy the demand of the rich. Michurin has created over one hundred varieties of fruits, among them pears that do not ripen until Christmastide (in boxes, in cellars) and that keep under the most primitive conditions until April.

"In Michurin's orchard in the stern Tambov Province, apricot, grape (four varieties), almond, walnut, mulberry, Damask rose, quince, rice, hemp, etc., etc., grow and bear profusely. And all this for the benefit of the working folk, for our rural population, for the peasant horticulturist, whose experience is small and whose knowledge limited.

"Luther Burbank tenderly nursed his fosterlings, Michurin trained his in spartan conditions, in order that his varieties might be thrown into any enviroment and yet produce the needed economic effect.

"Luther Burbank was a poor man when he began his work, but from the time he became an innovator he enjoyed all the bounties of American culture. Michurin—bear in mind the deplorable conditions of old Russia—lived in poverty bordering on penury. Yet, in his long life, full of struggle and disquietude, failures and disappointments, defeats and victories, Michurin has created that which may enrich not only the central belt of Russia, but the temperate zone of the whole world. In other words, Michurin is transplanting the South to the North.

"Luther Burbank and Ivan Vladimirovich Michurin are the opposite poles of horticulture, but they have much in common.

"Both began their work in early youth, both were poor, both were great thinkers, artists and inventors. Both have made magnificent discoveries in the realm of plant breeding.

"To Michurin, in particular, belongs the preeminent discovery of methods of horticulture, with the help of which it is very probable that in the near future man will be able to create not only new varieties, but even new species of fruit plants which will more fully answer to his life requirements, and which will be better adapted to the unavoidable vagaries of climate.

"Michurin is an honorary member of the Naturalists' Association of the Scientific Board of the People's Commissariat of Education, etc., etc.

"Michurin is now an old man. He is 72, but he is still creating, he still continues to tear veil after veil from the secrets of the plant world."

* * *

The silence of this night, which helps the mind to rest from the manifold, albeit petty vexations of the working day, seems to whisper to the heart the solemn music of the universal toil of humans, great amd small, the splendid song of the new era in history, the song which has been so boldly begun by the labouring folk of my country.

But, suddenly, in the brooding silence of the night, some idiotic hammer begins to beat starkly. One, two, three, ten, twenty strokes—and then there descends, like a lump of mud falling into crystal, translucent water, a savage howling, whistling, roaring, rattling, shrieking and grinding; inhuman voices rend the air, resembling the neighing of horses; one's ear is assaulted by the grunting of brass pigs, the blare of asses, the amorous quacking of gigantic frogs. All this insulting and insane cacophony is subordinated to a scarcely perceptible rhythm and, listening to this pandemonium for a minute or two, one involuntarily begins to imagine that it is the performance of an orchestra of lunatics, driven mad by sex, and conducted by a human stallion wielding an enormous phallus.

This is radio—one of the greatest discoveries of science, one of the secrets it has wrenched from ostensibly mute nature. The radio in the neighbouring hotel is entertaining the world of the fat men, the world of the marauders, conveying to them over the air a new foxtrot performed by a Negro orchestra. This is music for the fat men. In all the luxuriant cabarets of the "cultured" countries, fat men and women are lewdly wriggling their thighs to its rhythm, wallowing in obscenity, simulating the procreative act.

From time immemorial, the great poets of all nations and all eras devoted their creative powers to the inspired task of ennobling this act, of adorning it in keeping with man's dignity, so that he might not degrade himself to the level of the goat, the ox and the boar. Hundreds and thousands of magnificent poems have been written in praise of love. Love has been a stimulus to the creative powers of men and women. Love has made man a being immeasurably more social than the most intelligent of animals. The poesy of active, healthy, mundane romanticism in the relation of the sexes has been a factor of immense value in social education.

"Hunger and love make the world go round," Schiller said. Love is the basis of culture, hunger is the basis of civilization.

But along comes the obese marauder, the parasite who lives on the labour of others, the semihuman whose motto is, "After me, the deluge," and tramples with his fat feet on all that has been spun from the finest nerve tissue of the great poets, the enlighteners of labouring humanity.

He, the fat man, doesn't need woman as a friend and companion; to him she is a mere pastime, provided she is not a marauder like himself. Nor does he need woman as a mother, because to him, although he loves power, children are a nuisance. Ay, and even power he needs only, as it were, for foxtrots. And foxtrots have become indispensable to him, for your fat man is a poor male. For him, love is a dissipation; it is increasingly becoming a perversion of the imagination rather than the passionate urge of the licentious flesh it once was. In the world of the fat men, homosexual love is spreading epidemically. The "evolution" of the fat men is degeneration.

It is an evolution from the beauty of the minuet and the animated passion of the waltz to the lewdness of the foxtrot and the convulsions of the Charleston, from

Mozart and Beethoven to the jazz music of the Negroes, who no doubt laugh up their sleeves as they see their masters, the whites, evolving to that savage state from which the American Negroes have risen and which they are leaving farther and farther behind.

Culture is perishing!—howl the advocates of the power of the fat men over the labouring world. The proletariat is threatening to destroy culture!—they shriek. But they lie, because they cannot help seeing that it is the world-wide herd of fat men that are trampling upon culture, and they cannot help realizing that the proletariat is the only power capable of saving culture and of deepening and widening it.

An inhuman bass voice roars English words, one is deafened by a prodigious horn that is reminiscent of the shriek of a maltreated camel, a drum thunders, a pestilential pipe squeals, and one's ears are rent by the croaking and snuffling of a saxophone. Fat thighs sway, and thousands and tens of thousands of fat feet shuffle and stamp.

At last, the music of the fat men terminates in a deafening crescendo, in a thunderous clatter, as if a case of hardware had tumbled from the sky. And again the blessed silence, and one's thoughts return to home, from where Vasili Kucheryavenko, a rural correspondent, writes:

"In our hamlet of Rossoshinsk, with its three hundred households, there was formerly only one school; now there are three. We have a cooperative store, three clubrooms, a clubhouse, reading room and library, Party and Young Communist organizations, a Young Pioneer group, agricultural and rural correspondents' courses, a wall newspaper. Our villagers order books and subscribe to many newspapers and magazines. In the evening the clubhouse is always full, there you may see hoary greybeards and red-scarved Pioneers. The peasants readily subscribe to the government loan, even young schoolchildren. We had an old lady, 72 years old, who has just died. She used to say: 'I would join the Young Communists, but, alas, I am too old. Why did it all begin so late!' Before she died she gave orders to be buried in the soviet way, with banners. This grandma used to walk regularly several versts to the club and reading room and to meetings of the rural soviet. She was like a young girl. *Asia*, the American magazine, recently told of all this in an article about our village, illustrated by photographs."

This funny old grandma is remarkably significant. Of course, one old peasant woman doesn't make culture, but I know so many instances of such—how shall I say it?—amusing "rejuvenations" of village ancients, and they all point to one thing: the Russian people are growing younger. It is really wonderful to be living and working in our times.

(1928)

PROTEST AGAINST THE TRIAL
OF JOHANNES BECHER

TALENTED people are very scarce these days. Twentieth-century Europe produces them niggardly. And Johannes Becher is above all a talented man. I cannot judge the beauty and strength of his poetry, but I am sure it is not inferior to his prose. His *Levisite* (*The Only Just War*) is a fine book, the creation of a poet inspired by love and hatred.

Johannes Becher is facing punishment because he loves passionately and hates passionately.

He will be tried by worshippers of Christ, who was killed because he loved and hated.

In my opinion, Christian sirs—and I am an atheist, of course—there is a slight contradiction here. But, then, contradictions are so habitual with you that you probably pay no particular attention to them. When trying Becher you will be governed by a spirit of personal vengeance towards a man who had the audacity honestly, fearlessly and talentedly to tell you the truth.

I know the European bourgeoisie is not the least put out by its crimes. Can anything deter it after it has sacrificed millions of lives on the fields of France?

In his *Levisite*, Becher describes with overwhelming power how the finest elements of the working class are burned alive in clouds of poison gas, solely in order that war profiteers like Raffke and other monsters might burden the earth. The effect of four years of a most atrocious war is that some of the victors are bled white for years to come, while the vanquished have been robbed of their last shred. The only winner was the Third Party, and it is growing ever more stupid from pride, because it believes it is cleverer and stronger than anyone else. Overtly or covertly, all are working for a new holocaust, which promises to be even more senseless and idiotic than the last.

"War is a necessary factor in the development of culture, it is the supreme power and manifestation of the virility of our cultured nations," one of the "heroes" of *Levisite*, Bratz, remarks with consummate cynicism.

There you really have a fiend whose place is in jail. It is men like these who should be brought to trial.

If Johannes Becher is condemned, it will be tantamount to vindicating rascals and adventurers of the Bratz kidney.

It seems to me the bourgeoisie should have realized long ago that such "measures of self-defence" as the trial of Becher, or the murder of Sacco and Vanzetti after seven years of torment, cannot save it from irrevocable doom, but will only make it the more hated and thus accelerate its downfall.

The bourgeoisie has no longer anything to offer. It no longer possesses the means which formerly enabled it to keep the working masses in fetters. It now has no religion, no ideology, that might justify its crimes.

The only thing that still keeps it in power is its unscrupulous exploitation of scientific forces, which enrich its industry and technology.

But even that, of course, will not be for long: men of science have more than the customary perspicacity, and they will soon come to realize that in working for the parasites and "schiebers," they are working, not for "culture" but to the detriment of the people and of their own interests.

I appeal to all honest men and women to protest against the trial of Johannes Becher, whose only crime is that he is honest and talented.

(1928)

INHUMANITY

THE inhumanity of bourgeois Christian "culture" is eloquently and incontestably testified by the bourgeoisie's admission that wars are unavoidable, that the wholesale extermination of human beings is as inevitable as a "law of life."

There are wiseacres who allege that war breeds fearlessness, strength of will and other precious virtues. But we know that the revolting war of 1914-18, organized by the bourgeoisie, annihilated tens of millions of workers and peasants and bred on the blood of the slaughtered thousands of shameless parasites and beasts of prey—"schiebers," "nouveaux riches," "sharks."

The assertion that "war breeds heroes," that it inculcates fearlessness, only shows that the bourgeois philosophers and moralists cannot distinguish fearlessness from shamelessness and inhumanity.

Our times quite clearly reveal that apart from their direct aim—the economic plunder of the weakened enemy—wars between bourgeois states really do breed "fearless" people, champions of lawlessness, of inhuman government in "peace time." We see such people in the fascist organizations, in the German Stahlhelm, for instance, and in similar organizations in other countries.

"Peace time," as we know, is more and more definitely assuming the character of a continuous and bitter war of the master class against the working class.

Moreover, as the bourgeoisie morally degenerates, it rears an even larger number of thieves, swindlers and bandits. The banker breeds the bandit, we are told by the modern "Book of Genesis"—and it is undeniable.

The growth of crime in bourgeois countries necessitates a constant enlargement of the police force, which really does demand "fearless" men, men capable not only of beating up and killing workers, but of battling brigands. In Berlin, special "assault battalions" have been formed to protect the burghers from bandits. In the U.S.A. the burgher can insure himself against fraud and robbery. The premiums paid by insurance companies to victims of robbery amounted to 2,000,000 dollars in 1913, 4,500,000 dollars in 1920, and about 17,000,000 dollars in 1927. Chicago, a vast and rich city, is entirely under the sway of gangster organizations. President Hoover spoke in the Senate of the spread of crime. Of course, America is not the only country which is assiduously breeding offenders against the life and, chiefly, against the "sacred property" of the middle class. Europe does not lag behind her in this species of progress. The bourgeoisie is in dire need of "fearless" men.

And it goes without saying that war is profitable to the industrialists who, by the hands of their workers, manufacture guns and rifles for the mutual extermination of workers and peasants.

All this and much else, while it incontestably demonstrates the cynical inhumanity of the bourgeoisie, the criminality of its very existence, also speaks of its growing insanity and idiocy, which make its doom inevitable.

All my life I was a "pacifist." War only filled me with loathing, with shame for my fellow-beings, and with hatred for the instigators of wholesale massacres, for the destroyers of life.

But after the heroic war victoriously fought by the hungry, barefoot, seminaked workers and peasants of our country, and now that our working class is building amid incredible difficulties a new state, its own state, and is proving itself to be an intelligent and talented manager, I too have become convinced that a battle for life or death is inevitable.

And if a war should break out against the class by virtue of whose strength I live and work, I too will join its army as a rank-and-file soldier. I shall join it, not because I know that it will win, but because the great and righteous cause of the working class of the Soviet Union is my own legitimate cause, my duty.

(1929)

REPLY TO A QUESTIONNAIRE
OF AN AMERICAN MAGAZINE

You ask:

"Does your country hate America, and what do you think of American civilization?"

The very putting of such questions, and in such a form, smacks of a distorted, a truly American love of exaggeration and sensation. I cannot imagine a European putting such questions simply to "make money." As to your first question—and all the others, for that matter—permit me to say that I have no right to speak in the name of the 150 million citizens of my country, because I am not in a position to ask them what their attitude to your country is.

I presume that even in the countries whose blood your capitalists coin into dollars—in the Philippines, the South American republics, China—and even among the ten million coloured people in the U.S.A.—you will not find a single sensible man who will have the presumption to declare in the name of his people: "Yes, my country, my people, hate America, all its inhabitants, workers as well as billionaires, coloured people as well as whites; they hate the women and children of your country, its fields, rivers and forests, its beasts and birds, its past and its present, its science and its scientists, its magnificent technical achievements, Edison and Luther

Burbank, Edgar Allan Poe and Walt Whitman, Washington and Lincoln, Dreiser and O'Neill, Sherwood Anderson and all its talented artists, and that splendid romanticist, Bret Harte, the spiritual father of Jack London; they hate Thoreau and Emerson and everything that makes up the United States of America and all who inhabit those states."

I hope you do not expect to find an idiot capable of giving such an insane answer to your question, an answer so filled with hatred of human beings and culture.

However, I need not say that what you call American civilization does not appeal and cannot appeal to my sympathies. I think that your civilization is the most ugly civilization on our planet, because it has monstrously exaggerated all the diverse and shameful deformities of European civilization. Europe is tragically perverted enough by the cynicism of the class state, but it is still impossible to find in Europe such a pernicious and senseless phenomenon as your billionaires and millionaires, people who present your country with degenerates. You remember, of course, the case of the two rich Boston boys who murdered another boy out of curiosity? And how many similar crimes are prompted by "snobbery," by curiosity in your country? Europe, too, can boast of the downtrodden and defenceless condition of its citizens, but it has not yet gone to such shameful lengths as the murder of Sacco and Vanzetti. In France there was the "Dreyfus case," also a shameful affair: but in France, men like Émile Zola and Anatole France rose up in defence of the innocent man, and thousands followed their lead. An organization of manslayers resembling the Ku Klux Klan sprang up in Germany after the war; but there they were rounded up and put on trial. That is not the fashion in your country; there the Ku Klux Klan murders and cynically manhandles coloured people, even women, with impunity, just as governors of states wreak violence on Socialist workers with impunity.

There is no such disgusting thing in Europe as the baiting of "coloured" people, though it suffers from another shameful disease—antisemitism. However, America too is infected with this disease.

Crime is gradually increasing in Europe also, but it has not yet gone to the length of what—to judge by your newspapers—is happening in Chicago, where, besides the bandits of the stock exchange and the banks, bandits armed with guns and bombs rule the roost. Nor are the bloody affrays which prohibition gives rise to in your country possible in Europe. Nor would you find a city mayor who would publicly burn English classics, as the mayor of Chicago did.

I do not think Bernard Shaw would be entitled to answer an invitation to visit any other country as sarcastically as he did in reply to the invitation of the editor of the *Nation*, O. G. Villard, to visit America.

Capitalists are a revolting and inhuman tribe in all countries, but yours are the worst. They are apparently more stupidly greedy for money. Incidentally, my own private translation of the word "businessman" is—maniac.

Just think how idiotic and shameful it all is: our splendid planet, which we have learned with such difficulty to adorn and enrich—practically the whole earth— is in the greedy clutches of an insignificant tribe who are incapable of making anything except money! The magnificent creative power, the blood and brains of the scientists, engineers, poets and workers, who are the builders of culture, of our "second nature," are coined by these doltish people into yellow metallic discs and check slips.

What, besides money, do the capitalists breed? Pessimism, envy, greed and hatred, which will inevitably destroy them, but which, together with them, may in their explosion destroy a multitude of cultural treasures. Dire tragedy is what your morbidly hypertrophied civilization holds out for you.

Personally, of course, I am of the opinion that true civilization and rapid cultural progress are possible only where political power entirely belongs to the working people, and not to parasites who live on the labour of others. And, of course, I recommend that the capitalists be proclaimed a group of socially dangerous people, that their property be confiscated by the state, and that they be transplanted to some ocean island where they may be allowed to die out in peace. This would be a very humane way of solving a social problem, and entirely in the spirit of "American idealism," which is nothing but the most naïve optimism of people who have not yet lived through the dramas and tragedies which, taken together, are called the "history of a nation."

(1927-29)

THE BOURGEOIS PRESS[*]

THE rubbish you find in second-hand markets tells you of the way people lived yesterday; the advertisements and police items in the newspapers give a good insight into the way people live today. When I say newspapers, I am referring to the modern "organs of public enlightenment" in the "cultural centres" of Europe and America. I consider it just as useful to read the bourgeois press as to listen to the frank things servants have to say about the life of their masters. Diseases cannot, and should not, interest a healthy man, but the doctor is in duty bound to study them. The physician and the journalist have something in common: they both diagnose and describe diseases. Our journalists are in a better position than the bourgeois journalists, for they are well familiar with the general causes of social pathological phenomena. The Soviet journalist should therefore be as attentive toward the testimony of the bourgeois press as the physician is toward the cries and groans of a patient. If some talented person were to come along in our country and gather a sufficient number of facts from the police chronicle of the newspapers of any "cultural centre," and compare these facts with the advertisements of retail stores, restaurants and houses of entertainment, and with the descriptions of gatherings,

* Gorky did not complete this article.

receptions and public celebrations, and if he were to work up all this material, we should get a dazzling and staggering picture of the "cultural" life of present-day bourgeois society.

What do we find daily in the bourgeois press? Here, for instance, are some items it touched upon briefly in the past month of May.

"Reformatory Revolt"—fourteen boys run away from a reformatory, twelve are recaptured by mounted police, the whereabouts of the other two are unknown. "Another Minor Tortured." "Mother Slays Her Childern"—poisons two with gas; motive—starvation. "Another Gas Poisoning"—five asphyxiated: husband, wife, husband's old mother, three-year-old daughter, and baby. "Hunger Drives to Murder." "Another Woman Hacked to Pieces." "Accustomed to Jail"—a man released from prison after serving a five-year sentence goes to the police and says he is sick, cannot work and does not want to beg, and asks to be sent back to jail; the "just laws" of the bourgeois state do not permit this, so, being "accustomed" to jail, the man goes out and smashes a shop window and starts a fight with the police, and in this way gets what he wants. "Millionaire Pauper"—an old beggar, eighty years old, dies, and five million krone are found among his effects. "Lord Ashton, 89, Dies, Leaving £20,000,000." "Monster Trial"—three hundred persons in Lyons die from drinking water from contaminated city mains. "Huge Card Losses." "Several murders were committed yesterday in various parts of the city; the bandits got away safely." The word "safely" in this instance is not to be understood ironically, but as a sign of sympathy with the murderers' luck.

Then there are reports of more or less big cases of fraud, corruption, sexual depravity ending in suicide and murder. Of course, I have enumerated only an insignificant fraction of the items published in the course of the month—ninety per cent of the rest are of a similar criminal and pathological nature. All this is recounted very briefly, tersely and colourlessly; for the journalist to add a little animation or colour to his style, it is necessary for "another woman" to be hacked to pieces with unusually sadistic skill, or that the Düsseldorf murderer, Kürten, a worker, confess to fifty-three crimes and then "suddenly remark drily to the police investigator: 'What will you say if I now deny everything as just a hoax?'" That is a "sensation." But the work of the police in the bourgeois countries is becoming a series of sensations, and the case of Kürten should therefore not surprise the Soviet reader. You simply cannot understand why all this is published. The police chronicle evokes no "comment" in the bourgeois press. You feel that it has become commonplace, and that no one is outraged or alarmed by it. Formerly, before the war,* people were outraged. Sentimental individuals used to write milk-and-water articles on the "diseases of the social organism" and voice various sentiments, which were sometimes prompted by alarm, but more often by the irritation of "cultured" people disturbed by "abnormal facts."

Nowadays the bourgeois press is not interested in the commonplace tragedies of life, for the daily death of tens and hundreds of humble individuals has long become the customary order of things, it has no effect on the tenour

* The war of 1914-18.

of life and constitutes no menace to the people who want to live merrily and tranquilly. Luxurious cinemas are multiplying daily, and, still more luxurious restaurants, with jazz orchestras that shake the walls and ceilings. One is amazed by the abundance of advertisements of specifics against "lowered vitality" and the remarkably eloquent advertisements of venerealogists.

But you had this sensational stuff before 1914, you will say. Yes, but it was not so deafening. Now it seems that the bourgeois of the "cultural centres" have unanimously decided that

> *Life grows shorter and shorter,*
> *The days speed faster and faster.*
> *Then, let us all our days and nights*
> *Live merrier and merrier!*

This was preached from a cabaret pulpit by a spindle-shanked individual with a protruding stomach, heavily rouged cheeks and the insane eyes of a dope fiend.

I am laying on the colours too thick, you say? I have no desire to do so, because I know that dry rot is contagious. The colours of life are themselves becoming thicker and more lurid. Probably that is because the temperature of life is rising, and because the gaiety of the bourgeoisie is growing feverish. . . . The bourgeoisie tries to live gaily in order to drown a gloomy presentiment of its coming doom.

* * *

I think I know the work of the newspapermen of America and Europe pretty well. In my view they are journeymen, whose arduous and restless trade imbues them with a feeling of profound indifference to human beings; they very much resemble attendants in a psychiatric hospital, who are accustomed to regard patients and doctors alike as lunatics. This indifference explains the imperturbably dispassionate tone of their reports on the most diverse facts of life.

Here are some examples:

"A certain Hans Müller yesterday devoured 36 brace of sausages in 11 minutes for a wager."

"In 1928, 9,530 persons—6,690 men and 2,840 women—committed suicide in Prussia; 6,413 of the suicides were urban and 3,117 rural inhabitants."

"The mayor of Löwenberg, Silesia, decided to increase the city's revenue by introducing a tax on cats, but the city council turned down the proposal. The mayor has now resorted to a different device. He has traps set at night in the city park for prowling cats. The trapped animals may be redeemed by their owners at a ransom of three marks apiece."

"When bailiffs came to the parish of Niendorf, near Hamburg, to levy property for arrears of payments to the irrigation company, the peasants put up armed resistance and the bailiffs were forced to retire."

A "nocturnal ghost" is in the habit of visiting a pastor living in the vicinity of Berlin. After he had been awakened three times by its "indecent touch," he had the police called in. They found a hat under the pastor's window which is presumed to have been lost by the "ghost."

"Should women with bobbed hair be admitted to communion? This question was raised by a number of bishops, and was considered by the Vatican on May 24. The

College of Cardinals have answered the question in the affirmative. They do not find the wearing of short hair contrary to Christian morals."

Last year a newspaperman reported that the police figures show that in France about four thousand women disappear every year. Arrests of white slave traffickers were recently made in a number of French cities. The gang had sold 2,500 girls to brothels in the South American republics. A similar organization of traffickers in "human merchandise" operated in Poland. A French journalist, A. Londre, has made a thorough study of this branch of the slave trade. His book, *Criminal Trade*, was put out last year in our country by the Federation Publishing House. It is an extremely interesting book; it tells in detail of the way girls are decoyed and kidnapped, and of their "work" in the brothels of Argentina. But the most instructive thing about this book is that it does not contain a single expression of indignation.

On p. 10, Londre tells of his meeting with a white slave trafficker in the following words:

"Armand is a souteneur. . . . I know what his business is. He knows who I am. He trusts me and I trust him—like businessmen."

Exactly: like businessmen—and nothing more, though the "business" is inhuman and vile enough in all conscience.

But to explain Londre's mentality, it would be appropriate to cite the exact words of an American journalist:

"A policeman is not obliged to think whether the man he is escorting to trial or to jail is innocent or not. I bring before the court of society the same sort of people, and what has gone before or comes after doesn't concern me."

I heard this in New York in 1906, during a modest scandal staged by pious Americans. I had been driven out of two hotels. So I planted myself with my trunks in the street, and I decided to wait and see what would happen. I was surrounded by reporters, about fifteen of them. In their own, American, way they were good fellows. They "sympathized" with me, and were even, I thought, rather embarrassed by the scandal. One of them was particularly likeable, a hefty chap with a wooden face and comic round beady blue eyes of unusual brilliance. He was a celebrity. He was once commissioned by his paper to Manila, in the Philippines, to arrange the escape from jail of a girl-revolutionary, a nationalist, who had been imprisoned by the Spaniards and who was threatened with the death penalty. This fellow guessed that I was quite willing to let the scandal take its course. He persuaded the young writer, Leroy Scott, author of the novel *The Walking Delegate*, and his comrades of the Five Club to "take a hand in the affair." It later turned out that they could do nothing about it, but I was removed from the street to the "club"— the apartment where the five literary beginners lived in a "commune," and where Scott's wife, a Russian Jewess, was the housewife. The young writers used to gather in the evening in front of the fireplace in the "club's" spacious vestibule. Reporters came, and I talked to them about Russian literature, the Russian revolution, the Moscow insurrection (N. E. Burenin, member of the militant organization of the Bolshevik Central Committee, Scott's wife, and M. F. Andreyeva translated what I said into English).

The newspapermen listened, took notes, and, with a sigh of evident regret, said:

"It's all devilishly interesting—but it's not for our papers."

I asked why their papers could not tell the truth about events which very likely were characteristic of the future of the new age.

But they understood my question in their own simple way, as something purely personal. They said:

"We are all with you, but we can't do anything about it. You will not find or earn money for the revolution here. When the press reported that Roosevelt intended to receive you, the Russian ambassador interfered, and that stops your game. We see that it was not the photograph of Andreyeva the newspapers printed, and we know that your first wife and children are not living in poverty, but it is not in our power to expose it. They won't let you work for the revolution here."

"But why do they let Breshkovskaya?"

To this they did not reply. But they were mistaken: I was able to work, although I did less than I expected. (But that has nothing to do with the subject of this article.)

The journalists went on to acquaint me with the amazing power of the New York press. They gave some illustrations. A rich and influential philanthropical lady was accused by one newspaper of running a number of houses of prostitution. This was a first-class sensation. But a couple of days later this same paper printed the photographs of twenty-five policemen, who, it said, were the real organizers of secret prostitution, and not the highly respected lady in question.

"And what about the policemen?"

"They were dismissed, after having been suitably compensated. They will find jobs in other states."

Another instance. It was necessary to discredit a certain senator, so the story was printed that he was living on bad terms with his second wife and that his children, students, were at daggers drawn with their stepmother. The old man and his children wrote a denial. The paper printed it, but made a joke of it. The house where he lived was surrounded by reporters. . . .

(1930)

THE WISEACRES

CAN stupidity ever be said to be a "gift of nature"?

I am sure that it cannot, and that even cretins and idiots are created by that biology which is determined by "environment," by sociology.

Certain wiseacres assert that stupidity is a quality which nature bestows upon a man from the day of his birth and for his whole life, that nature consciously strives, as it were, to restrict the fruits of reason and the workings of the human imagination.

This fantastic idea was conceived in hoary antiquity by our hirsute ancestors, who were terrified by the inimical frenzy of the elemental forces of nature—earthquakes, floods, hurricanes, the alternations of cold and heat and the other malignities of the blind giant. Subsequently, wiseacres turned these fears into gods.

Stupidity is a malformity of the reason, which is induced, and is inducible artificially, by the pressure on the reason of religion, of the church—the weightiest of the weapons in the arsenal of the bourgeois state for the subjugation of the working masses. This is undeniable, and I do not in the least regret that on this point none of the wiseacres is capable of saying anything "new."

Stupid people are absolutely essential to the bourgeoisie; without them it could not lead its "beautiful life." The good thing about them is that their physical strength can be exploited with the greatest convenience. It is on the stupidity of the working masses that the power of world philistinism rests. The bourgeois system of educating the masses is a system of manufacturing idiots.

These incontrovertible truths are, I trust, well known to our Soviet, educated people. They know by what means the bourgeois state inculcates, implants and perpetuates stupidity. Thanks to the bold initiative of V. I. Lenin and the Bolsheviks, the vanguard of the working class, thanks to the work of the Communist Party and the efforts of the workers' and peasants' government, time-hallowed stupidity is disappearing pretty fast in the Soviet Union. The working folk have been awakened by these efforts to a growing consciousness of their importance, of their right to rule. The creative energy of the masses is more and more distinctly and convincingly proving itself to be a force that is perfectly capable of reconstructing the whole of life, from its foundations up. Thirteen years of this courageous and successful work have shaken, and are more and more obviously shaking, the ancient pillars of philistine bliss, which was so strongly cemented by the blood and sweat of the working people. Listening to the sound of the building of the new life in the Soviet Union, the whole working world is responding with a formidable echo, and is gradually organizing for the decisive battle for its liberty.

The object of this feuilleton is to discuss the stupidity of the wiseacres.

The wiseacre is above all an intellectualist. His outstanding characteristic is that with him, as with Hamlet,

Prince of Denmark, "the native hue of resolution is sicklied o'er with the pale cast of thought." Like Hamlet, he is an orphan: his mother—history—lives in wedlock with the capitalist, and his stepfather, albeit a scoundrel, encourages the arts, exploits science and pretends to be a cultured animal.

The wiseacre considers himself a master of culture, its "spiritual lever," the "salt of the earth," and so forth; in general, he thinks himself an "inimitable individual." He is not a "mere man," but the incarnation of the world's wisdom—the hub, so to speak, of the wisdom of the world. In "troubled moments of life," when hard realities wring from him a modicum of peurile sincerity, he calls himself a "convict chained to the wheelbarrow of history"—as a certain former "Spartacist" once put it. Another, a former Social-Democrat, said: "The bourgeoisie tyrannizes the workers, the workers tyrannize us, the intellectuals." Soviet journalists, who are in general barbarians, like all the people of the Soviet Union, sometimes call the wiseacres pimps. The pimp's profession is a disgraceful one—what he does is to find young girls and boys for the beds of rich old men and women. Needless to say, the activities of the leaders of European Social-Democracy coincide very fairly with this sort of occupation, but. . . . Here the wiseacres would probably find some sort of "but"—as for me, I have no inclination to look for one. And, indeed, the world, all reality, is built with strict logicality on "yea" and "nay," and "but," according to the law of logic, is the "excluded middle."

The wiseacre is convinced that the very best chair is the one in which he is accustomed to sit. He therefore insists that all should sit on chairs of the shape he prefers. Regarding all events from the standpoint of the comfort of his buttocks, the wiseacre, of course, cannot approve of anything that upsets the old piece of furniture in which his worthy posteriors repose.

For example: the Russian landlords of the days of serfdom loved to sit in Voltairean armchairs; then the intellectuals of the noble class conceived a fondness for the soft furniture of the idealist Schelling; they also sat on Fourier, Molleschott and Vogt, then transferred their seat to nihilism, then got to like Spencer, especially because he, among other things, said that from leaden instincts you will never get golden behaviour—a delightful aphorism which sanctions indifference to certain social ineptitudes, villainies and tragedies. But even Spencer proved to be uncomfortable, and the shifting of seats became more and more frequent. They sat on Marx—too hard! They tried padding Marx with Bernstein—nothing came of it! They sat on Nietzsche, then on Bergson— I omit a whole series of furniture pieces they tried. Now the wiseacres sit the devil knows where—many of them in exile. This process of shifting with increasing celerity from seat to seat is called the "history of the spiritual life of the Russian intellectual."

In exile, the wiseacres compose "Outlines of a Scientific-Religious Outlook," "A Gospel of Divine Justice," "Lives of the Saints," treatises on "The Orthodox Church's Worship of John the Baptist," and generally devote themselves assiduously to philosophical carpentry, trying to fashion something that can be sat in comfortably.

In the émigré press you may read imbecile disquisitions like the following:

"It is said that Abyssinian Orthodox priests dance when performing the liturgy. Evidently, in the soul of the Ethiopians—the Ethiopians whom Homer so respected that he always referred to them as 'the worthy men of Ethiopia'—in that soul the Orthodox religion has found a reflection different from the one it has found in our Russian soul.

"A Russian girl of our acquaintance who had been educated in a French Catholic nunnery recently complained to her mother:

" 'It's so terribly inconvenient taking a bath there; you have to sit in the bath in your chemise.'

" 'Whatever for?'

" 'That's what I ask. After all, you are alone in the bathroom, and the door is locked. But they say:

" ' "Alone? Of course, not. What about your guardian angel? Isn't he always with you?" '

"This charming childish naïvete of the Catholic nunnery appealed to me immensely. But is it anything like our idea of a guardian angel?"

And this was written by a former novelist, a man who in 1905 was a prominent contributor to an S.R. newspaper! O, the tragic ponderosity of posteriors!

But let us leave these comicalities, hard as it is to do so. I have just read Comrade S. B. Uritsky's excellent book, *The Sweeping Socialist Offensive*, and, having read it, I feel in a very cheerful mood.

In the old days there used to be a category of government clerks who were known as chancellerists. "Chancellerist" comes from the words "cane c'el aria"—dog in the open, that is, at the door or gate of the house. Chancellerists were called: "inky souls." The wiseacre is not quite like the chancellerist: his soul is bookish. But he also lives outside the gate of reality, and looks at it from under the gate.

The wiseacre has probably read at least sixteen thousand books on diverse subjects, and this semimechanical labour of appropriating the thoughts of others has developed in him a terribly exaggerated opinion of the power and scope of his own intellect. Of course, I would not deny a sack the right to be proud of the amount of grain stuffed into it. But one often observes that the broader the knowledge of a wiseacre, the wider and more convulsive is the amplitude of his fluctuations.

One knows of cases when a wiseacre, in his search for a comfortable seat to plant himself in, keeps shifting backward, and, from Marxism, lands into Orthodox obscurantism; beginning as a Bolshevik, he ends up as a church elder.

Some wiseacres hold that it is precisely in this frequent change of beliefs that freedom of thought is most fully manifested In the end, books seem to blind rather than enlighten the wiseacre, and the private workings of his soul are rarely well attuned.

Books to him are a source of contradictions, which agitate and torment him far more powerfully than the storms, tempests and hurricanes of social reality. Reality demands that books reflect its growth and movement, but as it becomes more tempestuous, more saturated with the energy of a new class, with its creative power, it tends to be rather scornful of books that reflect the reality of yesterday. But the wiseacres want reality to follow the books. One of them, writing to me recently from Leningrad, said quite seriously:

"The only thing we live by nowadays is politics. But politics, surely, are only the tactics of government administration, of government activity, and for this the tsar's Ministers and all the others who held key posts have answered before the Revolution. What, then, do we lack? We lack 'being.' Why? Because being is the corollary of a world outlook, and we have no world outlook!"

The "originality" of this thought is not exceptional: no, it is a very typical "manifestation" of that view of life which is got from under the gate. The wiseacre values books, he believes in them. But when he is told that among the worker and peasant masses of the Soviet Union the demand for books is growing by leaps and bounds, that 462,000,000 signatures were printed in 1927, and 1,365,000,000 in 1930—tell the wiseacre this, and he will not be happy. He will say: "Not the right kind of books are being published, they are not objective enough, and they are written by heretics, because materialism is a heretical and anticultural theory."

The wiseacre is firmly convinced that without his sagacious participation in the affairs of the world, the world will perish. But all he can contribute to the affairs of the world is drivel. He is absolutely convinced that he knows everything, and that everything to him is perfectly clear. Bookishness has killed in him the sense of modesty and the cautiousness of judgment characteristic of men who take an active part in the building of life and who regard it attentively and seriously. He writes from somewhere—Prague, say:

"I know very well that things in Russia are in an extremely bad way." Actually, he knows nothing, for he shuts his eyes to what ought to be known. He is absolutely unaware of the height to which the Soviet Union has been elevated by the activity of the working class and the advanced peasantry. He judges of a people of 160,000,000 in the same way as he would judge of the population of a small country town.

"The five-year plan is unfeasible," he croaks, although he should know that, on the initiative of the workers, the five years have been cut to four. In general, he refuses to recognize that an energy quite unknown to him, the wiseacre, an energy he has never observed anywhere, is operating in the Soviet Union—the free energy of workers and peasants who are coming ever more clearly to recognize that they are the sole lawful masters of their country, that they are working for themselves, and that they must work selflessly, manfully and to the top of their strength.

Only this consciousness can explain what would seem the incredible fact that the oil and peat industries have already attained 83 and 96 per cent, respectively, of the output they were to have attained by 1932/33, and this means that the workers in these industries are completing their five-year plan in two and a half years. The machine-building industry has already reached 70 per cent of its five-year target, and this means that the machine-building industry will complete its plan, not in five but in three years; and the same is true of electrical engineering.

What does this show? It shows what a mighty store of energy lies latent in the working class. And that the peasant no longer wishes to be a slave of the soil, dependent on the caprices of nature, is shown by the fact that 22 per cent of the peasant households of our country have united in collective farms. And this is only to be explained by the fact that the age-old prisoner of the soil has realized that nature must be combated with the help of machines, by assisting the soil with fertilizers—with the help of the most up-to-date cultural and scientific methods.

And there can be no doubt that the collective farms will grow. The peasant knows how to compare facts and draw conclusions from them. And the facts are such as these: "Krasny Partisan Collective Farm has calculated that when its harvest is distributed every collective farmer will receive no less than 700 rubles. This is an income beyond the dream of the individual peasant."

The energy of the workers and peasants is growing with astonishing speed. Even capitalists who are not fools do not deny this, although this growing energy threatens them with certain unpleasantnesses. But the wiseacre sticks to his position, because he has been rather hurt—he does not get enough eggs and butter with his breakfast, and he is sitting uncomfortably. "I cannot imagine how the semi-illiterate, drunken and lazy worker and the illiterate, debased muzhik can successfully compete with the capitalist. We know our country, we know the character of its man power, and we know that P. B. Struve is right when he says that the working class, as a creative force, can exist only in a capitalist state."

Staggering wisdom! I do not know when and where Struve wrote so amazingly of the working class, and whether he wrote this at all, or has been misquoted by my correspondents, who sign themselves "Honest Russians."

The knowledge of the facts these "honest Russian" wiseacres display is as profound as their wisdom. This wisdom, it seems to me, already smacks of the psychopathological. It is very strange that when they speak of "man power," of the worker and muzhik, the wiseacres forget the "female"—the new "man power," which is very much alive and also very energetic.

The mental befuddlement of the wiseacres assumes the most varied and curious forms. For example, when one of them was told that the cultivation of subtropical plants in the republics of Georgia and Abkhazia was developing with great success, and also that there are now, in 1930, 20,000 hectares of tea plantations on the Black Sea coast, as against 250 dessiatines before the revolution, he retorted with the question: "Surely, you don't intend to compete with China?" And that was all. Yet he is an educated man, a scientist, a specialist in botany!

The wiseacres are fond of boasting of their love and concern for the "people"; they are fond of recalling how they suffered when the "people" suffered under the incompetent and brutal rule of the landlords and capitalists. But now the workers and peasants have overthrown the rule of the landlords and capitalists and, having themselves become the masters of their land, are building in it a new system of state, and are teaching the workers of the whole world how to build Socialism. One would think that the "commiserators with the people's woes" might now abandon the sterile trade of mourners and commiserators, and that they might sit back quietly and admire the mighty self-initiative of the working people, their free creative labours in all fields of physical and intellectual endeavour. One would think that the wiseacres might now sing in chorus, "Lord, let now thy servant depart in peace," and, for the final composure of their souls, turn their thoughts to the grave. And high time too!

But the cultural advances and achievements of the "people" are beyond their ken. They are too busy recording with jesuitic meticulousness every deficiency, blunder, "breakdown"—everything which they learn from the "self-criticism" of the workers and peasants, and which, actually speaking, is not a "tragedy of misgovernment," but encouragement of the energy of the masses, education of the masses in self-initiative, inculcation of the consciousness in the working masses that they are responsible to the state for all their shortcomings, vices, mistakes, carelessness and overhaste. All this is incomprehensible and alien to the wiseacres, for what they are interested in is something else.

They write: "Ivan Ivanovich has been arrested, that paragon of nobility, whom we know as. . . ."

They peer from afar through the slits and gaps in the gate at the new history which the government, the will of the workers and peasants, is building, and think they know everything. There is only one thing, I am sure, that they do know well, and that is that wiseacres kindred to them in "spirit" are striving to the best of their feeble powers to reinstate philistinism, to restore the bourgeois system. And they probably feel that the more resolutely the workers' and peasants' government passes to the socialist offensive, the more diversely does the malice of the doomed philistine manifest itself. This malice creates its own atmosphere; naturally, some of the wiseacres are poisoned by it, and then it becomes necessary to ignore their nobility and deprive them of the opportunity to speak and act freely.

I am familiar with the exact words of one wiseacre, of the sincerity of which there can be no doubt. When he was asked why he had allowed himself to be "entangled in sabotage," he explained:

"Under the capitalist system we were in a certain degree higher officers in the service of capital, if it may be put that way. It was through us that capitalism practised the exploitation of the workers which is inherent and inevitable under capitalism, and this, in its turn, engendered a definite ideology, which sharply divided us from the workers and counterposed us to them."

And with this eloquent statement of a man kindred in "spirit" to the wiseacres, we may conclude.

OLD FELLOWS

THE editors of *Za Rubezhom* [*Abroad*] have received a
number of serious and edifying replies to the question-
naire in the first issue of the magazine. Among them was
one from "an office worker, a non-party Socialist, 60½
years old."

He does not so much reply to the questions, as over-
steps them, so to speak. First of all, he says that "it was
promised in the prospectus that the magazine would give
a truthful account of both home and foreign life." Here
he is mistaken: there is not a word in the prospectus to
the effect that· the magazine intended to give an account
of "home life"; the prospectus definitely says that the
magazine would treat of life "abroad," in conformity
with its title. The mistake may be attributed to the weakness of the old fellow's "non-party" eyesight—a defect
which at his age is incurable.

But in the sequel this mistake very definitely exposes
the old fellow's "inward nature." This old fellow is a
"humanitarian" it appears! He rebukes us for not saying
anything in our magazine about the "party purge," which
he, the old fellow, refers to as a "useless torture"—useless because, as he says, "you will not find any human
being without moral defects."

It should be remarked here that, politically, the "humanitarian" view of the defects of human beings has, under our conditions, a very serious practical significance: the "wreckers" speak frequently and convincingly in their frank testimony of how useful "defective," "morally unstable," "disloyal," "administratively unsuitable," "anti-Soviet-minded" individuals and ne'er-do-wells generally are for the business of state sabotage. It is precisely such individuals that are ejected from the Party by the purge, which the old fellow calls not only "torture," but "useless" torture, thereby admitting, it is to be presumed, that there is such a thing as useful torture.

Then the humane old fellow writes, very correctly, although not very literally: "Such deproletarization (?) as dekulakization is causing in the U.S.S.R. is to be found nowhere else in the sublunary world."

Yes, indeed, nowhere else in the sublunary world has the working class yet undertaken that necessary work which has been started so successfully in our country, the Soviet Union. But we are absolutely certain that **the entire mass of the working people will inevitably follow our good example**. And the import of this example is very simple and clear: the peasantry, the passive mass who were slaves of the elemental forces of nature, who for centuries were exploited, and who throughout the centuries continuously threw up brutal exploiters from their midst, must be placed in different conditions, must be re-educated to be masters of the soil instead of its slaves; in other words, the ground from which all the horrors of capitalism sprang must be destroyed. A contributor to the German Catholic paper *Neues Volk*, named Hammelrat, recently wrote of this gigantic work as follows: **"This is**

concentrated energy, which is shattering the old world and creating a new. Seven million peasant households, twenty million rural inhabitants, have taken to collective farming. The buttress of the collective-farm movement is the poor peasant. Here, in the collective-farm movement, the targets of the five-year plan have long been surpassed. . . . The Soviet press does not dilate on achievements, but keeps spurring them on. When it speaks of difficulties and failures, we should be moved to astonishment rather than to malignant triumph, for in this too is expressed that irrepressible energy which keeps driving things forward. And this youthful, insatiable energy is all-decisive. Russia is becoming increasingly independent of the rest of the world. This costs her big sacrifices, but the sacrifices are made. The five-year plan is predetermining the world politics of the coming decades."

This is said by a man who is not our friend, and who, moreover, is a Catholic, a member of the church, the head of which has proclaimed something in the nature of a crusade against our "non-party Socialist's" country and people. But the humane old fellow is not interested in the process of rebirth of his people, or in the titanic work being performed by the "concentrated energy" of the working class of his motherland. He tells us that sick "kulaks are rolled up in threes in matting and packed off"—presumably to the hospital.

The author of these lines has some idea of how matting is woven, and doubts whether there is any matting of the dimensions which would be needed to pack up three men together. This, of course, is a trifle—the matting, I mean—but such trifles are very characteristic, are always characteristic, of "non-party" denouncers and truth-lovers. When he asserts his truth, the truth-lover never hesitates to lie. The humane old fellow concludes his letter by appealing for "fulfilment of the promise to give a truthful and impartial account of life." The editors can only repeat what has already been said, namely, that they have made it their aim to give an account of life *Za Rubezhom* [*Abroad*]. Their aim is to show the reader that Europe, America and the foreign world generally are by no means living in a state of charming bliss, of tender mutual love between manufacturers and workers, landlords and peasants, employees and masters— in a word, in peaceful prosperity and undying joy. The editors will willingly deal with all worthy manifestations in foreign science, technology and art. The editors are well aware that so far they have not succeeded in doing their job as fully and as perfectly as they should.

But the editors do not promise the humane old fellow to deal with living and political conditions abroad impartially. To be impartial is to be dispassionate. But **we are passionate people, we hate passionately, and we shall be partial—take us at that or leave us!** Non-party old fellows from the ages of 18 to 70 and up—and party old fellows too for that matter—may fully slake their thirst for truth by reading our daily press, where the truth about Soviet realities is given passionately and ruthlessly. We know that this passionate ruthlessness in denouncing idlers, saboteurs, grabbers, botchers, fools, vulgarians and similar monstrosities puts new youth into the old fellows of all ages; we know that when they read of mismanagement and mistakes, of stupidities and villainies, they jubilate and dance on the edge of their graves. But we also know that our achievements are immeasurably greater than our shortcomings, and that the most fundamental achievement of all is precisely that "concentrated energy" which is capable of performing miracles.

The old fellow has considerably understated his age: he is not $60^1/_2$ but much older, even preposterously old. He is not the only one of his kind, and as a "type" belongs to that tribe of old fellows of whom the Neapolitan, Giordano Bruno, wrote in 1583:

"What is this peace and harmony they offer the unhappy nations? Is it not their wish, is it not their dream, that the whole world will, by acquiescing in their malevolent and haughty ignorance, assuage their evil consciences, when they themselves refuse to obey righteous doctrine?"

For this and many similar things written by Giordano Bruno in his books, *Exclusion of the Triumphant Beast* and *The Heroic Enthusiasm* the old fellows kept him in prison for seven years and then burned him at the stake. And one of the old fellows, Cardinal Gaspar Schoppe, declared over Bruno's ashes:

"Thus he has been consumed by fire and has died a miserable death. Methinks, he has now departed to those other worlds which he himself invented, to tell there of the way Romans deal with the impious."

As you see, four hundred years ago the old fellows were just as fiendish and evil as they are today. And just as Cardinal Schoppe rejoiced over the murder of Giordano Bruno, so our modern old fellows jubilate over the murder of Jaurès, Liebknecht, Rosa Luxemburg, Sacco and Vanzetti and the many others who were possessed of "heroic enthusiasm."

This monstrous longevity of the old fellows is not only deplorable but revolting. It shows how stagnant and inert is the life which produced the "old fellows," how slowly the "psychology of the individual" changes. But, on the other hand, it shows that the individual is growing more and more insignificant, and is less and less "influencing the course of history." This waning of the individual is excellently depicted in European literature: all in all, it provides a vivid commentary to the history of the growth, development and, then, evaporation of the energy of the bourgeois class.

Men of letters have created a number of monumental portraits of hypocrites, humbugs, fanatics, "profit-fiends" and similar pillars of the bourgeois world. In our day these pillars have all shrunken to the dimensions of a Briand, a Chamberlain and similar patchers-up of the chicken coop known as the bourgeois state. Our literary scholars would do a piece of work useful and essential for the education of our youth, if they were to write the biographies of some of these literary prototypes. They would be extremely interesting little histories of the degeneration of the individual. It would be convenient to take, for example, the type of Oliver Cromwell and to trace through a number of figures resembling him how this type has shrivelled to the dwarf dimensions of Alexander Kerensky.

The "great men" of the past are the blood ancestors of the present old fellows—that is indisputable. But this in no way enhances the size or importance of our old fellow, but only shows to what microscopic dimensions the "great ones" have shrunk.

Our old fellow is a petty individual, but he is also typical. His principal characteristic is a tender love for himself, for the "eternal truths" he has culled from various gospels, and for the "accursed problems" which cannot be solved by talk. Here, for instance, is an old fellow of 26 who writes: "Who am I that sits here and is doomed like all living things to die?"

This is the form the beautiful saying of Ecclesiastes takes today. And in the same way everything more or less brilliant is distorted by the idlers and drivellers, to whom, in the final analysis, nothing in the world is more interesting than their own corns. In fact, one of them literally writes: "We build universities and colleges, but we have not learned to cure a simple corn." Another, divinely majestic, proclaims: "Reality has parted ways with me, it has not understood me." Just imagine the cruelty of this capricious reality! *The individuality of the philistine is degenerating, and his thoughts are degenerating, cluttered up with rubbish and poisoned by a sordid way of life.* A crafty money-grabber, usurer, slave to wealth and, in the past, a builder of the iron cage of the state, the philistine has become a dwarf.

But tiny as he is, he is noxious, just as dust and the exhalations of marshes and the vapours of decaying organic matter are noxious. There are plenty of poisonous admixtures in the air we breathe. This is very harmful, and it must be fought in "never-ceasing combat." It would be well to write a history of culture as the history of the decay of the individual, as a description of its path towards death, and as a history of the rise of the new individual, which is assuming organic form in the fire of the "concentrated energy" of the builders of a new world.

(1930)

CYNICISM

Reply to a Correspondent

You ask: "Can it be that you, Maxim Gorky, are not outraged by the cynicism of modern life and that you sincerely rejoice at the despair of those who cannot see a way out of our sombre realities? Can it be that your philosophical calm is not disturbed by the endless tragedy of life?"

Permit me to tell you that I am least of all a philosopher, and that "calmness" is not characteristic of me at all. If I were a calm individual, then men of your type, those who think like you, would not be paying me so much attention, in which malice is so pitifully combined with obvious impotence of style and an illiteracy that is strange in intellectuals. I can only explain it by forgetfulness of the past.

Let us talk of cynicism. It so happens that "Cynicism" was the name of a short article published in 1908, in the symposium, *Literary Decadence*. This is the way it began.

"The pace of the world's life is speeding up, for the mighty tumult of a spring awakening is penetrating deeper and deeper into its secret recesses, and everywhere a rebellious tremor can be distinctly felt, as potential energy realizes its creative power and prepares for action. Slowly but surely the consciousness of the people is awakenin the sun of social justice shines ever brighter, and the breath of the coming spring is visibly melting the cold and heavy layers of hypocrisy and prejudice and exposing in all its shamefulness the ugly skeleton of modern society, that prison of the human spirit.

"Millions of eyes gleam with a joyous flame, everywhere flash the lightnings of wrath, illuminating the clouds, gathered through the ages, of folly and blunder, of prejudice and lies; we are on the eve of the festival of the universal rebirth of the masses.*

.   .   .   .

.   .   .   .

.   .   .   .

"Men who know that the people represent an inexhaustible well of energy, which is alone capable of turning the possible into the inevitable, dreams into reality —such men are happy. For they have always had a living creative sense of their organic ties with the people, and now this sense must grow, filling their hearts with a great joy and a thirst to create new forms for a new culture. The signs of the rebirth of humanity are evident, but the "members of cultured society" profess not to see them, which, however, does not prevent the philistines from sensing the inevitable approach of a world conflagration.

"Dull instruments of the process of accumulation of wealth**

.   .   .   .

they are condemned to defend their hopeless positions, and they hide in the narrow cage of their 'culture'—the name

* The dots represent the hoofprints of the tsarist censor.— *Maxim Gorky.*

** Again the hoofprints of the censor.—*Maxim Gorky.*

they give to the conviction which has been drilled into them and which deadens their souls, that the power of capital is eternally lawful and forever unshakable. They are now not even slaves of their master, but his domestic animals.

"Slaves are being reborn into men—that is the new import of life!. . ."

This was written by me—and, as you see, twenty-two years ago. I think that for those days it was not a bad article—incidentally, it was very flatteringly praised in a letter I received from Anatole France, a man who was not lavish in compliments. I should have liked to reproduce the article in full, maybe it would have convinced you that in these twenty-two years my attitude to people of your type has not changed very much, and that I can hardly be called a "betrayer of the finest precepts of the intelligentsia," and that I have "developed," not "thanks to their aid," but by withstanding their attempts to rear me in their own "likeness and image," that is, as a domestic animal or lap dog of capital. Of these roles, so beloved of the refined intelligentsia, I proved incapable.

I very much regret I cannot reproduce the article, "Cynicism," in full—I have not the rough draft, and as to the Russian text of my book, *Articles*, published in 1916 by Parus, the censor wandered through that like a hungry pig through a kitchen garden. But here is a piece which the censor did not devour:

"Cynicism also conceals itself under the mask of freedom, the search for full freedom—which is the most despicable of all its masks.

"Literature, as represented by its most talented devotees, attests that when, in his striving for full freedom, the philistine discloses his ego, his 'I,' a brute beast stands revealed before the eyes of modern society.

"This apparently is inevitable, and is independent of the will of the authors. Their efforts are worthy and clear—they want to present the edifying image of a man who is absolutely free of prejudices and traditions, which bind the philistines into a whole, into a society, that hampers the growth of the individuality—they want to create a 'good type' of hero who takes everything from life and gives nothing in return.

"Appearing in the pages of a novel, the hero more or less wittily demonstrates his right to be what he is, performs a number of feats to free himself from captivity to social sentiments and thoughts, and, if the surrounding personages do not strangle him in time, or if he does not kill himself, then by the end of the book he invariably appears in the sight of the philistine reader as a newborn pig—at the very best.

"The reader frowns, the reader is displeased. Where there is 'mine' there there must of necessity be an absolutely autonomous 'I.' But the reader sees that the full freedom of one 'I' necessarily demands the enslavement of all other personal pronouns—an old truth, which everyone tries hard to forget. The philistine sees this all too often, for in practical life, in the fierce daily struggle for a comfortable existence, man grows more and more cruel and terrible, less and less human. At the same time, brutes like this are necessary for the protection of sacred and blessed property.

"The philistine is accustomed to divide people into heroes and the mob; but the mob is disappearing, becoming transformed into socialist parties, and it is threatening to sweep the petty philistine 'I' from the face of the earth. The philistine calls in a hero to his aid—and there comes a stealthy and voracious being with the mentality of a wild boar or of a Russian bureaucrat.

"And for this monster, summoned to protect the sacred rights of private property, the sacred rights of the human individual do not exist: what is more, he looks upon private property itself with the eyes of a conqueror.

"On the one hand, the many-headed red hydra; on the other, a fiery and insatiable dragon with gaping jaws; and in between them bewilderedly staggers the tiny mannikin with his beggarly property.

"And although it is for him the chains of a convict, the yoke of a slave, he loves it, he serves it faithfully and is always prepared to defend its integrity and power with all the force of lying and cunning of which he is capable; he is always ready to vindicate the social order with every means—from God and philosophy to jails and bayonets!"

From this, I think, only one conclusion can be drawn, which is that I say the same today as I have always said.

My friend, and later my "enemy," Leonid Andreyev, in a letter he wrote to A. V. Amfiteatrov in 1913, called me a "knight of the proletariat." This was, of course, too ornate and flattering, but it was only said in order that he might follow it up with:

"He rolls the Sisyphus stone of realism uphill and down, and strings his miraculous and oracular dream of the proletariat on the four rules of arithmetic. After all, the only reality is that which I don't like; that which I like and want is never real."

This was printed in *Requiem*, a book published by Federation—and it was a very sad mistake on Andreyev's part. He should not have despised the four rules of arithmetic—nobody should—for these rules are the foundation of science. And as to the "miraculous dream" of a free proletariat, of the power of its creative will—in the Soviet Union this "dream" has become a heroic reality.

* * *

You write: "Our times are growing ever more cynical."

Perfectly true. I do not lay claim to being a prophet, but I consider myself not a bad observer. Twenty-two years have passed since I wrote of the cynicism of the bourgeois system, and now cynicism has developed in the bourgeois organism like a leprosy. But you have divined this too late, and your having divined it will scarcely help you to adopt a more honest and active attitude toward the historic task of the proletariat of the world. However, it would probably be useful to you if, instead of trying to inculcate in me the rules of meekness, you were to examine the world surrounding you more attentively. Look:

The imposing façades of the bourgeois states seem to have entirely collapsed, and anyone who has eyes to see may see what is going on within the stone cells of the European bourgeoisie. An economic crisis is rampant—a consequence of the marauders' morbid greed for wealth. Bank failure follows bank failure, and with the modest aid of members of governments and parliaments, the obedient servitors of capital, the bankers are robbing more and more assiduously. The luxury of bourgeois life in Europe and America is becoming more and more ostentatious, senseless and crude, and the amusements of the bourgeoisie are becoming more and more insensate and are more and more assuming the exclusive character of sexual perversion, of sexual depravity. "Industrial progress is the father of the worker," a certain newspaper sage recently said. He forgot to add that the bourgeoisie is the malevolent, stupid and dissolute stepmother of the working class. Millions of workers and their wives and children are starving, yet at the same time millions of tons of wheat cannot find a sale and are used to fuel furnaces. Here and there, capitalists save money by lowering wages, and say that government assistance to the workers must cease, for it perverts the hungry and turns them into idlers.

With a courage worthy of a far more active application, the hungry workers of Europe fruitlessly squander their energies exercising themselves in patience. Crime and suicide are growing in their midst; almost daily the newspapers carry reports of whole families poisoning themselves with carbonic acid gas because they are unable to stand the torment and humiliation of starvation any longer; and there are no few cases of fathers and mothers who, before putting an end to their own lives, cut the throats of their children, in order that they might not remain waifs and beggars in the bourgeois world.

Will you venture to deny that such facts are very numerous?

The leaders of Social-Democracy, those professional knight-errants of the welfare of the working class, those members of the Second International, which is dying from anaemia and ineptitude, forgetting in their old age who the ancient enemy of the working class is, would evidently like, but still hesitate, to say to their docile flock: "Eat as little as possible—better still, eat nothing at all, for our capitalist fatherland is in danger; the capitalist fatherlands of the workers of other nations are sharpening their knives against it."

And in order to divert the naturally keen interest of the workers of Europe from the Soviet Union, where the dictatorship of the proletariat has been established and genuine Socialism is being built at mighty speed, the Social-Democratic leaders, men like that decrepit old fellow Karl Kautsky, for instance, pour the sand of their lifeless philistine wisdom into the brains of the working class and cynically and ineptly slander the Communists, deriving the material for their slanders and mudslinging —material which they know to be rotten and false—from the bourgeois press, not shunning even the press of the Russian émigrés.

We find engaged in this business of fabricating lies and calumnies against the working people of the Soviet Union an unnatural and marvelous mixture of Russian generals who have been licked by the workers, theologians, bishops and contributors to Black-Hundred newspapers who have been expelled from the Soviet Union, former manufacturers and bankers and ex-radical writers of tsarist Russia—all the muck and trash that was swept out of our country by the hurricane of the great proletarian revolution.

The master of "Vatican City" has decided to take the lead of this Russian and European gang of enemies of the proletariat of all countries. He is to all appearances a very ignorant man—as an individual who believes he is the deputy of Christ, of the "god of love and humility," on earth, must be. He has ordered the priests to pray for "Russia's suffering people," of whose life and activities he has no clear idea; yet, on visiting Naples, this people, as represented by three hundred of its most energetic workers—most of them, by the way, non-party—exclaimed in sad surprise: "How great is the poverty here, how sickly the children, how awful the housing conditions of the workers!"

When I speak of the profound ignorance of the Soviet Union betrayed by the "big" and little men of Europe, its intellectuals, its press and its journalists, I am in no way exaggerating. And here is one of the proofs of this anecdotal ignorance. On January 1, 1931, the newspaper, *Il Mattino*, printed the following story from Vienna:

"BEARDS BECOME FASHIONABLE IN RUSSIA"

"The patriarchal beard, which annoyed Peter the Great so much that he ordered all the members of his court to shave them off, is again becoming the fashion in modern Russia. But not for aesthetic reasons, apparently. A little earnest thought will show that a long beard has many advantages: it saves expense on neckties, it warms the chest, it is a protection against colds, and at the same time it deprives the face of that bourgeois appearance which the absence of hirsuteness lends it. Only those unfortunates whom nature has blessed with red hair will be forced to sacrifice the growth on their chins, because in spite of the Bolshevik spirit, the people of Russia remain superstitious and believe that red-haired people bring ill-luck."

Idiotic anecdotes like this are printed almost every day in the European press—they are also printed in the celebrated Larousse dictionary. You will find in them, among other nonsense, items like these:

The samovar is a utensil for boiling water and has one or more faucets.

The Raskolniks are Russian sectarians. There are three types: Raskolniks, Rakolniks and Raskolnists.

Ivan III was known as the Good.

Ivan IV was nicknamed the Terrible because he flogged his wives to death.

General Denikin is a well-known general who fought the Bolsheviks on the orders of Kerensky.

An Italian newspaper recently carried a photograph of Dnieprostroy with the following legend: "New life in Siberia. View of Dnieprostroy on the River Ob, which will provide power and light for the city of Omsk."

All these are of course inconsequential trifles, but it is with rubbish like this that the heads of the European workers are stuffed day after day, and year after year. And people who are accustomed to declaiming about the "brotherhood of nations," "unity of nations," the "crisis of culture," seem to forget that ignorance is one of the greatest misfortunes of the world, and do not protest against, or even pay any attention to, the dissemination of ignorance.

And quite apart from this indifference to the spread of nonsense, lies and calumnies the European intellectuals voice no objection whatever to the multitude of very serious villainies and crimes that are committed against the working people in the bourgeois world. With childish naïvete, they continue, in your words, "to consider themselves the force that creates and guards European culture, which is founded upon Christian humanity, and which, after all, is advancing, and does seek for the truth of love, fraternity and equality."

It is to be gathered from this sentence that you are referring to the sinners in Dante's Inferno who advance with their faces turned backward.

I consider it absolutely shameless to talk so puerilely about the "universal truth of love" in our day, when the flames of national hatred kindled in Versailles are flaring ever higher, when the European capitalists are frantically arming for a new world shambles, and when hardly a day passes without workers being killed in the streets of the "world's cultural centres" merely because they want to eat. Far more honest than windbags of this type is the utterly brutalized General Ludendorff, who recently proclaimed his hatred for Jews, and now, in a letter to a Saarbrücken newspaper, says that "true Germans cannot be Christians."

That, at least, is consistent. And it is not the only fact testifying to the utter brutalization of the modern European generals of artillery, cavalry, politics, religion, and even science.

It is shameless and senseless to speak of a "universal truth," when in the sight of all a bloody conspiracy against the working people is being hatched with impunity, a conspiracy into which, in one way or another, the "democratic intelligentsia" will inevitably be drawn. The reality created by the capitalists, and by the philistines whom they drag after them like a dog on a chain, is so cynical as to lead one to think that the economic crisis is part of the grand conspiracy of capital against the working people, that the crisis is being artificially fostered, that an army of unemployed is being created in order to turn them into an army of soldiers. Fantastic, you say? Possibly. But it is more than possible that we shall witness another world slaughter of beggars engineered by the millionaires. I am not the only one who thinks so. There is professor of anthropology Leslie White, for instance, who, at an anthropological congress held in Cleveland in December, declared that war was inevitable, because capitalism is working for war as a means of solving the crisis. Suicide through war, White said, is a logical culmination of the capitalist system.

* * *

You say I do not see the truth? I see two.

One is your truth—senile, decrepit, blind in the left eye and toothless, which feeds on the offal it itself has excreted.

The other is young and audacious, and its energy is inexhaustible; it presses forward towards its lofty aim, never glancing backward; and sometimes it stumbles into the pitfalls malignantly and vindictively dug in its difficult path by the slaves of the old truth.

One of these truths is that in the Soviet Union the working people, guided by the Bolshevik Party and the workers' and peasants' government, are successfully building, under difficult conditions, a new state, their own state, a state of equals, and that this grand and courageous work is the beginning of the rebirth of the proletariat of the whole world, the beginning of a world Renaissance.

The other is the stupid, petty, malicious truth beloved of decadents inside and outside the Soviet Union. It vindictively points out that the 162 millions of the Soviet Union still do not dress in silk and velvet, that in the thirteen years of the dictatorship of the working class it has still not turned 25 million individualist small-property owners into Socialists. It is to these conclusions that all the petty carping of the partisans of the old, still living but rapidly dying truth of the poor in spirit boils down in the long run.

As you see, Mr. P. N., I know the truth.

(1931)

LOGIC OF HISTORY

The other day one of the White émigré papers printed the following item:

"New York, July 4. The fourteenth New York police magistrate in succession has been relieved of his duties for grave abuse of office—graft. In the past eighteen months more than half of the twenty-five New York police magistrates have been found to be criminals."

Three months ago this same paper reported that a judge in one of the American states was arrested for crimes of office, and that during his trial he admitted that in his period of activity as a combater of crime he had handed down no less than a thousand dishonest verdicts in return for bribes from relatives or friends of criminals.

A thousand crimes committed by one judge is of course a lot, but it should be remembered that Americans like to do everything on a grand scale. And in this case the White émigré press may be believed: it is a zealous, even a fierce, defender of the capitalist system, and it is therefore not in its interest to report unverified facts which compromise the system it admires.

Consequently, it reports these facts either from "inadvertence," or from stupidity, or because it is all one to it what it offers to its readers as long as they buy the paper.

It reports in a playful tone items like the following:

"A tramp was to have been brought before the Lyons court of correction on a charge of larceny. The gendarmes hesitated for a long time to bring the defendant into court, and only gave way on the insistent demand of the judge. The tramp appeared in court without his trousers. He said that he had torn them to pieces in protest against the unjust charge and had then swallowed a considerable part of the rags just to show 'what he was capable of if he was tormented any farther.' The judge ordered the tramp to be remanded to jail until he was fitted with another pair of trousers."

Very humorously told; although one suspects that the tramp is one of the new breed—a product of unemployment.

But let us return to America, to the judges who are being put in the dock in such large numbers. Not all of them are put in the dock, of course. State governor Fuller, for instance, the murderer of Sacco and Vanzetti, still continues to govern, if I am not mistaken. Nor has that judge been put into the dock who said publicly in a restaurant: "Within a minute three men will go to the electric chair. I'm not sure they're guilty, but let them burn as an example to others."

He was applauded by the people in the restaurant, I believe. We know that at this very moment eight young Negroes, mere boys, are awaiting death. They were accused of anarchism, although there was, and is, no evidence to support the charge. They too, evidently, are to be killed "as an example to others."

Actually speaking, the Italians Sacco and Vanzetti were likewise killed "as an example to others." Having been condemned to death, these martyrs were held in jail for seven years, a thing which was not done even in tsarist Russia. The proletariat of Europe protested against the sentence, so did the intelligentsia. But without avail. Sacco and Vanzetti were killed. No doubt the eight Negroes will also be killed, notwithstanding the protests of the proletariat of Europe and the Soviet Union.

It is necessary to protest against the cynical brutality of the capitalists, because this helps to organize the class consciousness and class solidarity of the proletarians.

But it would be naïve to think that these protests can have any influence on capitalist judges, who are men intoxicated with power, and who are becoming more and more intoxicated by an animal dread of social catastrophe. They sense that revolution will inevitably brush them away, wipe them from the face of the earth they are defiling. And there is nothing they can do but to be more and more ruthless towards the enemy while he is still insufficiently organized for the last, decisive fight. But the enemy is organizing, and that is why Severing, the Prussian Minister of the Interior, advises the police not to spare cartridges—the same advice that Trepov, Governor of St. Petersburg, gave in 1905.

On July 4, Severing sent a circular to all police offices, which said:

"The preceding circular permitted firing in the air, but from this it does not follow that only the firing of blank cartridges is sanctioned, and that the firing of live cartridges is forbidden. I shall not refuse to protect any man who resorts to firearms on the strength of this circular."

This proclamation makes it perfectly clear to every literate revolutionary that the Minister is prepared to kill, not eight, but eight hundred, eight thousand, and, if he can, eighty thousand workers. He is organizing his army for battle. And in this way he is teaching the German workers to organize. And they are organizing, leaving the ranks of the Social-Democratic Party for the Communist Party.

Everything is going as it should. The hour of the supreme battles, when the working people will destroy the parasites that prey upon them, is drawing near. As a judge, Communism has condemned the rest of the world to death; as the leader of the working masses, and by their hand, it will destroy it, and, as the organizer of labour energy, it will build a new world.

This is not the prophecy of a madman, nor is it consolation for the weak of spirit—it is the inevitable, incontrovertible logic of facts, the logic of history.

(1931)

REPLY TO A QUESTIONNAIRE
OF THE MAGAZINE "VU"

1. Is "another war" to be feared?

The governments of Europe are spending vast sums of the people's money on armaments. We know that even revolvers are not acquired for the ornamentation of drawing rooms, but for the purpose of murder or suicide—still less, then, is it to be presumed that armoured cruisers, submarines, tanks and the like are intended for the promotion of peaceful tourist traffic.

2. What causes may give rise to it?

The chief cause is the existence of capitalists, people with whom the passion for wealth has assumed the character of a disease, very much resembling satyriasis. How monstrous a thing it is that a small class—nay, a mere group—of maniacs have seized possession of the wealth of the earth and irresponsibly dispose of the lives of the peoples, that is, of the working masses, needs no demonstrating. The criminal activity of these people was accurately described 1,500 years ago by Lactantius, one of the "Fathers of the Church," who was known as the Christian Cicero. In the sixth chapter of his book, "On Righteousness," he literally says:

That which was formerly consumed in common, now often began to be amassed in the houses of a few; in order

to make others their slaves, some began to gather into
their own hands the prime necessities of life and diligently
hoard them, making the divine gifts of the earth their
own property solely to satisfy their gluttony and greed.
Then, under a false semblance of justice, they made un-
righteous laws to protect their rapacity and avarice from
the power of the people, doing so, now with the aid of
violence, now with the aid of wealth or of malevolence.
Having thus utterly departed from righteousness, they
sought to erect an arrogant and haughty inequality among
men, brazenly elevating themselves above others, and
began to distinguish themselves from them in attire and
weapons.

Besides Lactantius, the criminality of the capitalist
system was pointed out by all to whom the good habit of
honest thinking was not alien—for instance, by the econom-
ist Sismondi, a man who was very far from Socialism.
He, in the early nineteenth century, fully realized that
". . . a large part of the expenditure on social administration is designated for the protection of the rich from the
poor." We know that the testimony of these honest men
was substantiated scientifically and incontestably by Karl
Marx, and that, on the basis of the Marx-Engels philosophy
of history, and developing it to its logical conclusion,
Vladimir Lenin taught the Russian working class the direct and practical road to liberation from cruel captivity
to lunatics and incompetents.

It may now be legitimately said that the rich wage
wars—not only to strengthen their power over the poor,
but also against one another—with the hands of the poor
and with the help of men of brains, that is, with the
help of that section of the intelligentsia which serves the

inhuman aims of capital. This is one of the most disgusting spectacles in the world.

For instance, in August of 1930, a certain Englishman named Churchill said at a meeting of English manufacturers in the City:

"The English nation does not intend to surrender control over the life and development of India. The Round Table Conference has no authority to frame a constitution for India. No agreement reached at this conference will be binding on the British Parliament.

"Twenty-four thousand Indian politicians and their dupes are in jail. Disorders are put down resolutely and promptly. The British nation will not renounce its mission in India. We do not intend to forfeit this finest jewel in the British Crown. Loss of India would mean the end of the British Empire."

* * *

The Christian sentiments of the Archbishop of Canterbury should have been outraged by the cynicism of this speech. But they were not. The archbishop is also an Englishman, and also a cynic. He displays his official "humanitarianism" only when it is necessary and advantageous to his masters, as he did in the case of the Soviet Union.

Of the lunatics who direct the destinies of nations, the serenest is the King of Spain—he kills his people silently, whereas Pilsudski, for instance, in talks to newspaper reporters, formulates his "divine right" to kill in the words of a megalomaniac. He declares:

"I am one of those ultrastrong individuals—men, I would say, who are gifted with exceptional and extraordinary strength of will and decision."

This was no empty boast. He violently abused the Polish senators, calling them the most offensive names—which, incidentally, did not affect their "honour" or their health in the slightest. It might perhaps be wrong to call him a maniac if he confined himself to blackguarding senators, but in his actions he distinctly tends to imitate the Russian tsars.

Many other facts could be instanced to confirm the fundamental and monstrous fact—that nations are governed by men who have gone completely out of their senses. And it is quite obvious that so long as power over the life and will of nations is in the hands of these people, wars, and "peaceful plunder" in every form, and social cataclysms generally, are inevitable.

3. *What war will be like* was very eloquently described in August 1930 by one of France's former Premiers, M. Caillaux.

"Away with illusions! The last war was a war of heavy artillery, machine guns and submarines. The next war, if only mankind is mad enough to acquiesce in it, will be a war of chemicals and gas. In 1914-18 the combatants died by the million. In the year X—which I hope will never be entered in the calendar—civilian populations will be exterminated. No means exist by which the civilian population can be protected. There is now a gas which penetrates beneath the skin without making any lesion, quite unnoticed by the victim, but which after a time causes severe convulsions, and then leads to chronic and incurable madness. . . .

"It is not only for combatants that these tortures are designated, but, and principally, for the civilian population."

At the time, in August, M. Caillaux's words were confirmed by a leading military scientist, General Berthold Deimling, on the basis of a careful study of the air manoeuvres carried out that summer in Italy, France and Britain.

"Before the 'enemy' air raid on Lyons, gas masks were distributed to the population and arrangements made for the rendering of medical assistance. The city was protected by a special air squadron, electric searchlights and antiaircraft guns. Nevertheless, the attacking force penetrated to the city and bombed it. The recent manoeuvres showed that antiaircraft guns are not of much use, since the planes can always rise above or descend below shrapnel range. The English manoeuvres showed that the civilian population suffers more from the shrapnel splinters than the enemy."

4. *What the war of 1914-18 cost the people of France, and what they might have had if the war had not been* has been very well shown by *Vu*'s estimates, which set the expenditure at 887,000 million francs—all of it the working people's money, since there is no other money in the world. And how many healthy, socially valuable individuals were annihilated?

Every country, if I am not mistaken, has its laws for the prevention and punishment of crime.

One would think that the direct and logical conclusion from these threats of war should be that men who, for the furtherance of their own petty interests, plan the wholesale destruction of human beings should be isolated.

There are very humane ways of isolating such socially dangerous individuals: for instance, they might be deported to the Solomon Islands or to other places inhabited by anthropophagi. I am quite sure this proposal cannot be regarded as cruel, especially if it is applied to Messrs. Churchill, Chamberlain, the Archbishop of Canterbury, Poincaré and their ilk. The Archbishop of Canterbury has, of course, read his St. Jerome and remembers that this saint "when a youth himself saw in Gaul the Atticots, a British tribe who feed on human flesh." If the "arbiters of Europe's destinies" were sent to live with cannibals, they might revive their old tastes. But instead of suggesting some plan of isolating the criminals in accordance with the laws for the prevention and punishment of crime, Caillaux arrives at a totally unexpected conclusion: in his opinion, to save mankind we must follow the ancient Promethean myth: "If man wants to exist, he must bind the new Prometheus—science."

It is to this, to such sheer barbarity that the world is being led by the power of the capitalists, a class which is claimed by its ideologists to be the creator and guardian of culture. The capitalists find that science has already furnished them with adequate means for internecine warfare and for their own defence against the working class, and so—enough of science! It will not be surprising if Europe, like the U.S.A., produces its own "low-brow" Bryans, and if we shortly witness "monkey trials" in which the prosecutors are bishops.

I see no reason why the capitalists should not revive the Inquisition.

That capitalism is destroying culture is incontrovertibly shown by the intellectual impoverishment of Europe.

5. What can be done to avert war?

Just what has been done in the Soviet Union. To put an end to the vicious order of things, you have to begin somewhere. The working class began in the absolutely right way—by establishing their own power in the country. The results of its thirteen years' activity arouse the savage hatred of every scoundrel in the world, but they are arousing and will continue to arouse the active sympathy of the working masses of the whole earth and of all its honest men and women.

(1931)

ADULT SCHOOL IN SMOLENSK

I HAVE received your letter, Comrades.

The best, the strongest and most forceful thing in it is the following:

"Socialist emulation and shock work—that practical expression of the new attitude towards labour in our country—accelerate the tempo of construction and are moulding a new type of worker, one who works not for a master, but for himself and the whole working class."

Quite right, comrades! The Soviet Union is a vast body, composed of one hundred and fifty million units, who, by continually elaborating, exuding and injecting into life the powerful revolutionary energy of their will and reason, are creating new forms of state, a new culture. You are perfectly right, comrades: the culture being created by the working class and by that section of the peasantry which consciously and from conviction is marching shoulder to shoulder with the party of the Leninist workers—that culture demands primarily and principally a "new attitude towards work," as you say.

In what way must this new attitude reveal itself?

In a clear realization that in our country, the Soviet Union, there is no kind of work that is not necessary to the state, and that all forms of labour, whether in the laboratories of the scientists, in universities, on newspapers and magazines, in factory or workshop, in field or underground—all forms of labour deserve equal attention and respect and should be performed with equal energy.

In a clear realization of the necessity for a frugal attitude towards materials, and in a realization of the simple fact that the better, the more solidly and perfectly a thing is made, the longer it will serve and, hence, the sooner will this help to supply the country with the prime necessities of which there are still not sufficient for the needs of the population of our vast land.

In the realization that if a thing is made well and solidly, and will consequently serve people longer, this reduces expenditure of national labour, economizes working energy.

Hence, "the practical expression of the new attitude towards labour" demands a frugal attitude towards materials, machines and equipment, and a ruthless fight against the turning out of defective product. All this, of course, you know. And you also know that:

"The imposing tasks we have set ourselves in the five-year plan, and the high tempo of work, call for a rise in our general level of culture, and the speediest training of our own, proletarian specialists, on whom we may rely, and for whom the cause of the working class is their own cause."

Also correct, and very forcefully said! And, comrades, you have legitimate reason to note with pride that the process of raising "our general level of culture" is proceeding with astonishing speed. Thirteen years ago the overwhelming majority of the labouring folk of tsarist Russia might be called not only dumb, but deaf and dumb. The savage tyranny of the autocracy, the capitalists, the bureaucracy, the priests and the police, a tyranny backed by the bayonets of the downtrodden and brutified soldiers of the tsar's army, permitted the labouring people only to groan quietly and to speak of the bitterness of their life in whispers. The voice of the revolutionaries, especially of the most resolute of them, the Bolsheviks, reached the ears, and the mind and hearts, of the enslaved only slowly and with difficulty. The worker and peasant masses had but to raise their voice and hand, and hundreds of thousands of people were flogged with the knout or shot, as was the case in the Ukraine in 1902, in St. Petersburg on January 9, 1905, after the first revolution of 1905-06, in the Lena goldfields—always and everywhere!

It was necessary to live through the blood and misery of the four years of imperialist war, which destroyed or maimed more than ten million workers and peasants, before the working masses came to understand and appreciate the saving truth of the teachings of Vladimir Ilyich Lenin and his disciples. This invincible truth lent the worker and peasant masses, led by the Bolshevik Party, the strength to shatter and demolish the officer armies commanded by learned generals, and helped to eject from the Soviet Union the excellently trained armies of the "interventionists"—to repulse the onslaught of the European capitalists who had come to the aid of the expelled capitalists of tsarist Russia. All this you know very well, and I mention it merely in order to point out that since then only ten years have elapsed.

What have you achieved in this period?

A nation's cultural level is quite rightly measured by the number of books and newspapers it publishes. Before the revolution our illiterate, semiliterate, deaf and dumb labouring masses stood at a lower level than almost any country in Europe, with the exception of Italy and Spain. But in 1930 we occupied, I believe, one of the first places as regards the number of books and newspapers published. We are justified in saying that the entire people of the Soviet Union are very well familiar with what is going on in the world, and soon they will learn to speak intelligibly and reasonably of their needs. Illiteracy is being rapidly and successfully eliminated. With every year, the workers and peasants are promoting more and more of their own people to work in the administration, in the press, in literature, art, science and technology. The country speaks through the mouths of hundreds of thousands of worker and rural correspondents, army correspondents, youth correspondents and children's correspondents, and through the mouths of hundreds of thousands of "women delegates." We are entitled to be proud of the fact, of which there has been no precedent anywhere or at any time, that our Red Army is a cultural force, and not merely an organization created for the physical defence of the workers' and peasants' state.

But there is an even more graphic and incontestable index of the rapidity and success of our cultural growth. Before me lie some score and a half booklets published by the All-Union Central Council of Trade Unions, and a pile of books penned by our rapidly-growing army of "sketch-writers." Most of them are written by "shock workers," and are simple, lucid and vivid accounts of the way socialist emulation arose in mills and factories, in collective farms and agricultural communes, of the way shock brigades arose, and how Young Communists distinguished themselves in factories. They reflect the rapid spread of the patriotic and creative endeavour of the masses. These little books are themselves an act and product of the creative initiative of the masses. Why do I attach such great practical cultural significance to these booklets? Because in them is reflected the labour experience of the most energetic individuals and groups, and because they are published in hundreds of thousands of copies and will find their way into all the mills and factories of our country, will inform all the many millions of our workers and peasants of the instructive experience of individuals and groups. And this is bound to help to raise productivity of labour all over the Soviet Union. This seemingly small thing is convincing proof of how rapidly the realization is spreading in our country of the necessity to "overtake and outstrip" European capitalism in industrial might. And it is also indicative of the rapid growth of the collective, socialist mentality among the working masses.

I was very glad to read in your letter:

"The evening adult school named after you is doing great work in raising the general-educational and political level of the workers, and at the same time is preparing, in five groups, nearly 200 people to enter university and college."

That is splendid, comrades! Life is still rather hard, and we still lack many things, but we realize that nothing is beyond our power, that there are no obstacles we cannot overcome! All over the country warriors are being trained for industry, for Socialism; the physical might of the Soviet Union is growing together with its spiritual might; cultural forces are increasing and developing.

Well, you will ask, and how are our enemies outside the Soviet Union faring? If I were to tell you myself of the way they live, it would be said that I am "inventing." I will therefore allow them to speak for themselves. Here, for example, is what the monarchist newspaper *Vozrozhdeniye* says:

"Nothing speaks so eloquently of the distress of the Russian émigrés as the multiplicity of balls and concerts they arrange."

This, presumably, was written in melancholy irony, for this same newspaper prints the following gloomy verses by feuilletonist Lolo:

CHRISTMAS MEDITATIONS

At the "dawn" of exile days, we threw
Fate a challenge, at its dangers jeering,
Caring not whatever might ensue,
Destiny's grim jests but little fearing.

> *Fate revengeful drove sweet hope away,*
> *Dreams provided feeble consolation,*
> *Suffering held very life at bay,*
> *Days were spent in gloomy meditation.*

So the years stole by. We swore at grief,
Both in body and in spirit wasting,
Hearts pursued by fear—a furtive thief,
Gnawing pain and bitter anguish tasting.

> *Hair turned grey, we live in want and dearth,*
> *From festive song no consolation earning;*
> *Banished from the country of our birth,*
> *For its far-off shores we yet are yearning. . . .*

Still our thoughts and dreams upon it dwell,
Still we spin air castles in our prison,
Thirst for something—what, we know not well,
Put our faith in things that baffle reason.

Every year we brood, convention's slaves,
At the strangers' hollow merrymaking;
Ghosts of men, we're dancing on our graves,
Feigning mirth with hearts at point of breaking.

Verses like these are no rarity. Life is dull for the émigrés. Incidentally, they frequently and maliciously point to grammatical mistakes made by our young writers, yet they themselves are forgetting the Russian language and write like this: "The story well known from Dante's Inferno about the Florentine rogue who, adopting the guise of a dead rich man, bequeathed to himself, to the vexation of the absent relatives, all his propeity."

This is taken from *Rul*. There, too, we find that "a servant poured a pot with hot water on the robber." In Milyukov's *Posledniye Novosti* you may often meet sentences like "they all scattered, and the wolf himself among them," and "he ran after his daughter."

But murdering the Russian language, is, of course, not the principal occupation of the émigrés. Their time is chiefly devoted to zealously manufacturing lies and slanders about the Soviet Union; they assure one another that "the five-year plan has failed" and that "Russia is going to pieces," although European capitalists and economists are increasingly saying, and with increasing alarm, that "the five-year plan is succeeding," and that the

Soviet Union will soon be entirely independent of the European vampires.

In general, the émigrés are now an uninteresting lot, and nobody cares how they live. The European capitalists and parliamentarians are actively arming, and, it seems, are even more actively stealing.

Here, for example, is a story which appeared in *Rul* on January 7:

"ANOTHER GRAND SWINDLE IN FRANCE

"Paris, 7.1.31. The Oustric bank affair is assuming the character of a huge political scandal. Ex-Minister of Finance Reynaud compiled a list of eleven members of the Chamber of Deputies implicated in the Oustric affair, but his successor, the present Minister of Finance, Germain Martin, includes 45 names in the list, including ex-Premier Tardieu, Martin, chairman of the committee now inquiring into the Oustric affair, another Right leader of the Chamber and deputy for Paris, Taitinger, the leader of the League of Patriotic Youth, also Malvy, chairman of the Chamber of Deputies Finance Committee, and others. An entry has been found in the books of the Oustric bank showing that it paid Millaud, Tardieu's private secretary, 5,000 francs a month. In all, he received 120,000 francs. A receipt of the newspaper *Volonté* for 260,000 francs has also been found, as well as an order for 80,000 francs made out to the provincial paper *Echo du Sol*, organ of the Radical Durand, who was at one time Minister for the Interior. Some papers claim that Germain Martin's list is still far from complete and that it ought to include the present Minister of Agriculture, Victor Boret. The court investigator has established that Oustric paid 17,000 francs to Commissar of Police Benoît. Benoît is notorious as the commissar who arrested and beat up the shoemaker, Almazov. *Le Populaire,* organ of the Socialists, asserts that French holders of dubious foreign securities admitted to quotation in France under the pressure of bribed members of parliament have lost about 20,000 million francs. On the demand of the Ministry of the Colonies, two engineers, Giradon and Bussière, have been arrested in Paris, and a warrant has been issued for the arrest of Socialist ex-Deputy Lagrossilière, who represented Martinique. They are all accused of bribing government officials. In December 1929, the colony of Martinique was granted a credit of 200,000,000 francs for construction work. The accused founded a construction company with a capital of 500,000 francs. This company, which was financed by the Oustric bank, secured contracts with the help of colossal bribes. The bank of Inard, in Draguignan, has failed, declaring a deficit of 11,000,000 francs. The owner of the bank has committed suicide."

And here is an even more interesting story from *Il Mattino*:

"SENSATIONAL SCANDAL IN AMERICA

"London, 19.1.31. A big sensation was caused in America by a report on the results of a search made by the Chicago police in Rex Hotel, belonging to Al Capone the bandit,* and chiefly frequented by the city's

---

* Don't think that the word "bandit" is a printer's error for "banker." No, for some years past Chicago has been in the power of two gangs, one headed by Al Capone and the other by Diamond. Both engage in large-scale bootlegging, both have committed many murders, fight pitched battles with the police and so on.—*Maxim Gorky.*

criminal underworld. Lately, because o. inter-gang strife, the only patrons of the hotel were Al Capone's followers, who came there to report on their activities.

"Only now have the police decided to take energetic measures. At first the search yielded no results, but later two secret safes were found in the wall of one of the rooms. When they were opened they were found to contain packages and bundles of cheques and promissory notes.

"The packages were examined with the object of finding Al Capone's correspondence with accomplices, and weapons. Nothing of this nature was discovered, but the cheques and promissory notes yielded unexpected results. The cheques were signed by well-known high-placed American politicians, and show that not only officials in all branches of American government and administration were implicated in the activities of Al Capone's gang, but even leading personages in Washington.

"The discovery reveals that Al Capone's gang had close contacts with police officials, prominent politicians and persons in high administrative posts, some of them so highly placed that their names cannot be mentioned.

"The news has caused a sensation in political circles and panic among Al Capone's followers.

"(When the first police report was published, showing how far the corruption in the highest classes of society has gone, a large number of speakeasies, where, with the tacit consent of the police, the indigestible products of distilleries which fake fashionable drinks were sold, began to close down.)"

The parenthesis is an insertion in the news message by *Il Mattino*.

"A full description of the contents of the safes will be published within a few days, but presumably a censorship will be established in order to keep the scandal within bounds and to keep too heavily compromised members of high society out of trouble." (*Il Mattino*, January 20, 1931.)*

In the United States, they sometimes get up to amusements like the following:

"A Negro in a Missouri town has been lynched by a mob. He was dragged from the jail to the old schoolhouse, lifted to the roof and tied spread-eagle to the rafters. The whole building was then drenched with kerosene and set afire. The Negro was burned alive as the building was consumed by the flames."

Such are the uses to which Americans sometimes put schools!

Let us conclude these excerpts from foreign newspapers with the following jolly little item from *Vozrozhdeniye*:

"Present-day Berlin is a city of supreme contrasts—external magnificence and an extraordinarily severe internal crisis.

"Someone in Berlin has thought up a smart advertising stunt which probably has no parallel even in America. One of the department stores keeps a special staff of shoplifters. Usually, a middle-aged woman is chosen for the job. The 'shoplifter' spends the whole day in the store. Her business is to be caught stealing. She is instructed in advance what exactly she is to take on the particular day—an umbrella, or a piece of material, or even a radio

* No description of the contents of the safes was published. Al Capone was arrested more than a year after the search.— *Maxim Gorky.*

set. The 'shoplifter' is publicly denounced by one of the shop assistants. Of course, a crowd gathers. The 'culprit' is surrounded by irate middle-class fraus thirsting for blood. Usually they are almost ready to have her lynched, but at the critical moment the department manager appears on the scene and loudly exclaims:

" 'Madam, you have stolen such-and-such an article. It evidently appeals to your fancy. Well, take it and go your way in peace. We sell our goods so cheaply that it is all the same to us whether they are taken for nothing or paid for.'

"That is one side of Berlin life. Here is another. . . .

"These big department stores barely manage to keep afloat, because of high taxes. The celebrated Admirals-Palast Music Hall has gone bankrupt and is being sold literally for a song. And banker Goldschmidt, a man known to the whole German financial world and owner of one of the biggest banks in Berlin, the other day went to bed and put a bullet through his heart. A note was found on his table, saying: 'All my money is gone. . . .' "

Note that in the last item, the job of "shoplifter"— a fine job, what?—is spoken of in a tone of amusement, as a "smart stunt," and the failure of the music hall and the suicide of the banker with obvious regret.

Well, comrades, that should be enough, I think. There is no end to filthy muck of this sort, and it nauseates one to talk of it. My cordial greetings. Good cheer!

(1931)

THE LEGEND OF "COMPULSORY LABOUR"

"THE economic crisis is steadily spreading." "Unemployment is assuming the proportions of a world calamity." "Starvation is causing an epidemic of workers' suicides and crimes against property, and prostitution, including child prostitution, are increasing." "*No less than one thousand American workers* die of starvation daily."

These are not my words, I have taken them from bourgeois newspapers. The capitalists are saying with increasing unanimity, that they have not the means to feed the workers and that state aid to the unemployed cannot be thought of. The President of the U.S.A. refused to endorse a Red Cross allocation in aid of the unemployed, for this, he said, would be a "socialist measure." In Peremyshl, the manager of the labour exchange told an unemployed deputation: "We have no funds. All I can offer you is some money to buy a rope to hang yourselves with."

A prominent German politician put it even more eloquently and cynically: "Twenty million Germans will have to perish because the state cannot feed them." The savage roar of despair of this servitor of capitalism called forth no "comment" in the bourgeois press, which, the lie and slander specialists assert, enjoys "freedom of speech." Nor did this roar awaken any response in the noble hearts of the "humanitarian" intellectuals, nor in the empty souls of the lords, bishops and diverse adventurers who irresponsibly and criminally direct the life of the working class of Europe, America, Asia and Africa. The workers of the world have another opportunity to convince themselves that to expect help from the capitalists, from the bourgeoisie, from humanitarian "freedom of speech" is as hopeless as to expect to get milk from a bull. It is high time the proletarians of all capitalist countries understood that the words, "the workingmen have no country," contain a stern and incontestable proletarian truth. This truth was proclaimed in his day by Karl Marx; it was repeatedly stressed by Vladimir Ilyich Lenin, the founder of Bolshevism. Bourgeois "thinkers," defenders of the power of the capitalists and of economic slavery for the working people, contested this truth. But the time has now come when the capitalists themselves, and not in word but in deed, affirm that the workers are indeed aliens in the lands of their native tongue, that the capitalist system can do nothing for the tens of millions thrown out of employment by its senseless passion for profit, and that twenty million must "perish."

These "bold" words burst from the throat of a German cynic, but, needless to say, they were sympathetically received by all the cynics of Europe and America, by the "masters" of the proletarians. It is high time the proletarians of all countries awakened to the meaning of the words "economic crisis." That meaning is simple and clear: the economic crisis was brought about by capitalist greed, by the anarchy of production, by the utter indifference of the commanding class to how the working people live. Today there are no bourgeois thinkers who, for all their dexterity in distorting the truth, can refute this fact or conceal its tragic significance.

Facts are facts. The capitalist system has created conditions under which tens of millions of people are bereft of work and must "perish" of starvation. This is all the more incontrovertible since it is confirmed by the organizers of starvation themselves.

The organizers of starvation refuse to aid the starving workers; they are concerned with something which to them is far more important than the fact that the unemployed are dying of starvation. What concerns them is the problem of how, and to whom, to sell the grain they have amassed without loss. They are doing everything in their power to keep the grain of the Soviet Union out of the European and American markets.

They could give enough bread to the workers, but that, of course, would not solve the crisis, and, what is more, it is not what they are after. All their energies and attention are bent in another direction.

It is a fact that in the Soviet Union there is no unemployment—on the contrary, there are not enough workers for building a state on genuine socialist lines. It is very likely that in the near future the Soviet State will have to turn to outside sources in order to make good the deficiency of labour power; in part it is already doing so.

Since this fact is incontestable evidence of the rational nature of the socialist economic system, the capitalists had to invent the vile slander about "compulsory labour" in the Soviet Union. To give the capitalists the lie and refute this despicable calumny is quite useless, because the capitalist as a rule is not a man, but a "trust," that is, part of a soulless, mechanically-operating machine, driven by the forces of greed and envy. And no matter what the trustified press, which has been bought body and soul, liver and lights, by the bourgeoisie, may say, no matter how eloquently and verbosely it may talk about "slave labour" and "compulsory labour" in the Soviet Union, its venal words cannot gloss over, cover up and conceal from sight the fact that it is precisely the forces of capitalist greed and envy that is destroying culture, reducing life to anarchy, and more and more definitely leading to the senseless exhaustion of the physical strength of the labouring people.

The utter senselessness and criminality of capitalist "management" is best brought out by the fact that labour, the creator of values, is being increasingly diverted to "war industry," that is, to the production of instruments for the slaughter of human beings and the destruction of genuine labour values, cultural values, whose purpose it is to improve the conditions of human life and labour. It is high time the workers of Europe understood that, essentially and in the final count, capitalism compels them to work for destruction. This is not a "paradox": wars are instigated in the interests of trade; the more you destroy, the more you sell. The war of 1914-18 increased the number of millionaires.

The legend fabricated by the capitalists about "compulsory labour" in the Soviet Union has as its ultimate aim a piratical attack upon the Soviet Union—an attack in which the capitalists will compel their unemployed proletarians and poverty-stricken peasants to take part.

In that case the proletariat of Europe would have to take up arms against its most advanced detachment, against the workers and peasants of the Soviet Union, who, by supreme exertion and with amazing enthusiasm, are courageously and successfully building a socialist state, and are thereby working in the interest of the proletarians of the whole earth—for the realization of socialism in a country with a population of 160,000,000 will mean the ultimate collapse of capitalism throughout the world.

Is it necessary to tell you, the workers of Europe and America, that it is precisely this fear of their doom that is the root and origin of the hatred entertained by the capitalists for the Soviet Union? Or that it is precisely from this fear and this hatred that sprang the legend of "compulsory labour," as well as the legend about dumping? They invented the story about "dumping" because they do not want to give the hungry cheap bread, because they do not want to "incur a loss," when there is grain in such abundance that it is allowed to rot and is used as fuel for locomotives. The story about "compulsory labour" has been invented with the purpose of organizing an economic blockade of the Soviet Union, with the purpose of creating difficulties for the proletariat of the Soviet Union in the organization of their state, with the purpose of preventing the realization of the five-year plan and the collectivization of agriculture, of weakening the Soviet Union and hurling you against its people and turning the whole Land of Soviets into a colony of European capital. All this is so simple that a child can understand it. And you must understand it too. It is high time!

In the game started against the workers and peasants of the Soviet Union, it is you that are the heaviest losers.

"Compulsory labour"? In the Soviet Union labour is obligatory, for the basic maxim of Socialism, properly understood, is: "he who does not work, neither shall he eat." Under Socialism everyone must work, and there is no place for marauders or parasites; and there must not be the conditions that might produce marauders, parasites, idlers, self-seekers, adventurers and similar scum. In the Soviet State, compulsory labour is not practised even in houses of detention; there illiterate criminals are obliged to learn to read and write, and peasants are allowed leave to go home and work their land and see their families.

How high the human being is valued in the Soviet Union is perhaps best shown by the existence of the labour communes, all the members of which are former "socially dangerous" individuals.

In the Soviet Union, the process of cultural regeneration of the worker and peasant masses, who are extremely diversified in their national composition, is proceeding with amazing rapidity. No one could have believed that this process would proceed so rapidly and so successfully that even the nomadic tribes of the Central Asiatic steppe-land would freely and willingly join the majestic movement. In the Soviet Union people who want to work, and who realize the lofty aim of labour in the Union of Socialist Soviets—such people, whoever they may have been in the past, are surrounded by the Soviet workers' and peasants' state with the greatest solicitude and attention.

In bourgeois society, a man who errs from the right path is bound to fall, struck down by the "law"; he is cast out of "society" and is trampled down by the hoofs of the middle class, or he joins the ranks of the professional criminals, the offenders against the "sacred institution" of private property. Of course, there are incorrigible criminals in the Soviet Union too. For instance, two murderers and a raper of minors recently fled from a northern lumber camp to England. It was they who told Lord Newton and some bishop the story that "compulsory labour" was practised in the lumber camps. As we know, the lords and bishops were not fastidious and reiterated the lies of the murderers and raper in the British Houses of Parliament.

One would think that even a man with the rank of a lord or a bishop is not bound to be unnaturally stupid. Their stupidity is obviously unnatural, because they pretend to be excessively stupid, since they find this to their advantage. Actually, they are just normally stupid, as befits lords and bishops, who are Englishmen into the bargain, that is, men with whom hypocrisy is a sort of hobby.

To demonstrate that complusory labour cannot exist in a country where the workers and peasants are the masters, where they are sparing no effort to create a socialist culture, where group and individual labour emulation is in full spate, where such a thing as "shock work" is possible, and where the workers, in their eagerness to accelerate and expand production, themselves better the plans of their government with their own production and financial counterplans—to demonstrate the impossibility of compulsory labour under such conditions would be tedious and profitless. Those for whom slandering the Soviet Union is a necessity will not, of course, believe any proofs. They realize full well what a menace to them the building of Socialism is, and they have to assert that the five-year plan is being carried out by compulsory labour, and not by the class reason and disciplined will of workers and peasants who are working for themselves and who know that they themselves are their own rulers.

Capitalism, for its part, realizes full well that it is precisely the knowledge of this that explains the mass influx of shock workers into the Party after the discovery of the wide-flung conspiracy of the "wreckers," who wanted to sell and betray the Soviet Union to the European capitalists. The capitalists have long since realized that the Bolsheviks are by no means just a "handful" of men who have seized political "power," but a good ten million politically educated people, and that the ideological and practical, the cultural and labour influence of these millions is spreading to all the rest of the population with amazing speed. The capitalists guess that the time is not so far off when all the labouring folk of the Soviet Union will become "Bolsheviks"—that they are no longer to be broken, and that their example will be followed by all the "starvelings of creation."

The capitalists—whose power rests on slave labour not only in the colonies, but in their own countries, where they beat up and shoot down unemployed and strikers in the streets almost daily—say that compulsory labour is abhorrent to Christian morals. They are lying, of course. But they refute their own lies. Here, for example, is an amendment the Americans introduced to section 307, art. 664, of their customs regulations—it deserves careful perusal:

"Washington, Feb. 12. An amendment adopted by the House of Representatives Tariff and Finance Committee to section 307 of the Tariff Act reads:

"'All goods, wares, articles, and merchandise mined, produced or manufactured wholly or in part in any foreign country by convict labour or/and forced labor or/and indentured labour under penal sanctions shall not be entitled to entry at any of the ports of the United States, and the importation thereof is hereby prohibited, and the Secretary of the Treasury is authorized and directed to prescribe such regulations as may be necessary for the enforcement of this provision. The provisions of this section relating to goods, wares, articles, and merchandise mined, produced, or manufactured by forced labour or/ and indentured labour, shall take effect on April 1, 1931; *but in no case shall such provisions be applicable to goods, wares, articles, or merchandise so mined, produced, or manufactured which are not mined, produced, or manufactured in such quantities in the United States as to meet the consumptive demands of the United States.'*"

As you see, it is not a question of morals, but whether it is profitable or not profitable.

* * *

In the despicable business of creating an atmosphere of lies and slanders around the Soviet Union the capitalists have the zealous assistance of the "Socialists" of the Second International; and the most zealous are the Germans. And this is quite understandable: whereas the workers "have nothing to lose but their chains," the German Socialists may lose something far pleasanter than chains. The fact is that the German Social-Democrats are, primarily and principally, 300,000—if not more—government, municipal and trade union officials. They are in power, and they want to retain their positions. They call themselves Socialists, but they look on quite coolly at the sale of municipal enterprises to private interests—and that alone is a sufficiently graphic illustration of what their "Socialism" is worth. And as to the attitude of these "Socialists" to the workers, this is well demonstrated by a fact like the following. The employees of the Leiser chain stores came out on strike. *Vorwärts,* organ of the Social-Democratic Party, printed an article entitled, "Illegal Strike," and Leiser had it posted up in his stores as proof that he, the boss, was in the right. Quite clearly, "Socialists" of this type can have no liking for the Soviet Union. And they particularly dislike the Communists, which gives rise to cases like the following. A Communist happens to be working in the offices of a district cooperative society, and is hence, as it were, a black sheep. He is told that if he does not want to lose his livelihood, he must leave the Communist Party and join the Social-Democratic Party. Being a family man, he yields to pressure, and the "Socialist" party gains a member and the party treasury a few extra marks—and probably a certain amount of cash goes from the treasury for the support of the *Sotsialistichesky Vestnik,* a sheet published by Dan, Abramovich and similar gentry which teems with malicious lies about the Soviet Union. And it is conceivable that the German Social-Democratic workers are, without themselves knowing it, helping the spread of lies and slanders about the Soviet Union and its workers' and peasants' government.

* * *

The socialist press is the favourite source of information of the press of the Russian Whiteguard émigrés, although they themselves are no mean hands at the manufacture of lies and slanders. Truth to tell, their products are becoming shoddier and shoddier. For example,

Professor Milyukov's paper says that upward of 600,000 exiles are living in Solovki.

This would be terrible, if it were not a sheer lie. The biggest of the Solovki islands is 23 kilometres long, and 15 kilometres broad. Nearly a quarter of this area is covered by lakes. The next largest island after the Bolshoy Anzersky is three times smaller. One of the islands is entirely given over to the breeding of sable, fox and polar fox, and scarcely a dozen people live on it. The other islands are smaller still and uninhabited. Naturally, you couldn't put 600,000 people on these islands; they would probably not hold 20,000.

In this same paper an overenergetic and not very intelligent old lady calculates that in the Soviet Union there are fifteen million people without jobs. This in a country where labour exchanges are being closed down because they have nobody to cater for, in a country which is experiencing a shortage of labour!

A certain physician writes to the monarchists' newspaper that "foreigners find it hard living in the collective farms." What foreigners? How did they get into the collective farms?

Speaking of the circulation of Soviet newspapers, they cut the figures to a fraction, and omit to say, for instance, that *Krestyanskaya Gazeta* is printed in 2,500,000 copies, and besides publishes other periodicals for the peasant population in no less than 3,000,000 copies: the children's paper *Druzhniye Rebyata*—750,000; *Gazeta dlya Nachinayushchikh Chitat,* a paper for beginners who have just learned to read—750,000; *Na Strazhe*—450,000; *Kustar i Artel*—200,000, and the magazines: *Krestyanka,* for peasant women—80,000; *Krestyanskaya Molodyozh,* for the peasant youth—40,000; *Izba-Chitalnya*—40,000; *Dere-vensky Teatr*—20,000; *Selkor*—12,000, and others with circulations running into tens of thousands. The humourous magazine for peasants, *Lapot*, has a circulation of 245,000. Take the central newspapers of the Soviet Union: *Pravda* has a circulation of 1,530,000, *Izvestiya*—1,100,000, *Komsomolskaya Pravda*—567,000.

The émigrés know that these are the true figures. But they have to lie. Lies and slander are their only weapons. Similar falsehoods by people who have been brutalized by the "tedium of life" may be found in any of the émigré newspapers. This is the way they inform the European bourgeois and "socialist" press. But sometimes they feel themselves that their mendacity is going to the length of absurdity, and then you get oddities like this. The Berlin *Rul*—for some reason, one of the most embittered, and a very silly and vainglorious sheet—prints the following piece of self-adulation:

"In connection with the diverse rumours prompted by the latest events in Moscow, the authoritative *Kölnische Zeitung* cites extracts from the Paris *Croix*, which draws attention to the false information proceeding chiefly from Riga and Revel and contrasts it with the h o n e s t i n f o r m a t i o n g i v e n b y c e r t a i n n e w s p a p e r s, n o t a b l y t h e B e r l i n *R u l*, which has facilities for receiving information from Russia, and which, thanks to its literary experience, which goes back to the days when *Rech* was published in St. Petersburg, is able to distinguish false news from true."

Rul has more than once been convicted of lying even by émigré newspapers. For example, Milyukov's Paris paper showed that the "Red Commander" letters were fabricated in the offices of *Rul,* and fabricated very clumsily.

All these are insignificant motes, but when there are many motes they form a cloud of dust, and people who sincerely want to know the truth about life in the Soviet Union have to peer through a murky pall. But it is not so much these people that matter as the working masses of Europe and America—it is the proletariat that this cloud of slanders and lies is intended to blind. The legend about "compulsory labour" has been invented not only with the purpose of economically blockading the Soviet Union, but also in an attempt to discredit the socialist constructive efforts of the Soviet workers and peasants in the eyes of the proletarians.

They are being gradually prepared for a new holocaust. The Social-Democrats drove them to the field of death in 1914, the Socialists fired on the workers in the streets of Berlin in 1918—this is well worth remembering.

I recently heard a gramophone record of a song by Negro singers. It contains the following words:

> *We're going to fight again, somewhere,*
> *And again we don't know why.*

If the proletarians of Europe and America do not want to be slaughtered again by the tens of million, they ought to know where they are being driven, and why, and they ought to know whom they should follow.

(*1931*)

REPLY TO AN INTELLECTUAL

You write:

"Many European intellectuals are beginning to feel they are people without a country, and our interest in life in Russia is growing. Nevertheless, it is not clear to us what is going on in the Soviets."

What is going on in the Soviet Union is a struggle waged by the organized will of the working masses against the elemental forces of nature and against those "elemental" forces in man which, essentially, are nothing but the instinctive anarchism of an individuality moulded for centuries by the pressure of the class state. This struggle is the fundamental feature of current life in the Soviet Union. He who sincerely desires to grasp the profound significance of the revolutionary cultural process going on in former Russia, will properly understand it only if he looks upon this process as a struggle for culture and for the creation of culture.

You people of the West have adopted an attitude to the peoples of the Soviet Union which I cannot call worthy of men who consider themselves the vehicles of a culture that is compulsory for the whole world—for it is the attitude of a shopkeeper to his customer, of a creditor to his debtor. You remember that tsarist Russia borrowed money from you and learned to think from you, but you forget that the loans brought fat interest to your manufacturers and merchants. You forget that in the nineteenth and twentieth centuries Russian science poured its mighty stream into the general current of European scientific research, and that now, when your creative art is manifestly and regrettably drying up, you live by the strength—by the ideas and images—of Russian art. You will not venture to deny that Russian music and literature, alongside with Russian science, long ago became the possession of the entire cultured world. One would think that a people which in the course of one century elevated its intellectual creative powers to a level equal to that which Europe achieved only in the course of many centuries—that this people, now that it has obtained the opportunity for free creative endeavour, deserves more thorough study and closer attention than it receives from the intellectuals of Europe.

Is it not time for you squarely to face the fact that the European bourgeoisie and the peoples of the Soviet Union are working for different aims? Surely, it is already clear enough that it is not the interests of the "nation as a whole" that the political leaders of Europe serve, but only the interests of mutually contending capitalist groups. This strife between traders who are absolutely unaccountable to their "nations" has led to such crimes against humanity as the European shambles of 1914-18; it has accentuated the "elemental forces" of mutual distrust among nations, it has converted Europe into a series of armed camps, it is squandering vast quantities of the national labour, gold and iron on the manufacture of weapons for the wholesale slaughter of human beings. This mutual strife of the capitalists aggravates the world economic crisis, which, by sapping the physical strength of the "nation," retards the growth of its intellectual forces. This strife of the marauders and traders is paving the way for a new world war. Ask yourself why all this is so. And, generally, if you sincerely desire to cure yourself of your distressing perplexities and of your passive attitude towards life, ask yourself some most elementary questions of a social nature, and, without allowing yourself to be distracted by words, seriously ponder over the purposes of the existence of capitalism, or, rather, over the criminality of its existence.

You, the intellectuals, "treasure culture, whose importance to all mankind is undeniable." Do you? You see with your own eyes that, in Europe, capitalism is daily and incessantly destroying this culture you treasure, and, by its inhuman and cynical policy in the colonies, is undoubtedly creating an army of enemies of European culture. While, in the black and the yellow continents, this "culture" of the marauders is training thousands of similar marauders, it should not be forgotten that in these continents there are still several hundreds of millions of despoiled and embeggared. The Indian, the Chinaman, the Annamite bow to the guns, but this does not mean that they worship European culture. And they are beginning to understand that in the Soviet Union another culture, different in form and in meaning, is in the making.

"The East is peopled by pagans and savages," you say, and, in illustration of the savagery of the East, you refer to the status of the oriental woman. Let us discuss this question of savages.

On the music hall stages of Europe tens and hundreds of women are made to display their nakedness. Does it not seem to you that making a public diversion of the naked female body should call forth some protest from the mothers, wives and sisters of the European intellectuals? It is not from the "moral" standpoint that I refer to this cynical diversion, but from the standpoint of biology and social hygiene. To me, this despicable and vulgar diversion is an undoubted proof of the fact that the European bourgeoisie is sinking into savagery and decadence. I am convinced that the conspicuous and rapid growth of homosexualism and lesbianism, which is due to economic causes—the high cost of maintaining a family—is accelerated by this loathsome public humiliation of women. All too many are the symptoms of the growing savagery of bourgeois Europe, and it is not for you to speak of the savages of the East. The peasants of those of its tribes which now form part of the Soviet Union are superbly learning to appreciate the value of true culture and the profound importance of the role of woman in life. The value of true culture is appreciated by the workers and peasants of the Chinese provinces where Soviets have already been set up. The Indians will learn to appreciate it too. The entire labouring folk of our planet must learn where lies the true path to their freedom. And it is for this freedom they are fighting in all parts of the earth.

In the capitalist world, the struggle for oil, for iron, for armaments needed for another massacre of millions and millions of human beings, for the right of a minority politically and economically to oppress the majority, grows fiercer and fiercer. This brazen, cynical and criminal struggle waged by a small group of people who have gone savage in their lust for senseless accumulation of wealth, has the blessing of the Christian Church, the most hypocritical and iniquitous of all the churches of the earth. This struggle has completely killed and annihilated the "human-ism" which cost the intelligentsia of Europe so dear, and of which they were so proud. Never before have the intelligentsia so clearly betrayed their impotence and so shamelessly revealed their indifference to life as they do now, in the twentieth century, which is so replete with tragedies created by the cynicism of the ruling classes. In the political sphere, the thoughts and sentiments of the intelligentsia are dominated by adventurers, obedient instruments of the will of capitalist groups, who, bartering everything that is to be bought and sold, actually, in the final analysis, barter the energies of the people. The concept "people," as I use it here, includes not only the workers and peasants, but also the petty officials and the army of "servants" of capital and the intelligentsia generally —who are still a fairly colourful patch on the filthy rags of bourgeois society.

* * *

Absorbed in their verbal search for the "universally human," the intellectuals of the diverse tribes and tongues look upon one another through the prism of their national and class prejudices and preconceptions. As a consequence, the defects and shortcomings of their neighbours interest them far more than their virtues. They have flogged one another so often that they no longer know who has been flogged most and hence deserves most respect. Capitalism has imbued them with a sceptical distrust of one another and astutely plays on this.

They failed to grasp the historical import of the October Revolution, and had neither the moral strength nor the desire to protest against the bloody and piratical

intervention of the capitalists in 1918-21. When the authorities in the Soviet Union arrest a professor, a monarchist
or a conspirator, they protest; but when their capitalists
violently coerce the peoples of Indo-China, India or Africa, they are indifferent. If a score or two arrant criminals
are shot in the Soviet Union, they cry "Atrocity!" but if
thousands of absolutely innocent people are exterminated by guns and machine guns in India or Annam, the
humane intellectuals preserve a discrete silence. They are
still incapable of appreciating the results of the thirteen
years' work of the active forces of the Soviet Union. In
parliament and the press, politicians keep hammering it
into their heads that the work of the Soviet government
amounts solely to the destruction of the "old world,"
and they believe that this is so.

But the fact is that in the Soviet Union the working people are rapidly absorbing all the finest, all the
indisputably precious treasures created by universal culture—and are not only absorbing but multiplying them.
The old world, of course, is being destroyed, for the individual must be liberated from the diverse restrictions
it imposes to intellectual growth, from captivity to class,
national and ecclesiastical ideas and superstitions. The
fundamental purpose of the cultural process in the Soviet
Union is to unite the people of the whole world into a
single entity. This work is prescribed and dictated by
the whole course of man's history—it is the beginning
of a world, not only a national, renaissance. This was
the dream of isolated individuals, of Campanella, Thomas
More, Saint Simon, Fourier and others, at a time when for
the realization of this dream the industrial and technical
requisites did not yet exist. Today these requisites do exist,

the dream of the utopians has been given a scientific foundation, and the work of realizing this dream is being accomplished by the many-millioned masses. Another generation, and in the Soviet Union alone there will be some two hundred million workers in this field.

People believe when they are unwilling or unable to understand.

Class instinct, the mentality of the small proprietor, the philosophy of the blind defenders of class society induce the intellectuals to believe that in the Soviet Union the individual is crushed and oppressed, that the industrialization of the country is being effected by compulsory labour, in the way the pyramids were built in Egypt. This is not merely a lie, it is so obviously a lie that it can be taken as the truth only by people absolutely devoid of individuality and utterly debilitated, by people whose intellectual power and critical faculties are completely run down and exhausted.

The legend that the individual is crushed is definitely refuted by the rapid increase in the numbers of talented individuals in all branches of endeavour—in art, in science, in technology. And it could not be otherwise in a country where the entire mass of the population is drawn into the process of culture-making.

Of the twenty-five million "private owners"—the semiliterate and illiterate peasants who were debased and downtrodden by the despotism of the Romanovs and the oppression of the landed bourgeoisie—twelve million have already appreciated the wisdom and advantage of collective farming. This new method of work is freeing the peasant from his conservatism and anarchism, from the zoological qualities of the small owner. It leaves him with considerable free time, and he uses this leisure to educate himself. This year (1931) fifty million adults and children in the Soviet Union are receiving tuition, and it is planned in the course of the year to print 800 million books—3,500 million printed signatures. There is already a demand for 5,000 million signatures, but the mills are unable to supply enough paper. The thirst for knowledge is growing. In these thirteen years scores of scientific research institutes, new universities and polytechnics have been founded in the Soviet Union, and they are all brimful of young students; the worker and peasant masses are continuously advancing thousands of disseminators of culture from their midst.

Has any bourgeois state ever made it its aim, is any bourgeois state capable of making it its aim, to introduce the entire mass of the working people to culture? History's answer to this simple question is in the negative. Capitalism promoted the intellectual development of men of labour only to the extent that it was necessary and advantageous for the advancement of industry and trade. Capitalism needs men only as a more or less cheap source of power and as defenders of the existing order. Capitalism has never understood, and is incapable of understanding, that the aim and purpose of genuine culture is to facilitate the development and accumulation of intellectual energy. In order that this energy may develop continuously, and help man as quickly as possible to master the forces and gifts of nature, the maximum amount of physical energy must be freed from working senselessly and anarchically for the narrow and selfish interests of the capitalists, marauders and parasites on labouring humanity. The idea of the human individual as a repository of vast stores of intellectual energy is quite alien to the ideologists of capitalism. In spite of all its verbal subtleties and embroideries, the ideology of the defenders of the power of the minority over the majority is essentially zoological.

The class state is built on the model of a zoo, where all the animals are confined in iron cages. In the class state the cages, more or less skilfully constructed, are ideas; they keep men divided and make it practically impossible for them to develop a consciousness of the unity of their interests, or the growth of a united, genuinely universal human culture.

Would I deny that in the Soviet Union the individual is restricted? Of course not. In the Soviet Union the will of the individual is restricted whenever it is inimical to the will of the masses, who are conscious of their right to build new forms of life, and who have set themselves an aim beyond the power of any individual, even if he be a supernatural genius. The advanced detachments of the workers and peasants of the Soviet Union are marching to their lofty goal, heroically bearing on the way a host of personal discomforts and inconveniences.

The individualist insists on his fictitious freedom, on that accustomed independence he has been induced to feel by centuries of education within his iron cage. The cages in which the writers, journalists, philosophers, officials and the other smoothly polished parts of the apparatus of the capitalist system are enclosed are of course more comfortable than the cage of the peasant. His sooty and dirty hut, his "private enterprise," keep him in a continual state of self-defence against the caprices of the elemental forces of nature and the tyranny of the capitalist state, which pares him to the bone. Psychologically, the peasants of Calabria and Bavaria, of Hungary and Brittanny, of Africa and America, differ very little from one another, if one excludes differences of language. All over the globe the peasants are almost equally helpless and equally infected with zoological individualism. In the Soviet Union the peasant is adopting collective forms of labour and is gradually throwing off that specific mentality of the slave of the soil, the eternal captive of propertied pauperdom.

Individualism results from pressure on man from without, from class society; individualism is the futile attempt of the individual to protect himself from tyranny. But, surely, self-defence is nothing but self-restriction, since the state of self-defence retards the growth of intellectual energy. This state is equally harmful to society and to the individual. The "nation" spends billions arming itself against neighbour nations, the individual spends the greater part of his energy defending himself against the tyranny of class society. "Life is struggle"? Yes, but it should be a struggle of men and mankind against the elemental forces of nature, a struggle for mastery over them. The class state has turned this noble struggle into a despicable fight for command of the physical energy of men, for the purpose of their enslavement. The individualism of the nineteenth- and twentieth-century intellectual differs from the individualism of the peasant not in essence, but only in its forms of expression: it is more colourful and smoother polished, but it is equally zoological, and equally blind. The intellectual lives between the anvil of the people and the hammer of the state: in general, of course, his condition of life is hard and tragic, because reality is usually hostile to him. That is why it so often happens that the captive mind of the intellectual extends the discomfort and hardship of his conditions of life to the whole world, and the outcome of his objective experience of life is philosophical pessimism, practical scepticism and similar mental distortions. We know that the home of pessimism is the East, especially India, where the caste system of society has been carried to fanatical lengths.

The reality of class society restricts the free growth of the individuality, and the individuality therefore seeks position and repose beyond reality. In god, for example. The toiling folk, in their search for an explanation of the beneficent or baleful manifestations of the elemental forces of nature, incarnated them, in their splendid pagan manner, in the images of beings resembling humans but more powerful than any human. The people endowed their gods with all their own virtues and vices. The gods of Olympus and Asgard are magnified humans. Vulcan and Thor are smiths, similar to any ordinary smith, only stronger and more skilful. The religious creations of the working people are simply art creations; there is nothing mystical about them, they are fully realistic and undivorced from actuality; they definitely reveal the influence of labour activity, and, essentially, their purpose is to encourage labour. In the poetic creations of the people one observes a consciousness of the fact that, when all is said and done, reality is created, not by gods but by the labour energy of man. The people are pagan. Even 1,500 years after Christianity became the state religion, the gods, as the peasant conceives them, are still the ancient gods: Christ, the Madonna, the saints walk the earth and interfere in the working life of the people just as did the gods of the ancient Greeks and Scandinavians.

Individualism arose from "private enterprise." Clan added to clan formed a collective. The individual who, from one cause or another, severed himself, broke away, from the collective, and, hence, from actual, perpetually recreated reality, made for himself a god, a single, mystical god, beyond the grasp of reason, a god whose purpose was to justify the right of the individual to independence and power. Mysticism was necessary because the right of the individual to be a sovereign, an autocrat, cannot be explained by reason. Individualism endows its god with the qualities of omniscience, omnipotence and superintelligence, in other words, with the qualities which the human individual would himself like to possess, but which develop only in the reality created by collective labour. This reality always lags behind and falls short of man's reason, because the reason which creates it is always slowly, but continuously, perfecting itself. If this were not so, people would of course be content with reality, and contentment is a passive state. Reality is created by the inexhaustible power of man's rational will, and there is never a moment when its development ceases. The mystical god of the individualists has always been immobile, inactive, creatively lifeless; and he cannot be otherwise, since he reflects the inherent creative impotence of individualism. The history of the sterile fluctuations of the religious metaphysical thought of the individualists is known to every educated person. In our day the impotence of these "intellectual" fluctuations has become indisputably clear, and betrays the utter bankruptcy of individualist philosophy. But the individualist still continues his fruitless search for answers to the "enigmas" of life. And he seeks for them, not in labour activity, which is developing in all its aspects and with revolutionary speed, but in the "recesses of his ego." He continues to stand guard over the beggardom of "private enterprise," and has no desire to fructify life. He is entirely taken up with introspection, as a means of self-defence. He does not live, but hides, and his "intellectual activity" is very reminiscent of the activity of a certain biblical personage—Onan.

By meekly submitting to the precepts of the capitalist state, the intellectuals of Europe and America—the writers, the journalists, the economists, the adventurers who were once Socialists, the dreamers of the Gandhi type— are, knowingly or unknowingly, helping to guard the foundations of the bourgeois class system, which definitely hampers the onmarch of the universal cultural process. In this process an increasingly active part is being played by the will of the working masses to create a new reality. The intellectuals think that they are protecting "democracy," although it has already demonstrated and continues to demonstrate its impotence, that they are protecting "freedom of the individuality," although it is shut up in a cage of ideas which restrict its intellectual growth, that they are protecting "freedom of speech," although the press has been captured by the capitalists and can only serve their anarchic, inhuman, criminal interests. The intellectual works for his enemy, for the master is and always has been the enemy of the worker, and the idea of "class collaboration" is as naïve and senseless as friendship between the wolf and the sheep.

The intellectuals of Europe and America are working for their enemies. This is shown very distinctly and nakedly by their attitude toward the revolutionary cultural process begun by the worker and peasant masses of the

Soviet Union. This process is proceeding in an atmosphere of frenzied hatred on the part of the European bourgeoisie, and under the threat of a piratical attack by the latter on the Soviet Union. The pressure of these two factors explains practically all the adverse facts which the enemies of the Soviet workers and peasants are so fond of stressing.

Particularly zealous and malicious in recording these adverse features in Soviet life are the Russian émigré politicians, the men who supply the information to the European bourgeois press. Who are they, these émigrés? The majority of them are political failures, ambitious, petty individuals, but men with "great hopes." Some of them would like to be Masaryks, Briands or Churchills, many of them Fords, but the thing about them all is that they tried to "bite off more than they could swallow." Their moral, and intellectual, worthlessness is known to me of old. They revealed it as far back as 1905-07, after the first revolution. They then gave daily demonstrations of their incompetence in the Duma, and betrayed it to the full in 1914-17, when they came forward as "champions" against the "autocracy," but not, it goes without saying, against imperialism. They gained a certain popularity as moulders of the political consciousness of the petty and big bourgeoisie—in a word, they are ideologians of the middle class. "When there is no fish, a crab will serve," the saying goes. In Russian life, theirs was the backward gait of a crab. This is characteristic of the majority of intellectuals in times of revolution.

But their shameful role is not confined to perpetual political "changes of landmark" and forgetfulness of "Hannibal vows." In 1917 and after, together with the surviving tsarist generals, who despised them as renegades and "enemies of the tsar," they served the oil, textile and coal magnates, the big millers and landlords. Russian history remembers them as traitors to their people. For four years they betrayed and sold their people to your capitalists, Messieurs the intellectuals of Europe. They helped the Denikins, Kolchaks, Wrangels, Yudeniches and other professional manslaughterers to wreck the economy of their country, already devastated by the four years of a war which was a disgrace to all Europe. With the help of these contemptible individuals, the generals of the European capitalists and the generals of the tsar exterminated hundreds of thousands of Soviet workers and peasants, burned hundreds of villages and Cossack hamlets, destroyed railway lines, blew up bridges, damaged everything they could, with the object of utterly weakening their country and delivering it into the hands of the European capitalists. Ask them why they massacred the people and wrecked their economy, and they will shamelessly tell you: "for the good of the people"—taking care to omit to say why, then, the "people" ejected them from their country.

Since 1926, they have assisted in the hatching of numerous plots against the workers' and peasants' state. Of course, they deny they had any share in these crimes, although the plotters, their friends, have admitted that they gave information to their press throwing "a deliberately false light on Soviet activities," and, it goes without saying, the plotters, in their turn, were guided by the press of the betrayers of their country.

Messrs. Europeans, your humanitarian feelings are outraged by the deserved punishment meted out to the forty-eight sadists, organizers of starvation? Very strange!

How is it you are not outraged by the almost daily murders of absolutely innocent workers by the police in the streets of your cities? The forty-eight degenerates are more loathsome than the Düsseldorf sadist, Kürten, who was nine times sentenced to death. I do not know what were the motives of the Soviet authorities for not committing these plotters to trial, but I can guess: there are crimes whose villainy is much too attractive to our enemies, and to teach our enemies villainy would be too naïve. Incidentally, if I were a German citizen I would protest against the public trial of Kürten, because class society has produced, and produces, too many sadists, and I see no reasons that would justify the necessity for the public propaganda of sadism or for perfecting the technical qualifications of criminals. It is permissible to ask: why do European intellectuals stand up for "freedom of the individual," when the individual happens to be Prof. S. F. Platonov, for instance, a monarchist, but are indifferent when the individual happens to be a Communist?

If you want to have an accurate idea of the depths of bestiality to which the Russian émigrés have sunk, read the appeal for funds for the fight against the people of the Soviet Union printed in the Paris organ of the monarchist émigrés, *Vozrozhdeniye*.

This infamous undertaking is headed by "The Blessed Metropolitan Antonius, President of the Synod of Archbishops of the Orthodox Church of Russia Abroad." Here are this fiend's own words:

"By virtue of the power granted me by God, I bless all weapons raised against the satanical Red government, and remit the sins of all who, in the ranks of the insurrectionary levies or as individual people's avengers lay down their lives in the cause of Russia and Christ. And, above all, I bless the weapons and the militant work of the National Brotherhood of Russian Truth, which for many years, by word and by deed, has been waging a stubborn fight against the Red Satan in the name of God and Russia. May the mercy of the Lord sustain all who join the ranks of the Brothers or who come to the aid of the Brotherhood.

"Metropolitan Antonius"

It is quite clear that the Metropolitan, the leader of a Christian church, is giving his sanction to violation of the will of the people and to terroristic acts. Does it not appear to you that such appeals, such condonence of murder by a churchman whom malevolence has obviously driven to idiocy, are not quite in place in the capital of a "cultured state"? Don't you think you ought to cry "Quiet!" "Lie down!" to "His Blessedness." Is not this savage outburst on the part of a Russian priest a sign not only of the bestialization of the Russian émigrés, but also of the extreme and absolutely disgraceful indifference of the European intellectuals to social ethics and social hygiene? Yet you talk about the "savagery of the East."

You believe what the Russian émigrés say. Well, that, of course, is your "personal affair"—but I doubt whether it is your right. I doubt it because you are clearly not interested in what the other side, the workers' and peasants' government, has to say. The Soviet press does not conceal objectionable features in our present-day realities; its principle is the sternest self-criticism, and it is not afraid of washing any dirty linen in public. It is working with the masses, the millions, who are still not very literate—for which, of course, they cannot be blamed. But honest people should remember that the not very literate may easily make mistakes. And it should be known that the majority of the slanders and lies which the émigré press disseminates, and which are its comfort and mainstay, are based on facts taken from Soviet self-criticism.

I, personally, both in the press and at meetings in Moscow and Leningrad, have protested against inordinate self-criticism. I know how greedily, how lasciviously, the émigrés pounce upon everything that might offer them the least grain of comfort in their morbid resentment against the workers and peasants of the Soviet Union. Some time ago I wrote an article for the Soviet press on an edition of Brehm which had been spoilt by an old, but careless and not very literate, writer. The editor of the émigré *Rul*, Josif Hessen, a very stupid and ludicrously irate old fellow, wrote an editorial in which he exclaimed with comical exultation: Why, even Gorky criticizes the Soviet regime! He knows very well that I never hesitate to tell the blunt truth to people who work carelessly, unscrupulously or in general badly. But he, like every other émigré "politician" for that matter, cannot help lying.

There is a peculiar kind of "truth," which serves as spiritual nourishment only for misanthropes, for sceptics whose scepticism is based on ignorance, or for indifferent individuals who seek a justification for their indifference. It is an old, putrid, moribund truth—offal for swine. This truth is being vanquished and destroyed by the work of the advanced detachments of builders of the new culture in the Soviet Union. I see for myself and know very well how it hampers the work of honest people.

But I am opposed to its being used to sustain and comfort men who have been deservedly degraded by history.

"Are there any discontented workers and peasants, and what is the cause of their discontent?"—you ask. There are discontented, of course, and it would indeed be an extraordinary miracle if after only thirteen years of work, 160,000,000 people had succeeded in satisfying all their needs and desires. What dissatisfaction there is, is precisely due to the fact that thirteen years are too little for the machinery of government to be able to satisfy the rapidly growing cultural requirements of the working masses. Many things are still scarce, and there are quite a number of people who grumble and complain. These complaints might be called ridiculous, because they are premature and ill-considered; but I would not call them ridiculous, because one definitely discerns in them the firm conviction that the regime is capable of satisfying all the needs of the country. Of course, that section of the well-to-do peasants who believed that the revolution would make them big landed proprietors, landlords, and bring the poor peasants under their power and will, are not only discontented but actively resist the work of the Soviet government. It goes without saying that this section of the peasantry are opposed to collectivization and are in favour of individual farming, wage slavery and all the rest that would inevitably lead to the revival of capitalist forms of life. But the day of this section of the peasantry is over, their resistance to collective farming is hopeless and only continues by inertia.

The more active sections of the worker and peasant masses do not complain—they work. They know very well that they themselves are the government, that everything they need and desire can be satisfied only by their own efforts. It is precisely this consciousness of power and omnipotence that has called forth such phenomena as socialist emulation, shock work and the other indisputable symptoms of creative fervour, of labour heroism. It is thanks to this consciousness that many plants have completed their five-year plan in two-and-a-half years.

The workers understand the chief thing—that the power is in their hands. In bourgeois states, the laws are made up above, in the parliaments, and are made for the purpose of consolidating the power of the ruling class. Legislation in the Soviet Union is initiated at the lower rungs, in the rural soviets and in the factory committees, and if you follow the course of any legislative act you will easily see that not only is its purpose to satisfy the actual needs of the working masses, but that it is clear evidence of their cultural growth.

The worker and peasant masses of the Soviet Union are all gradually beginning to realize that their material enrichment and cultural development are being artificially and malignantly retarded by the capitalists of Europe and America. This realization of course greatly contributes to the growth of their political consciousness and the consciousness of their own strength.

If, instead of listening to talebearers and believing traitors, the intellectuals of Europe and America seriously and honestly pondered over the historical significance of the process which is unfolding in the Soviet Union, they would understand that its import is that 160,000,000 people are acquiring the indisputable treasures of universal human culture, that they are working not only for themselves, but for all mankind, by demonstrating to it the miracles that can be performed by a rationally organized will to live.

In the final analysis, it amounts to this: do the intellectuals of Europe and America want another world holocaust, which will reduce their numbers still more and weaken and brutify them still further? The worker and peasant masses of the Soviet Union do not want war; they want to build a state of equals. But if they are attacked, they will fight to a man, like a single entity, and they will win, because history is working for them.

(1931)

CAPITALIST TERROR IN AMERICA
AGAINST NEGRO WORKERS

THE capitalists and their obedient servants—the Social-Democrats and fascists, the Churchills and Kautskys, the old men driven half-crazy by fear of a social catastrophe and the astute young men who aspire to be big parasites, the "pen gangsters and press pirates," all the biped scum bred by the capitalist system, all the vermin in human shape without which capitalism cannot exist—accuse the "Bolsheviks" of the Soviet Union of wanting to "destroy culture." The bourgeois press has been issued the slogan by its masters: "The fight against the Bolsheviks, the fight against Communism, is a fight for culture!"

The capitalists, needless to say, have something to fight for. Their "culture" consists of a series of institutions which act quite freely with the object of defending and justifying the absolute and unlimited power of a parasitic minority over the labouring majority: the workers and peasants, and the petty bourgeois, who live by performing wretched little jobs for the big bourgeois. Their culture consists of schools where lies are told, of churches where lies are told, of parliaments where, too, lies are told, of a press which lies and calumniates. Their culture is the police, who have the right to manhandle and slay workers. Their culture has developed to an incredible height—to a continuous and daily war against the workers, who do not want to be robbed, do not want to be beggars, do not want their wives prematurely to lose their health and become old women at the age of thirty, their children to die of starvation and their daughters to prostitute themselves for a crust of bread, and who do not want crime—prompted by unemployment—to spread in the working people's honest midst.

In effect, the cultural life of bourgeois states amounts chiefly to street fighting between police and workers, to increasing suicide from starvation, to the spread of petty larceny owing to unemployment, to growing prostitution. This is no exaggeration: the "police chronicle" of all the bourgeois newspapers is filled with facts of this kind. The "cultured" bourgeois world lives in a continuous state of war with the working class, and the war grows more and more sanguinary every day. A minority fighting for the right to rob the majority with impunity—that, in a nutshell, is the whole cultural life of the present-day world outside the Soviet Union. In their war against the poor and hungry, the rich and well-fed try to weaken the working class in its striving to organize for the world-wide decisive fight, by tearing from its midst, flinging into jail or killing its most active individuals, and at the same time they try to intimidate the mass of the workers by condemning to death innocent men, of which the murder of Sacco and Vanzetti was an example.

Just now, in America, in the town of Scottsboro, a tragedy is being enacted which is reminiscent of the case of these two Italians who, after they had been sentenced to the death penalty, were kept in jail for seven years waiting to be burned in the electric chair. Against this murder of two innocently condemned men, the humanitarians of all Europe and its working class protested; but the protest did not produce a single crease in the wooden faces of the American millionaires. In Scottsboro, eight young Negroes have been condemned to death. They too are quite innocent. They were seized by the police at random, they were unacquainted with one another; nevertheless they were sentenced to death. This was done in order to intimidate the Negroes; this murder is a "precautionary measure." It is being committed because the Negro masses are being drawn more and more into the revolutionary movement and are taking their place side by side with the masses of white workers. They are beginning to take an active part in the struggle against American imperialism. Scared by the spread of the rebel spirit among the thirty million Negroes—workers and farmers—the bourgeoisie are doing their utmost to crush the growing fighting strength of the Negro masses. And the weapon they use is—white terror.

This is clearly to be seen in the bloody events at Camp Hill, Alabama. This case has added new fervour to the campaign the working class of the world is waging against lynching and in defence of the American Negro workers, and has laid additional stress on its importance.

This year the Negro share croppers of Tallapoosa County, Alabama, formed their own organization. It is militant, and is taking an active part in the Scottsboro campaign. A fortnight ago it called a meeting of its members in a church to protest against the Scottsboro case. The landowners mustered four hundred police and armed fascists, who attacked the church. In the course of the affray, Ralph Gray, the leader of the organization, was severely wounded and was carried home by his comrades. When the fascist ruffians learned that Gray was still alive, they surrounded and broke into his home and shot him in his bed, in the presence of the doctor who was tending his wounds. The fascists wrecked many a Negro hut in their hunt for officials of the organization. Four Negroes were carried off to the woods and lynched. Fifty-five Negroes have been arrested on a charge of "manslaughter." Five leading officers of the organization are accused of "attempted murder." Sheriff Young, the ringleader of the fascist band, was severely injured while the heroes were endeavouring to defend themselves.

Take the jail in Harlan County, Kentucky, in the very heart of the East Kentucky mining region, which is a source of wealth to some of the biggest corporations in the country, and which has only hunger, poverty and death to offer to the miners and their families. In the dark dungeons of this jail lie nearly a hundred miners. Some of them are charged with manslaughter, and are menaced with the death penalty. Many of them are accused of "belonging to organized bands," others of "criminal syndicalism," because they addressed meetings. Three months ago the miners went on strike in an attempt to improve their miserable conditions. Governor Sampson brought out the constabulary against the strikers, and the mine owners set gangs of armed fascists, sheriffs and police against them with orders to crush the strike with heavy guns and bombs. Thirty-one persons—eighteen miners and thirteen soldiers and fascists—were killed. The miners captured six guns with ammunition, raided a company store and seized provisions for their starving families.

Eighteen miners are threatened with the death penalty, fifty with long terms of imprisonment. Sixteen miners' homes were burned down. Miners' families are being evicted from their homes to this day.

In Pennsylvania, West Virginia and Ohio, forty thousand miners are on strike, the majority of them Negroes. Most of the six hundred miners arrested on July 6 were Negroes. When they were arrested they were beaten up and tortured.

The American section of the International Labour Defence is giving world prominence to the Scottsboro case. For the first time since the American Civil War, the brutal exploitation of the Negro masses by the ruling class of the United States is receiving international publicity and condemnation. The demand made by the American section of the ILD that execution of sentence be postponed for ninety days was supported with a storm of protest all over the world. From the U.S.S.R., Britain, France, Australia, Cuba, Austria, Germany and many other countries came thousands of resolutions demanding the release of the eight Negro Scottsboro boys. American consulates in Germany and Cuba were besieged by thousands of demonstrating workers.

The eight Negro Scottsboro boys are lying in prison with the electric chair before their eyes, and with the daily reminders from the wardens that they will soon be burned in it.

"The world-wide campaign must be intensified. No meeting or demonstration should be held, no leaflet, no ILD paper should be issued without containing an appeal to the masses to raise their voice against the white terror American imperialism is resorting to in order to stifle the mounting indignation of the Negro masses in the United States." (From an appeal by the ILD to all its sections and organizations.)

When the proletariat of all countries protests against the killing of its brothers, it is not, of course, because it reckons on persuading the capitalists not to kill. The capitalists cannot be "humane"—everything human except the brute beast in man is alien to him. If he donates dollars squeezed out of the workers to universities, he does so in order to strengthen his power. The teachings of Marx and Engels are not taught at his universities, and anyone who were to suggest that lectures in dialectical materialism should be given to students would be kicked out at once. It is the duty of the proletarian to protest against these murderers, but he should know that the murderers cannot stop murdering, and that they will murder the finest of his fellows. The capitalist protects his dollars, and to him dollars are always more precious than any individual, no matter who that individual may be. The proletariat should know that Rosa Luxemburg and Karl Liebknecht were not killed by soldiers, but by the capitalists, and that it was not a half-crazy woman that fired at Lenin, but a mechanical instrument of a definite system of thought—an instrument of the vile, inhuman bourgeois way of thinking.

The proletarians should know that between them and the capitalists no agreement—"compromise" or truce— is possible. It is time the proletarians knew this. And it should also be firmly remembered that in 1914 the proletariat of Europe and America was betrayed to the capitalists by the Social-Democrats, and that this cost the workers thirty million lives. They should not forget that that "bloody hound," Noske, is also a Social-Democrat. And, in general, they should not forget the crimes committed against the working class by its diverse enemies, by traitors and scoundrels. All this must be remembered in order that the bloody villainies of the past may not be repeated in the future. And all this is easy to remember. One has only to watch the vile and atrocious activities of the Second International Socialists and all that the European capitalists are contriving against the Union of Socialist Soviets.

The workers of Europe and America should realize that when they work in war industries they are manufacturing rifles, machine guns and guns to be used against themselves. The capitalists will not themselves go and fight if they make up their minds to start war on the Soviet Union—they will send their workers and peasants to the fields of death, to fight the workers and peasants who have abolished capitalism in their own country. Every capitalist war means suicide for the working class.

The working class of Europe and America should protest against individual murders of workers by the capitalists. It should protest, because this helps to foster in it the sentiment of international class solidarity—and the broadening and deepening of this sentiment is something the working class of Europe and America needs very badly. But even more solid, resolute and stormy should be its protest against every attempt on the part of the capitalists to engineer another world slaughter of workers and peasants.

The best, the surest and most practical way of preventing such a slaughter is for the socialist workers to go over en masse to the Communist Parties.

The Third International is a real leader of the workers, because it is a workers' international. It will not betray them. It recognizes the necessity for only one war—a war of the proletarians of all countries against the international capitalist gang, against those who live on the labour of others.

(*1931*)

TO THE WORKERS OF MAGNITOSTROY
AND OTHERS

DEAR COMRADES,

Thanks for your invitations to visit the sites of the industrial fortresses you are building. I should very much like to see you working on the erection of these gigantic plants, to talk to you and to learn something from you. But I have no time for travelling; I am engaged on work which in due course, I hope, you will appreciate as useful to you. You know yourselves that every man must do his job to the best of his ability and with all the energy he can muster. The best of you know this very well, and their labour heroism is an example to all the working people of the Soviet Union. It is an example to me too. To us time is precious, not a single minute must be wasted in vain. The tasks we have to accomplish are enormous; never before has any nation in the world set itself such difficult aims and tasks as the working class of the Union of Socialist Soviets has set itself and is accomplishing.

We have to destroy as speedily as possible the entire old order and create absolutely new conditions of life, such as do not exist anywhere else. We have to equip our peasant millions with machines, to lighten their back-breaking toil, to make the soil more fertile, to learn to control drought and other caprices of nature that kill the crops in our fields; we have to lay millions of kilometres of good road, to do away with overcrowded and dirty villages, to build for the tillers of the soil fine towns, with schools, theatres, public baths, hospitals, clubs, bakeries, laundries—everything which makes up the riches of the town, and which from time immemorial created the distinction between the customs, habits and way of life— the "spiritual make-up"—of the urban dweller and the rural dweller. This pernicious distinction, forced upon us by past history, we must destroy root and branch. And we must train ourselves to be qualitatively different: we must tear the "old Adam" out of our souls by the roots we must foster in ourselves greater confidence in the all-conquering power of rational labour and technology, we must become unselfish individuals and educate ourselves to look upon everything socialistically, we must rate our petty personal interests below the grand tasks whose accomplishment demands that we work to build the first state in the world where people will not be divided into classes, into rich and poor, masters and workers, and where the chief cause of all the miseries and sufferings of man—the lust for private property, the foundation of envy, greed and folly—will have disappeared. We are building a state in which each will work according to his ability and receive according to his needs, where every man will feel himself the master of all the wealth of his country, and where the opportunity for the free development of all his capacities will be open to everyone. We want to create a new man—and have already begun to create him.

* * *

I see from some of the letters I receive that not yet all by far realize that personal egotism is the parent of villainy, that not yet all by far have grown tired of the petty and stupid life their grandfathers and great-grandfathers lived. There are quite a number of people among you, comrades, who are poisoned by the past—the countryside keeps pouring them in an ever-increasing stream into your midst. But yours is a healthy environment, one that can cure even arrant individualists: you are gradually infusing into them your labour energy, and it is no longer true to say that "only the grave can cure" social hunchbacks—they are being cured by the socialist heroism of the working class. However, you must never cease to hammer it into the people of the old world that the only way in life open to their grandfathers and great-grandfathers was the despicable and narrow way to wealth. Along this way they could advance only on the backs of the poor, of their class brothers. That is the way their grandfathers and great-grandfathers did climb to wealth, forfeiting their conscience and adding to the burden of oppression of the poor by the rich. Wealth grows like mildew, and the richer a man was, the less he resembled a human being, and the more greedily he squeezed rubles out of the poor, together with their flesh and blood.

We can see to what lengths the capitalists of Europe and America have gone: they have grown gorgeously and fabulously rich, and have amassed thirty-five million unemployed. Thousands of rich men roll in gold, while millions of poor men die from starvation. Just figure: if each of the thirty-five million unemployed could spend at least a ruble a day on himself, how much profit would flow into the pockets of the capitalists? But the fact is that, while there are things to sell, there is nobody to buy. The capitalists refuse to sell cheap, they prefer to annihilate surplus commodities so that their price might not fall. This is atrocious, but it is a fact. On August 14, the European papers carried the following story from America: "New York, August 12. The U. S. Department of Agriculture has recommended the governors of the fourteen cotton states to destroy one-third of the 1931 crop in order to raise the price of cotton." This story is not an invention. It is corroborated by the American newspapers, and one of them, the *Washington Post*, even remarks that it is a humiliating commentary on the present mental state of America and the state of her productive forces, and an indication of how ignominously the system of regulating supply and demand has collapsed that, with superabundance on the one hand and dire need on the other, valuable products have to be destroyed. What, the paper exclaims, has happened to the productive forces of America, if wheat and cotton have to be burned or allowed to rot in the fields at a time when millions of citizens are forced to go without either?

It used frequently to be said that the only explanation of the criminally inhuman deeds of the capitalists is that they are mad, that passion for wealth, for the amassing of money, has driven them out of their minds. This was said in order to "strengthen the impression," to more clearly stress the shamelessness of the plunderers of the world. But even this is justified by the facts. *Vozrozhdeniye,* the Paris monarchist émigré paper, reports the following fact: "John O'Bannon, a millionaire, brought suit in a New York Court for the annulment of a medical order committing him to a lunatic asylum. The millionaire told the court the story of his life. He began by inventing a substitute for leather, floated a company, and made a fortune of fifteen million dollars. Feeling nervously run down, he applied to the doctors, who declared him insane and ordered him to be put in a lunatic asylum. He made another two million dollars in a short time while he was already in the madhouse. He demonstrated his business talent even in the psychiatric hospital by suggesting to the director various projects for running it more efficiently and profitably. The court questioned several medical experts, but they all affirmed that this outstanding businessman was mad after all, and he was sent back to the psychiatric hospital."

There is only one inference to be drawn from this, and that is that the capitalist methods of robbing the workers have become so simple that even a downright madman can appropriate millions. The capitalist economic system is becoming more and more frankly and brazenly a system of banditry, and conditions of life are more and more acquiring the character of undisguised anarchy. The newspapers recently carried the following story from America:

"Not only Chicago, but every more or less big city in the United States deserves to be called a gangsters' paradise. This is quite frankly admitted in the report of the Wickersham Committee, which was appointed by President Hoover to investigate prison conditions and the police system."

"In practically all the big cities," the report calmly relates, "the police are allied with the criminal world. In cities where the chief of police is obliged blindly to obey the mayor, and where that official is a political creature of murderers and scoundrels of every description, police practices are bound to sink to the level of the elements who influence them." What this leads to might be seen in the case of Chicago, New York and San Francisco, where bandits robbed and killed whomever they wished in broad daylight.

During a recent shooting affray between police and bandits in the streets of Chicago, four children were killed. Generally, in this little war between the qualified bandits—the police—and the ordinary bandits, no consideration is shown for the passer-by, and if policemen happen to kill a bystander it is not punishable as "manslaughter through carelessness."

The capitalist world is dying, rotting to death. It has no longer any powers of recuperation within it, they have evidently been used up to the last drop. It keeps going mechanically, by inertia, relying solely on the brute force of the police and the army—a not very reliable force, because the majority of the soldiers are proletarians, and although their minds are stuffed with the rubbish of middle-class prejudices, in the given conditions their political, class revolutionary consciousness is bound to grow. A world social revolution is not a fantasy; it is something inevitable, something that is already maturing. In Europe, besides the police, the capitalists are supported by the Social-Democratic "leaders" and by a section of the workers, duped by these "leaders," who are out for power and glory. These "leaders" are behaving more and more disgracefully. For instance, Lord Lothian, on his return to England after visiting our country with George Bernard Shaw, said:

"In the Russian revolution are implanted ideas which will immensely influence the future development of mankind. The question is how to apply them in our country," i. e., in England. Vandervelde, the head of the Social-Democrats, wrote an article against Lord Lothian in which he said that "if the privileged world begins to think like him, the overthrow of capitalism will come very soon." It is not joy that rings in these words of the "leader" of the working class; they express the obvious sadness of an old lackey who is afraid that any moment his master will be knocked off his perch. "Socialists" who admonish capitalists, "you are not sticking firmly enough to your class position," fully deserve the shameful stigma of betrayers of the working class. What is it, after all, that these "Socialists" are saying? What they are saying is: "better that millions of workers starve, than that the millionaires live in discomfort." The capitalist world is rotting, and the fetid poison of its decay infects all who voluntarily or involuntarily serve its inhuman interests, its—already impotent—passion for minting the flesh of the workers and peasants into gold. And the "Socialists in words" whom until recently the working class considered its friends and leaders are also rapidly rotting. Now the workers, in their fully warranted indignation and disgust, smash the windows of the editorial offices of the Social-Democratic *Vorwärts*, where sits that pitiful old fellow, Kautsky, who was once a prominent teacher of the European proletariat. Now the working people of the world are coming to realize that they have only one friend, teacher and leader who will not betray and sell them. That leader lives and works in the Socialist Soviet Union, and is not an individual, but a collective of many millions, firmly cemented by the consciousness of their historical class mission.

There are people in the Soviet Union who, having said, "our country is passing through an era marked by an unparalleled upsurge of creative energy," at once begin to play down that energy. They do this from various motives, but one motive is common to them all—doubt in the strength of the working class. It is to be presumed that this doubt and scepticism find a reverberation even in the workers' midst, because, together with collective letters from heroes of socialist emulation, I sometimes receive letters from individuals in which this disbelief of people in their own strength, this doubt of the possibility of consummating the great work which has been begun, this doubt in ultimate victory, is also clearly betrayed. I would remind these people of what Comrade Stalin said in one of his speeches, which he always bases on verified facts, on the facts of the creative initiative of the collective of ordinary "manual workers," the many millions of builders of Socialism. We have, he said, all the objective conditions for victory, and everything depends on our will and reason. What is the meaning of these words?

It is, comrades, that you have taken into your hands the power over the richest country in the world, a country whose visible natural wealth is already immeasurable, though we have still inadequately explored its riches and have begun to exploit only a tiny fraction of them. Almost daily, our scientists who are investigating the treasures hidden in the bosom of the earth discover vast new deposits of coal, metallic ores and mineral fertilizers needed to enhance the fertility of our fields. It is as if the earth senses that its lawful master has been born, a genuine and intelligent master, and is opening up its recesses and unfolding its riches before him.

From a simple button or match to a harvester combine or airplane, everything is produced by man. All the secrets of life, all its enigmas, are solved by human labour energy. Hence the only thing is to develop and intensify this energy—in other words, it is up to you!

The capitalist world, the world of the marauding individualists, had no need to be particularly energetic in exploring and opening up the treasures of the earth. The marauders preferred to grow rich by plundering the cheap living energy, the energy of the workers. You are building a state in which coercion of man and senseless squandering of his energy for the sake of the most insane and vulgar luxury, the maintenance of huge armies and the dissipation of valuable metals for the manufacture of weapons of mass slaughter, for wars, is absolutely impossible. You are building a state in which all people have an equal right to develop their talents and abilities, and the road to science and art is wide open to all, a state in which there is no master class, but everyone is a master and the equal of all.

This is a big thing, a difficult thing, and I know, of course, that your life is still hard. But you are free to make your life easier, and you alone can do it. You still lack much, but you alone can produce everything you lack. Your enemies in your midst, the people of the old world, are still squealing and grumbling, insinuating vile philistine thoughts into your minds and trying to imbue you with disbelief in the grand significance of your labours, doubt in the inevitability of your victory—and you alone can and should eradicate this vermin, this wretched debris of the old world.

Your strength is invincible, comrades. You proved this in the class battles of the civil war, and you are demonstrating it daily now by your heroic labour. Your strength is invincible, and it makes your triumph over all obstacles certain. You must overcome them all—and you will. I cordially grasp your mighty fists.

(1931)

ON WHOSE SIDE,
"MASTERS OF CULTURE"?

Reply to American Correspondents

YOU WRITE: "You will probably be surprised by this message from people across the ocean with whom you are unacquainted."

No, your letter did not surprise me; I get such letters quite frequently. And you are mistaken when you refer to it as "original"—outcries of alarm from intellectuals have become quite common these past two or three years. This is natural: the chief job of the intellectual has always in effect been to adorn the existence of the bourgeoisie, to console the rich in their moments of vulgar tribulation. Handmaidens of the capitalists, the intellectuals, or the majority of them, assiduously patched with white thread the philosophical and religious habiliments of the bourgeoisie, which have long grown soiled and threadbare and which are plentifully stained in the blood of the working people. To this day they continue to busy themselves with this difficult, but not very praiseworthy and absolutely sterile task, betraying an almost prophetic prevision. For example, even before the Japanese imperialists proceeded to dismember China, the German Spengler, in his book *Man and Technique*, voiced the idea that the Europeans of the nineteenth century had committed a most serious blunder in imparting their knowledge and technical experience to the "coloured races." In this view Spengler is supported by your American historian, Hendrik van Loon; he also holds that equipping the black and yellow peoples with the experience of European culture was one of the "seven fatal historical mistakes" of the European bourgeoisie.

And now we observe a desire to correct this mistake; the European and American capitalists supply the Japanese and Chinese with money and arms and help them to destroy one another, and at the same time send their fleets to the East in order, at a convenient moment, to show their mighty armed fist to Japanese imperialism and proceed together with the brave rabbit to share the skin of the slain bear. Personally, I think the bear will not be slain, because there are one or two things the Spenglers, van Loons and similar consolers of the bourgeoisie who dilate on the dangers menacing European-American "culture," forget to mention. They forget that the Indians, the Chinese, the Japanese, the Negroes are not socially monolithic and homogeneous, but are split up into classes. They forget that against the venom of the selfish thoughts of the European and American philistines, the antidote of the teachings of Marx and Lenin has been elaborated and is having a very healthy action. It is possible, however, that they have not really forgotten this, but only keep a tactful silence about it, and that their cries of alarm regarding the downfall of European culture are due to their realization of the impotence of the poison and the potency of the antidote.

Ever greater grow the numbers of those who howl that civilization is perishing, and ever louder their howls.

In France, some three months ago, ex-Minister Caillaux publicly lamented the insecurity of civilization.

"The world," he cried, "is suffering from the tragedies of abundance and distrust. Is it not a tragedy that wheat has to be burned and bags of coffee thrown into the sea, when millions of people have not sufficient to eat? As to distrust, it has done harm enough already. It caused the war and dictated the peace treaties, which can be rectified only when distrust disappears. If trust is not restored, all civilization will be endangered, because the peoples might be tempted to overthrow an economic system to which they attribute all their ills."

One must either be an arrant hypocrite or utterly naïve to speak of the possibility of mutual trust among the marauders who are today so frankly baring their talons and fangs at one another. And if by the "people" is meant the working people, then every honest man must admit that the workers are absolutely right in "attributing" to the idiocy of the capitalist system the ills with which this system rewards them for their wealth-creating labour. The proletarians are more and more clearly realizing that bourgeois realities are, with awful fidelity, justifying the words said by Marx and Engels in their *Communist Manifesto*:

"It [the bourgeoisie] is unfit to rule because it is incompetent to assure an existence to its slave within his slavery, because it cannot help letting him sink into such a state, that it has to feed him, instead of being fed by him. Society can no longer live under this bourgeoisie, in other words, its existence is no longer compatible with society."

Caillaux is one of the hundreds of old fellows who continue to affirm that their bourgeois idiocy is the wisdom bestowed on man for all time, that he will never invent anything better, never go beyond it, never rise to higher pinnacles. And it was not so very long ago that the consolers of the bourgeoisie cited their science as proof of their economic wisdom and its stability.

Now they would exclude science from their vile game. On February 23, this same Caillaux, speaking in Paris before an audience of ex-Ministers, men like Paul Milyukov and have-beens generally, said, in imitation of Spengler:

"Technology in many cases gives rise to unemployment, turns the wages of discharged workers into extra dividends for the shareholders. Science 'without conscience,' science not warmed by 'conscience' works to man's detriment. Man must curb science. The present crisis is a defeat for human reason. Sometimes there is no bigger misfortune for science than a great man. He advances theoretical postulates which have meaning and significance at the particular time they are advanced, as in the case of Karl Marx, let us say. They are correct in 1848, or 1870, but are quite incorrect in 1932. If Marx were alive today he would not write as he did."

In these words, the bourgeois acknowledges that the intelligence of his class is debilitated and bankrupt. He recommends "curbing science," forgetting how much strength it has lent his class for the consolidation of its power over the labouring world. What does "curbing science" mean? Denying it freedom of research? There was a time when the bourgeoisie very bravely and effectively resisted the attacks of the Church on freedom of science. In our day bourgeois philosophy is gradually reverting to what it was in the most gloomy period of the Middle Ages—the handmaiden of theology. Caillaux is right when he says that Europe is menaced with a reversion to barbarism, as Marx, of whose teachings he is ignorant, predicted; yes, it is absolutely undeniable that the bourgeois of Europe, and of America, the mistress of the world, are with every year becoming more ignorant, intellectually emaciated and barbarous—and they themselves, as represented by you, realize it.

The idea of the possibility of a reversion to barbarism is most "fashionable" among the bourgeoisie nowadays. The Spenglers, the Caillaux and similar "thinkers" reflect the state of mind of thousands of philistines. This state of alarm arises from a presentiment of the doom of their class—from the fact that all over the world the revolutionary sense of the working masses in the justice of their cause is growing. The bourgeois would prefer not to believe in the revolutionary cultural development of the working people, but they see and feel it. It is an all-embracing process and superbly justified. It is a logical and inevitable development of the whole labour experience of mankind, of which the bourgeoisie's historians tell so edifyingly. But since history, too, is a science, it too must be "curbed," or—simpler still—its existence must be forgotten. This is the advice given by Paul Valéry, the French poet and academician, in his book, *Review of the Contemporary World*: he wants us to forget history, which he quite seriously blames for the calamities of the nations. He says that, by recalling the past, history gives rise to fruitless dreams and robs people of their tranquility. By people he means, of course, the bourgeoisie. Valéry is probably incapable of seeing any other people on earth. This is what he has to say about history, of which the bourgeoisie until very recently were so proud, and which they wrote so skilfully:

"History is the most dangerous of all the products elaborated in the chemical laboratory of our intellect. It stimulates dreams, it intoxicates nations, arouses in them false memories, exaggerates their reflexes, inflames their old wounds, robs them of tranquility and drives them to mania—megalomania or persecution mania."

In his capacity of consoler, he is, as you see, very radical. He knows that the bourgeoisie wants to live tranquilly, and that it considers itself entitled to destroy tens of millions of people so that it may live a tranquil life. It can easily, of course, destroy tens of thousands of books—for the libraries, like everything else on earth, are also under its control. Does history prevent a tranquil life? Then, away with history! Withdraw from circulation all books on history! Let it not be taught in the schools! Proclaim study of the past socially dangerous and even criminal! Let people with a propensity for historical research be proclaimed abnormal and have them deported to uninhabited islands.

The chief thing is tranquility! And that is the concern of all the consolers of the bourgeoisie. But to achieve tranquility, as Caillaux says, there must be mutual confidence among the capitalist marauders of the different nationalities; and for the establishment of confidence, it is necessary that the doors of other lands—China, for instance—be opened wide, so that they may be plundered by all the marauders and shopkeepers of Europe. But the shopkeepers and marauders of Japan want to shut these doors to all but themselves, on the ground that China is nearer to them than to Europe, and that it is more convenient for them to rob the Chinese than the Indians, whom the "gentlemen" of England are accustomed to rob. Rivalry in plunder gives rise to antagonisms, which are fraught with the alarms of a new world war. What is more, as *Gringoire*, a Paris magazine says, "the Russian Empire has been lost to Europe as a normal and sound market." It is in this that *Gringoire* sees the "root of the evil," and, like many other journalists, politicians, bishops, lords, adventurers and swindlers, it insists on the necessity for all-European intervention in the Soviet Union. Then, unemployment is steadily growing in Europe, and so is the proletariat's revolutionary sense of the justice of its cause. It all comes to this, that there is very little chance of the establishment of "tranquility," and even, it seems, no place at all for it. But I, not being an optimist, and knowing that the cynicism of the bourgeoisie is unbounded, am prepared to recognize that there is one way by which the bourgeoisie may endeavour to clear itself a place for a tranquil life. Racist Deputy Berger hinted at this possibility in a speech in Cologne on February 19, when he said:

"If, after Hitler comes to power, the French attempt to occupy German territory, we shall cut the throats of all the Jews."

When the Prussian Government learned of this statement, it forbade Berger to make any more public speeches. This aroused a storm of indignation in the Hitler camp. One racist paper writes: "Berger cannot be accused of inciting to unlawful actions: we shall cut the throats of the Jews on the basis of a law which we shall pass when we come to power."

This statement should not be regarded as a joke, as a German "witz." In its present state of mind the European bourgeoisie is quite capable of "passing a law" not only for the wholesale extermination of Jews, but for the extermination of all who think differently from it, and, above all, of all who do not act in accordance with its inhuman interests.

*   *   *

Entrapped in this "vicious circle," the intellectual consolers gradually lose their faculty for consoling, and themselves come to stand in need of consolation. They even turn for consolation to people who refuse to dispense alms on principle, because the bestowing of alms establishes the right to do so. The talent for "beautiful lying," which is their basic talent, is no longer capable of concealing the ugly cynicism of bourgeois reality. Some of them are beginning to feel that to amuse and console people who are fatigued from the exertion of plundering the world and who are alarmed by the growing sharpness of the proletariat's resistance to their villainous aims, people with whom an insensate thirst for wealth has assumed the character of raving lunacy and manifests itself in socially destructive forms—that to console and amuse such people is becoming not only a fruitless occupation, but one dangerous to the consolers themselves.

One might also point to the criminality of consoling dejected robbers and assassins. But I know that this argument will touch nobody's heartstrings—for it would be moralizing, and moralizing has been tabooed as supererogatory. Far more to the point is the fact that in the present-day world the intellectual consoler is becoming that "middle" to which logic sternly denies existence.

An offspring of the bourgeoisie and a proletarian in social status, he seems to be awakening to the humiliating tragedy of his position as a servant of a class that is doomed to perish and, like the professional bandit and murderer, fully deserves to perish. He is beginning to realize this because the bourgeoisie is ceasing to need his services. He is continually hearing men of his fraternity trying to curry favour with the bourgeoisie by asserting that there is an overproduction of intellectuals. He sees that the bourgeois is more readily inclined to turn for "consolation" to charlatans who prophesy the future than to philosophers and "thinkers." The European newspapers are crammed with advertisements of chiromants, astrologers, casters of horoscopes, fakirs, yogis, graphologists, spiritualists and other mountebanks who are more ignorant even than the bourgeois themselves. Photography and the cinema are killing the art of painting, and artists, in order not to die of starvation, exchange their pictures for potatoes, bread and the cast-off clothing of the middle class. One Paris paper printed the following cheerful little item:

"Distress is very severe among Berlin artists, and there is no sign of alleviation.. There is talk of organizing artists' mutual aid, but what help can people give one another who earn nothing and who have no prospect of earning anything? Berlin art circles accordingly hailed with enthusiasm the original idea of a woman artist named Annot Jacobi, who suggests a system of direct barter. Let coal dealers supply fuel to artists in exchange for statues and pictures. Times will change, and the coal dealers will have no cause to regret their bargains. Let dentists exercise their art on artists. A good picture is never amiss in a dentist's waiting room. Butchers and dairymen should jump at the opportunity to do a good deed and at the same time acquire real art without cash outlay. A special bureau has been set up in Berlin to develop Annot Jacobi's idea and put it into practical effect."

The paper that reports this system of direct barter does not say that it is also being practised in Paris.

The cinema is gradually destroying the high art of the theatre. There is no need to dwell on the corrupting influence of the bourgeois cinema, because it is perfectly evident. Having exhausted every sentimental theme, it is beginning to make an exhibition of physical malformity.

"Metro-Goldwyn-Mayer's Hollywood studios have collected an original troupe for work on the film 'Freaks.' It includes Ku-ku, the bird-girl who has a great resemblance to a stork; P. Robinson, the skeleton man; Martha, who was born with one arm and skilfully knits lace with her feet. The studios have acquired Shilze, the 'pin-headed woman,' who has a normal body but an extraordinarily tiny head resembling a pin; Olga, a woman with a luxurious masculine beard; Josephine- Joseph, half-woman, half-man, the Hilton Siamese twins, dwarfs and Lilliputians."

The Barnays, Possarts, Mounet-Sullys and other artists of this category are no longer needed; they are being ousted by the Fairbanks, Harold Lloyds and other jugglers, headed by the monotonously sentimental and dreary Charlie Chaplin, just as classical music is being ousted by jazz, and Stendhal, Balzac, Dickens and Flaubert by the diverse Wallaces, men with a faculty for telling how police detectives protect the property of big robbers and organizers of wholesale murder by catching petty thieves and murderers. In the field of art, the bourgeois is quite satisfied with collecting postage stamps and tramway tickets, or at the best, with collecting fake old masters. In the field of science, the bourgeois is interested in the cheapest and most convenient ways and methods of exploiting the physical energies of the working class; science exists for the bourgeois only to the extent that it is capable of contributing to his enrichment, regulating the functions of his stomach and intestines, and stimulating his sexual vigour. The bourgeois is incapable of understanding that it is the fundamental mission of science to promote intellectual development, to aid the repair of the human physique which capitalist oppression has undermined, to convert inert matter into energy, to study the mechanism of the structure and growth of the human organism. In all this the modern bourgeois is as little interested as the savage of Central Africa.

Seeing this, some intellectuals are beginning to realize that "creative culture"—which they considered their business, the product of their "free thought" and "independent will"—is no longer their business, and that culture is not an inherent necessity for the capitalist world. The events in China have reminded them of the destruction of the University of Louvain and its Library in 1914; the other day they learned of the destruction by Japanese guns in Shanghai of the T'ung tsi University, the Naval College, the School of Fishery, the National University, the Medical College, the Agricultural and Engineering Colleges and the Workers' University. No one is outraged by this barbarous act, just as no one is outraged by the curtailment of allocations for cultural institutions, which goes hand in hand with the steady increase of armaments.

But, of course, only a very small section of the European and American intellectuals feel that they must inevitably come under the "law of excluded middle" and are exercised by the question of whose side to take: whether, in accordance with old habit, the side of the bourgeoisie against the proletariat, or, as honour dictates, the side of the proletariat against the bourgeoisie. The majority of the intelligentsia continue to be content with serving capitalism—a master who, fully aware of the moral flexibility of his servants and consolers, and seeing the futility and sterility of their reconciliatory work, is beginning openly to despise them and already entertains doubt as to whether the existence of such servants and consolers is necessary.

I often receive letters from specialists in consoling the middle-class philistines. I shall quote one of them I received from Citizen Sven Elverstad:

"Dear Mr. Gorky,

"Terrible confusion and dismay, bordering on despair, now reigns all over the world, caused by the dreadful economic crisis which has stricken all countries of the earth. This world tragedy has prompted me to institute in the *Tidens Tegn*, the newspaper with the largest circulation in Norway, a series of articles with the object of infusing new spirit and hope into the millions of victims of this dreadful catastrophe. I have accordingly seen fit to apply to writers, artists, scientists and politicians with the request to give their opinion on the subject of the tragic condition of the people in the past two years.

Every citizen in every country is faced with the alternative: either to perish under the drastic blows of a cruel fate, or to continue to fight in the hope of a happy solution of the crisis. Everyone needs the hope that the present gloomy situation will end happily, and it will burn brightly in the bosom of each on reading the optimistic opinion of a man to whose words all are accustomed to listen attentively. I therefore take the liberty of requesting you to let me have your view on the present situation. It may not be more than three or four lines, but it will undoubtedly save very many from despair and imbue them with strength to face the future courageously.

> "Yours respectfully,
>
> "Sven Elverstad"

There are still plenty of people like the author of this letter, people who have not lost their naïve faith in the healing virtue of "two or three lines," in the virtue of a phrase. This faith is so naïve, it can hardly be sincere. Two or three phrases, or two or three hundred phrases will not infuse new life into the decrepit bourgeois world. Every day, in all the parliaments of the world and in the League of Nations, thousands of phrases are uttered, but they do not console or reassure anyone, do not inspire anyone with hope in the possibility of checking the elemental growth of the crisis of bourgeois civilization. Ex-Ministers and other idlers tour the cities urging bourgeois society to "curb" and "discipline" science. These people's pratings are immediately seized upon by the journalists—men to whom "it's all the same, all a tedious game," and has been for a long time. And one of them,

Emil Ludwig, writing in a serious paper, the *Daily Express*, advises mankind to "get rid of the specialists." And the petty bourgeois listens to and reads this vulgar nonsense, and draws his conclusions from it. And if European bourgeoisdom should decide that it is necessary to close the universities, it will not be surprising. Incidentally, it might argue the following fact in support: in Germany 6,000 posts requiring a university diploma fall vacant annually, but the German universities turn out some 40,000 graduates every year.

You, Citizens D. Smith and T. Morrison, are mistaken when you ascribe to bourgeois literature and journalism the role of "organizer of cultivated opinion." This "organizer" is a parasitic growth which endeavours to cover up the sordid chaos of reality; but it does so less effectively than ivy or weeds, for example, cover up the rubbish and debris of ruins. You have a poor knowledge, citizens, of the cultural role of your press, which unanimously asserts that "the American is before all an American," and only after that a man. The German racist press, in its turn, teaches that a racist is before all an Aryan, and only after that a physician, geologist or philosopher. The French journalists argue that a Frenchman is before all a victor, and he must therefore be more strongly armed than others—referring, of course, not to the arming of the brain, but only of the fist.

It would be no exaggeration to say that the European and American press is zealously and almost exclusively engaged in depressing the cultural level of its readers, which is low enough as it is without its help. Serving the interests of the capitalists, their employers, and possessing the faculty of inflating a fly to the dimensions of an

298

elephant, the journalists do not make it their aim to subdue the swine, although, of course, they see that the swine have gone raving mad.

You write: "When we were in Europe, we realized with deep bitterness that the Europeans hate us." This is very "subjective," and while subjectivism enabled you to discern a part of the truth, it concealed from you the whole truth: you failed to observe that all the bourgeois of Europe live in an atmosphere of mutual hatred. The spoliated Germans hate France, which, suffocating from a surfeit of gold, hates the British, just as the Italians hate the French, and all the bourgeois unanimously hate the Soviet Union. The three hundred million Indians are fired with hatred of the English lords and shopkeepers, the four hundred and fifty million Chinese hate the Japanese and all Europeans, who, being accustomed to rob China, are also prepared to hate the Japanese, who consider that robbing the Chinese is their exclusive prerogative. This hatred of all for all is growing and becoming ever denser and more pungent, it is swelling among the bourgeois like a festering sore, and it will of course burst, and then possibly the best and most healthy blood of the peoples of the earth will flow in rivers again. Besides millions of the sturdiest individuals, war will destroy an enormous amount of wealth and the raw materials from which it is made, and will result in impoverishing the health of mankind and its metal and fuel resources. It goes without saying that war does not eliminate the mutual hatred between the national groups of bourgeoisie. You consider yourselves "capable of serving universal human culture," and feel yourselves "obligated to protect it from sinking into barbarism." That is very good. But ask yourselves the simple question: What can you do today or tomorrow to protect this culture, which, incidentally, never was "universally human," and cannot be when there are national-capitalist state organizations which are absolutely unaccountable to the working people, and which hound one nation against another?

Ask yourselves, for instance, what you can do to counteract such culture-destroying phenomena as unemployment, or the emaciating effect of hunger on the health of the working class, or the spread of child prostitution? Do you understand that emaciation of the masses means the emaciation of the soil from which culture springs? You are probably aware that the so-called "cultivated stratum" has always been a product of the masses. You should know that very well, because Americans are in the habit of boasting that in the U.S.A. newspaper boys can rise to the dignity of presidents.

I mention this only to note the astuteness of the boys, and not the talents of the presidents—about which I know nothing.

There is another question you would do well to ponder over: do you believe that the four hundred and fifty million Chinese can be turned into slaves of European and American capital, when the three hundred million Indians are beginning to realize that the role of slaves of Britain has by no means been ordained for them by the gods? Just consider: a few tens of thousands of marauders and adventurers want to live in tranquility for ever at the expense of the energies of a billion toilers! But that is normal, you say? It was, and it is normal, but will you have the hardihood to say that it ought to be? The plague was also regarded as almost normal once, in the Middle

Ages, but now the plague has practically disappeared, and its role on earth is being performed by the bourgeoisie, which is contaminating the whole coloured world, infecting it with a profound hatred and contempt for the white race. Does it not appear to you, the protectors of culture, that capitalism is provoking race wars?

* * *

You accuse me of "preaching hate," and advise me instead to "propagate love." You presumably think me capable of adjuring the workers: Love the capitalists, for they devour your strength; love them, for they fruitlessly dissipate the treasures of your earth; love these people who squander your iron on the making of the guns which destroy you; love the scoundrels thanks to whom your children are wasting away from starvation; love those who destroy you in order that they may themselves live in ease and satiety; love the capitalist, for his church keeps you in the darkness of ignorance.

Something similar is preached by the Bible, and, recalling this, you refer to "Christianity" as a "cultural lever." You are very much behind the times; honest people have long ceased to speak of the cultural influence of the "gospel of love and meekness." It is inappropriate and impossible to speak of this influence in our day, when the Christian bourgeoisie inculcates meekness both at home and in the colonies and compels its slaves to love it with the help of "fire and the sword," which it employs with greater energy than it ever did before. Nowadays, as you know, the sword has been replaced by machine-guns and bombs, and even by the "voice of God from on high." A Paris newspaper reports:

"In their war with the Afridis, the British have thought of a stunt which serves them in good stead. A body of rebels are taking refuge on a plateau amid inaccessible mountains. Suddenly a plane appears above them flying at a very great height. The Afridis jump for their weapons. But no bombs fall. Instead, words pour down from the plane, and a voice from heaven, speaking persuasively in their vernacular, urges them to lay down their arms and cease their senseless contest against the British Empire. There have been quite a number of cases when, startled by the voice from heaven, the rebels really did give up the fight.

"The voice of God expedient was repeated in Milan on the anniversary of the founding of the fascist militia, when the whole city heard the Divine Voice pronouncing brief words of praise of fascism. Milanese who had had occasion to hear General Balbo speak recognized his baritone in the voice from heaven."

Thus a simple expedient has been found for proving the existence of God and utilizing his voice for the subjugation of savages. It is to be anticipated that God will one day be heard over San Francisco or Washington, speaking in English with a Japanese accent.

You hold up as an example to me the "great men, the teachers of the Church." It is really funny, your saying this seriously. Let us not ask how, of what and why the great churchmen were made. But before leaning for support on them, you would do well to test their firmness and stability. In your disquisitions on the "Church" you betray that "American idealism" that can spring only from profound ignorance. In the present instance, your ignorance of the history of the Christian Church can only be explained by the fact that the inhabitants of the U.S.A. have never known from their own bitter experience that the church is an organization for coercing the mind and conscience of man, and have never experienced this as poignantly as the inhabitants of Europe. You should acquaint yourselves with the bloody affrays that took place at the œcumenical councils, with the fiendishness, ambitiousness and selfishness of the "great Church teachers." You would learn quite a lot in particular from the story of the charlatanry at the Council of Ephesus. You should do some reading on the history of heresies, acquaint yourselves with the extermination of "heretics" in the early centuries of Christianity, with the Jewish pogroms, with the massacres of the Albigenses and the Taborites, and with the bloody policy of the Church of Christ in general. Interesting for the under-educated is the history of the Inquisition, but not, of course, as given in the account of your fellow-countryman, Washington Lee, which was approved by the censorship of the Vatican, the initiator of the Inquisition. It is quite presumable that if you were to acquaint yourselves with all this, you would arrive at the conviction that the Church Fathers worked very zealously to consolidate the power of a minority over the majority, and that if they fought heresies, it was because the heresies originated among the working masses, who instinctively sensed the mendacity of the churchmen. They preached a religion for slaves, a religion which the masters never accepted otherwise than through misunderstanding or from fear of the slaves. Your historian, van Loon, claims in an article on "great historical blunders" that the Church had to fight against, and not for, the teachings of the Gospels. He says that Titus committed a supreme blunder in destroying Jerusalem—for the Jews, driven out of Palestine, dispersed over the whole earth, and it was in the communities they founded that Christianity ripened and grew; and Christianity was no less fatal to the Roman Empire than the ideas of Marx and Lenin are to capitalist states.

So, in fact, it was, and so it is: the Christian Church fought the naïve communism of the Gospels—this is the sum and substance of its whole "history."

What is the Church doing in these days? Above all, of course, it prays. The Archbishop of York and the Archbishop of Canterbury—the man who preached something in the nature of a "crusade" against the Soviet Union—these two archbishops have compiled a new prayer, in which English hypocrisy is consummately combined with English humour. It is a rather longish compilation, constructed on the style of the prayer "Our Father." The archbishops appeal to God in the following words:

"Concerning the policy of Our Government for the restoration of credit and prosperity, Thy will be done. Concerning all that is being undertaken for the future constitution of India, Thy will be done. Concerning the forthcoming disarmament conference and all that is being undertaken to establish peace on earth, Thy will be done. Concerning the restoration of trade, credit and mutual amity, give us this day our daily bread. Concerning the cooperation of all classes for the common weal, give us this day our daily bread. If we have been guilty of national pride and have found greater satisfaction in ruling over others than in assisting them to the best of our ability, forgive us our sins. If we have displayed selfishness in the conduct of our affairs and have placed our interests and the interests of our class above the interests of others, forgive us our sins."

A typical prayer of frightened shopkeepers! In the course of it they pray God about a dozen times to "forgive" them their "sins," but not once do they say that they are willing or able to cease committing them. And only in one instance do they ask God's "forgiveness":

"That we have succumbed to national arrogance, finding satisfaction in ruling over others, and not in the ability to serve them, O Lord, forgive us!"

Forgive us this sin, but we cannot cease from sinning— that is what they say. But this prayer for forgiveness was rejected by the majority of the English clergymen; they considered it would be awkward and humiliating for them to read it.

This prayer was to be "offered up" to the throne of the British God on January 2, in St. Paul's Cathedral, London. Clergymen who did not find the prayer to their liking received permission from the Archbishop of Canterbury not to read it.

So you see what vulgar and stupid comedies the Christian Church has come to be capable of, and how amusingly the clergy have degraded their God to the level of a senior shopkeeper and participator in all the commercial transactions of the best shopkeepers of Europe. But it would be unfair to speak only of the English clergy, and to forget that the Italian have founded a Bank of the Holy Ghost, and that in France, on February 15, in Mulhouse, as the Paris newspaper of the Russian émigrés reports:

"The police authorities ordered the arrest of the manager and salesman of a bookshop run by the Catholic Union Publishing House, which is directed by Abbé Egy. The shop sold pornographic photographs and books imported from Germany. The 'goods' have been confiscated. Some of the books are not only pornographic, but abuse and revile religion."

Facts of this kind could be cited by the hundred, and they are all indicative of one thing: that the Church, the servant of its patron and master, capitalism, is infected with the same diseases that are destroying capitalism. And if it may be assumed that there was a time when the bourgeoisie did "reckon with the moral authority of the Church," it has to be admitted that this was the authority of a "policeman of the spirit," the authority of one of the organizations which served for the oppression of the working people. The Church "consoled," you say? I don't deny it. But this consolation is one of the methods of extinguishing reason.

No, preaching to the poor to love the rich, to the worker to love his master, is not my trade. I am not capable of consoling. I know too well and have known for too long that the whole world is permeated by an atmosphere of hate, and I see it becoming ever denser, ever more active and beneficent.

It is time you "humanitarians who want to be practical men" realized that two hates are operating in the world: one arose among the marauders, from their mutual competition, as well as from their fear of the future, which is fraught with inevitable doom for the marauders; the other— the hate of the proletariat—springs from its loathing for life as it is, and is being ever more brightly illumined by consciousness of its right to rule. These two hates have developed to such a pitch of intensity that nothing and nobody can reconcile them, and nothing but the inevitable battle between the classes that are their physical exponents, nothing but the victory of the proletarians, can rid the world of hate.

You write: "Like many others, we think that in your country the dictatorship of the workers leads to coercion of the peasants." I would advise you to think like the few—like those, still very few, intellectuals who are already beginning to understand that the teachings of Marx and Lenin are the pinnacle attained by the scientific thought that studies social phenomena honestly, and that only from the pinnacle of these teachings is the direct road to social justice, to new forms of culture, plainly visible. Make a little effort and forget, if only for a while, your kinship with the class whose whole history is one long tale of physical and spiritual coercion of the mass of labouring humanity—the workers and peasants. Make this effort, and you will understand that your class is your enemy. Karl Marx was a very wise man, and it would be a mistake to think that he appeared in the world like Minerva from the head of Jupiter. No, his teachings are just as much a coping-stone placed by genius on scientific experience as the theories of Newton and Darwin were. Lenin is easier than Marx, and, as a teacher, no less wise. They will show you the class you serve, first in its power and glory; they will show you how, by means of inhuman coercion, it worked to build, and did build, a "culture" that suites it out of blood, cant and lies; and then they will show you the process of decay of this culture. Its subsequent, present-day, corruption you can see for yourselves—after all, it is precisely this process that inspires the alarm that finds expression in your letter to me.

Let us talk of "coercion." The dictatorship of the proletariat is a temporary thing; it is necessary in order to re-educate and convert the tens of millions of former slaves of nature and of the bourgeois state into the one and only master of their country and of all its wealth. The dictatorship of the proletariat will cease to be necessary when all the working people, all the peasantry, will be living in equal social and economic conditions, and when it will be possible for every individual to work in accordance with his abilities and receive in accordance with his needs. "Coercion," as you and "many others" conceive it, is a misunderstanding; but more often it is a lie and calumny against the working class of the Soviet Union and its party. "Coercion," as applied to the social process going on in the Soviet Union, is a term used by the enemies of the working class with the object of discrediting its cultural work— the work of regenerating its country and organizing new economic forms.

In my view, it would be right to talk of compulsion, which is an entirely different thing from coercion; for, surely, you do not coerce children when you teach them to be literate? The working class of the Soviet Union and its party are teaching the peasantry to be socially and polit-ically literate. Just in the same way you, the intellectuals, are compelled by somebody or something to feel the tragedy of your position "between the hammer and the anvil"; you, too, are taught the elements of social and political literacy by somebody—and that somebody, of course, is not I.

In all countries the peasantry—the millions of small owners—constitute a soil from which marauders and para-sites spring; capitalism, in all its monstrous ugliness, grew from this soil. All the energies, abilities and talents of the peasant are absorbed in his concern for his beggarly property. The cultural idiocy of the small owner is fully equal to that of the millionaire—you, the intellectuals, should see and feel this very well. In Russia, before the October Revolution, the peasants lived in seventeenth-century conditions, and this is a fact which even the Russian émigrés will not venture to deny, even though their incensement against the Soviet regime has assumed ludicrous and preposterous proportions.

The peasants must not be fourth-rate, semisavage people; they must not be a prey of the astute muzhik, the landlord and the capitalist; they must not slave like convicts on tiny, highly-divided plots of exhausted land that is incapable of feeding its beggarly, illiterate owner— who is not in a position to manure his land, employ machines for its cultivation, or to develop the science of agriculture. The peasants must not justify the dismal Malthusian theory, at the bottom of which, in my opinion, lies the fiendishness of clerical thought. If the peasants, in their mass, are still incapable of understanding the reality and humiliation of their position, it is the duty of the working class to imbue them with a consciousness of it, even by compulsion. However, there is no need for this, because the peasant of the Soviet Union, who suffered the torments of the shambles of 1914-18, and who was awakened by the October Revolution, is no longer blind and is capable of thinking practically. He is being supplied with machines and fertilizers, the road to all schools is open to him, and every year thousands of peasant children enter on the careers of engineers, agronomists and physicians. The peasant is beginning to understand that the working class, as represented by its party, is striving to create a single master in the Soviet Union, a master with 160,000,000 heads and 320,000,000 hands—and that is the chief thing he needs to understand. The peasant sees that everything done in his country is done for all, and not for a small group of wealthy people; the peasant sees that in the Soviet Union only that is being done which is useful to him, and that the country's twenty-six agricultural research institutes are working to enhance the fertility of his land and to lighten his labour.

The peasant does not want to live in squalid villages, as he has done for centuries, but in agricultural cities, where there are good schools and crèches for his children, and theatres, clubs, libraries and cinemas for himself. The peasant is conceiving a growing thirst for knowledge and a growing taste for cultivated living. If the peasant did not understand all this, then the work in the Soviet Union would not in these fifteen years have achieved the magnificent results that have been achieved by the combined energies of the workers and peasants.

In the bourgeois countries, the working people are a mechanical power, and, in their mass, are ignorant of the cultural significance of their labour. The bosses in your country are the trusts, organizations of plunderers of the national energies, of parasites on the working people. Warring among themselves, operating with money and trying to ruin one another, they engineer tragic stock-exchange swindles—and now, at last, their anarchism has plunged the country into an incredible crisis. Millions of workers are dying of starvation, the health of the nation is being fruitlessly dissipated, infant mortality is growing disastrously, suicide is on the increase, and the basic soil of culture, its living human energy, is becoming exhausted. And, notwithstanding this, your Senate turned down the La Follette-Costigan bill for the appropriation of 375 million dollars for immediate aid to the unemployed, while the *New York American* publishes figures showing that in New York 153,731 unemployed and their families were evicted from their homes for non-payment of rent in 1930, and 198,738 in 1931. In New York, in January of this year, hundreds of unemployed were evicted from their homes daily.

In the Soviet Union, the administrators and legislators are the workers and that section of the peasantry who have come to understand the necessity for abolishing private ownership of land and for socializing and mechanizing the cultivation of the fields, who have come to understand that they must psychologically remake themselves into workers of the same kind as those that work in the mills and factories, in other words, they must become the genuine and sole masters of the country. The number of peasant collectivists and Communists is growing continuously. It will grow still faster as the new generation rids itself of the heritage of serfdom and of the superstitions born of centuries of slavish existence.

In the Soviet Union the laws are made from below, they originate among the working masses, and flow from the conditions of their vital activity; the Soviet Government and the Party formulate and legislatively enact only that which matures in the processes of labour of the workers and peasants—labour, whose principal aim is to create a society of equals. The Party is the dictator only to the extent that it is the organizing centre, the neuro-cerebral system of the working masses; the aim of the Party is to convert as swiftly as possible the largest possible proportion of physical energy into intellectual energy, so as to provide freedom and scope for the development of the talents and abilities of every individual and of the entire mass of the population.

The bourgeois state, being committed to individualism, assiduously educates the youth in the spirit of its own interests and traditions. That, of course, is natural. But we find that it is precisely among the youth of bourgeois society that anarchist ideas and theories most frequently arose and arise—and that is unnatural and indicative of the abnormal and unhealthy state of an environment in which people are stifled, and consequently begin to dream of the total destruction of society in order to achieve unlimited liberty for the individual. As you are aware, your youth not only dream of this but act accordingly: in the press of Europe we find more and more frequent reports of "pranks"— pranks of a criminal nature—played by your and its bourgeois youth. These crimes are not prompted by material want, but by the "tedium of life," by curiosity, by an urge for "thrills," and at the bottom of all these crimes lies a very low opinion of the individual and his life. Absorbing into its midst the most talented progeny of the workers and peasants, and compelling them to serve its interests, the bourgeoisie boasts of the "freedom" of the individual to attain a "certain personal prosperity"—a comfortable den, a snug hole. But you will not deny, of course, that in your society thousands of talented people perish on the way to vulgar prosperity, being incapable of overcoming the obstacles placed in their way by the conditions of bourgeois life. The literature of Europe and America is full of descriptions of gifted people who come to a fruitless end. The history of the bourgeoisie is the history of its spiritual impoverishment. What talents can it boast of in our times? It has nothing to boast of but diverse Hitlers, pigmies stricken with megalomania.

The peoples of the Soviet Union are entering an era of renaissance. The October Revolution aroused tens of thousands of talented people to vital activity, but they are still all too few for the accomplishment of the great aims the working class has set itself. There are no unemployed in the Soviet Union, and everywhere, in all spheres of human endeavour, the forces are still inadequate, although they are increasing with a speed never and nowhere witnessed before.

You, the intellectuals, the "masters of culture," would do well to realize that once the working class takes political power into its own hands, it will open for you the broadest opportunities for creative cultural endeavour.

See what a stern lesson history administered to the Russian intellectuals: they refused to side with their working people, and now they are rotting in impotent fury, putrefying in exile. Soon they will become totally extinct, and will be remembered only as traitors.

The bourgeoisie is inimical, and can no longer be anything but inimical, to culture—this is a truth that is confirmed by bourgeois reality, by the whole practice of the capitalist states. The bourgeoisie rejected the Soviet Union's project for general disarmament, and this alone is sufficient to justify us in saying that the capitalists are socially dangerous people, that they are preparing for a new world war. They are keeping the Soviet Union in a tense state of defence, compelling the working class to spend a vast amount of precious time and material on the production of weapons of defence against the capitalists, who are organizing to attack the Soviet Union and to turn this huge country into their colony, their market. The peoples of the Soviet Union have to spend on self-defence against the capitalists a vast amount of energy and means which might with undeniable benefit be used to promote the cultural regeneration of mankind, for the construction process in the Soviet Union is of importance to all mankind.

The putrid environment of a bourgeoisie gone crazy from hate and from fear of the future is producing increasing numbers of idiots who have absolutely no idea of the significance of what they are crying. One of them turns to the "gentlemen, the rulers and diplomats of Europe" with appeals like this: "The time has come for Europe to use the yellow race to crush the Third International." It is quite likely that this idiot blurted out the dreams and intentions of "gentlemen," of "diplomats and rulers," of his own kidney. It is quite possible that there are "gentlemen" who are seriously thinking of doing what this idiot cried aloud. Europe and America are ruled by irresponsible "gentlemen." The events in India, China, Indo-China may well contribute to the growth of racial hatred towards the Europeans and the "whites" in general. This will be a third hate, and you, the humanitarians, would do well to ponder whether you, or your children, need it. And what good are you likely to derive from the preaching of "race purity"—that is, again of race hatred—in Germany? Here is a specimen:

"Sauckel, the Nazi leader in Thuringia, has ordered the National-Socialist group in Weimar to protest against the arrival in that city of Gerhart Hauptmann, Thomas Mann, Walter von Molo and Professor Henri Lichtenberger of the

Sorbonne for the forthcoming centenary of the death of Goethe. Sauckel accuses them of non-Aryan extraction."

And it is likewise high time for you to decide the simple question: on whose side are you, "masters of culture"? Are you with the handiworkers of culture, and for the creation of new forms of life; or are you against them, and for the perpetuation of a caste of irresponsible marauders, a caste which has decayed from the head downward, and which continues to function only from inertia?

(1932)

THE OLD AND THE NEW MAN

THE nineteenth century has been loftily styled the "age of progress." The title is deserved, for in that age reason, scientific research into the phenomena of nature and the subjugation of its elemental forces to economic interests, attained an unprecedented pinnacle and produced many a "technical marvel." Reason studied organic life and discovered the invisible world of the bacteria—a discovery which is not being utilized to the full because of the shameful and cynical conservatism of social class conditions. In the Russian translation of Wallace's *The Twentieth Century*, it is said that the eagle flight of man's thought had in this century majestically and proudly revealed to him his strength.

But alongside with scientific thought, another line of thought was no less active. It produced among the bourgeoisie the mental state known as "Weltschmertz"—the philosophy and poesy of pessimism. In 1812 Lord Byron published the first cantos of his *Childe Harold*, and shortly after the philosopher and poet, Giacomo Leopardi, Count of Monaldo, began to preach that knowledge only discloses the impotence of reason, that all is "vanity" and that the only truths are suffering and death. The idea was not new; it was very beautifully formulated by Ecclesiastes, it was preached by Buddha, it burdened the minds of Thomas

More, Jean Jacques Rousseau and many other men of great intelligence and talent. It would be hardly right to attribute the resurrection of this idea by Byron and Leopardi solely to the grief felt by the feudal nobility at having been vanquished by the bourgeoisie; but it goes without saying that, together with the aristocracy's land, the bourgeoisie also inherited some of its ideas, for ideas possess the pernicious faculty of outliving the conditions that gave rise to them.

The tenacity of pessimistic ideas may well be explained by the fact that this philosophy is in its very essence profoundly conservative, and, by asserting the senselessness of being, it satisfies the requirements of not very penetrating minds and tranquilizes the lovers of tranquility. This tenacity is also attributable to the fact that the circle of consumers of ideas is extremely small and circumscribed, and does not abound in originality or boldness of thought.

In the nineteenth century it was the Germans who were the most assiduous purveyors of pessimistic ideas to Europe. Not to mention the Buddhist philosophy of Schopenhauer and Hartmann, the anarchist Max Stirner, in his *The Ego and His Own*, is nothing but a profound pessimist. The same must be said of Friedrich Nietzsche, the exponent of the bourgeois yearning for a "strong man"— a yearning which, degenerating and regressing, shifted its ideal from the celebrated Frederick the Great to Bismarck, to the semi-imbecile Wilhelm II, and in our day to that obvious lunatic Hitler.

For the first twelve years it was Bonaparte, the "Little Corporal," who was the model of a "great man" for the European bourgeoisie. The influence of his semifantastic career on the thoughts and sentiments of several middle-class generations has not been sufficiently investigated, although it is precisely Bonaparte who most convincingly shows how necessary it is for the middle class to bank on a "hero," and how inevitable the downfall of the hero is.

The role of the "hero" as the maker of history was very elegantly, although rather hysterically, argued by Carlyle. He was believed, but this did not prevent the heroes from shrinking to the dimensions of a Clemenceau, Churchill, Woodrow Wilson, Chamberlain and similar "leaders of cultured humanity"—as these individuals are called by their lackeys.

The employers are more reserved about the heroes who work in their service, because each of the groups of employers that started the shambles of 1914-18, knowing that "war breeds heroes," expected to get an Alexander the Great, or a Tamerlane, or at least a Napoleon, but got instead Joffres, Pershings and Ludendorffs. To "return to our muttons"—in the line of German pessimists should be mentioned Weininger, author of the gloomy book, *Sex and Character*, and Spengler, author of *Decline of Europe* and *Man and Technique*.

The "decline of Europe," i.e., its spiritual debilitation, the emaciation of its talents, the poverty and wretchedness of its organizing ideas, are all phenomena characteristic not only of Europe, but also of both the Americas, ay, and of the whole world. The bright stars in the bourgeois heaven have faded!

The Forsytes in England, the Budenbrooks in Germany, the Babbits in the United States are clearly incapable of breeding "heroes," and are forced to contrive them out of petty adventurers.

In the country where once the nebulous geniality of the optimist Dickens eclipsed the healthy criticism of Thackeray, the morose voice of Thomas Hardy was lately stilled, and now such books, so bitter, so full of dreadful despair, as Richard Aldington's *Death of a Hero* have become possible. The twentieth-century literature of France has not even risen to such heights of artistic generalization as were achieved by Galsworthy, Thomas Mann and Sinclair Lewis. Romain Rolland, author of the splendid epic *Jean Christophe*, a man of courage and integrity, has to live outside his country, driven from it by the brutish obtuseness of the bourgeois. France has lost thereby, but the world of the working people has gained. The French rentier lives like a boa constrictor that has swallowed too much food, is unable to digest it, yet is afraid that everything it has not yet managed to devour may be devoured by other beasts of its kind. Intellectual poverty, of course, does not impede the customary and senseless urge of the shopkeepers to seize new fertile territories and to enslave colonial peoples. But the fatty degeneration that comes from gold weighs ever more obscenely and oppressively on the brain of the bourgeoisie. The spiritual impoverishment of Europe is an astonishing spectacle, although more and more people are appearing in it who are ashamed of living in the cynical conditions created by the shopkeepers, and who realize that in banking on "heroes," on individualism, the shopkeepers have lost.

To the question—what did the social culture of Europe achieve in the nineteenth century?—there is only one possible answer: it enriched itself to such a disgusting extent that it became perfectly obvious to all that its wealth was the cause of the unparalleled poverty of the working class. So deep a gulf has been dug between the working class and the bourgeoisie that it is absolutely inevitable that the bourgeoisie must tumble into it.

And that, of course, is the right place for it. "Culture" will suffer thereby? Revolutions have never been pauses in the history of the cultural growth of man; revolution is a process of summoning new creative forces into being.

The cultural revolutionary process is developing rapidly in the territory of the former Russia of the Romanov tsars and of the semiliterate hucksters who bartered away the treasures of their country to the European capitalists and plundered the peasants and workers, who were delivered into the power of ignorant priests, extinguishers of reason.

It would be appropriate here, I think, to recall my own life, which gives me the right to be regarded as an informed and truthful witness.

For nearly fifty years I observed the life of people of various classes. Not placing too much trust in my own immediate impressions, I checked them by studying the history of my people and comparing it with the history of the peoples of the West. I was sufficiently "objective," even when I felt that objectivism was retarding my understanding of the elementary "truths" of life, was deflecting the development of my knowledge of the world from the straight line.

It is not easy to apprehend that at the bottom of objectivism lies that urge which is inherent in the majority of people, if not to reconcile, at least to equilibrate facts which are intrinsically irreconcilable. This should be well understood by people in whose country the doctrine of compromise was invented, and where only a few intellectuals, specialists in elucidating the secrets of life, are beginning only after the infamous war of 1914-18 to understand that it is not reconciliation that contradictions demand, but a study of their causes.

I affirm that the life of the worker and peasant of tsarist Russia was incomparably harder than that of any of the labouring classes of Europe. The labouring class of Russia was more downtrodden and ignorant.

The pressure of the state and the church on human will and reason was more oppressive, more crude and crippling in Russia than in Europe. Nowhere did talented individuals perish in such numbers and so surely as in the Russian land. I am not a "blind patriot of my country," and I am certain that I am well familiar with the "soul of the people." This "broad" and capacious soul was saturated and poisoned by dark and ugly superstitions and savage prejudices born of the primitive conditions of life. Incidentally, one should study it not from Turgenev, Tolstoy or Dostoevsky, but from its folklore—its songs, tales, proverbs and legends—from its domestic and religious rites, from its sects, its handicrafts, its industrial arts. This alone will give an idea, in all its fullness and sadness, of the dreadful ignorance of the people, and at the same time of its astonishing, multiform and profound talent.

The aristocratic writers of the first half of the nineteenth century wrote very compassionately of the peasantry, depicting them—the "god-people"—as mild-hearted, lyrical, dreamy and submissive to fate; what was needed was to persuade the government that the muzhik was also a human being, and that it was time to remove the yoke of slavery—of serfdom—from his neck and to educate him. This propaganda of primitive humanitarianism was continued by the bourgeois intellectuals of the second half of the century, who painted the muzhik in the same bright and tender colours as he was painted by Turgenev, Tolstoy and others. One might say that the aristocrats wanted to have the muzhik liberated only in order to obtain a rather more productive labourer, and the bourgeois because they wanted to utilize his strength in the fight against the autocracy.

At the end of the century, with the development of industry, "legal Marxists" appeared among the bourgeoisie. These were a species of domestic fowl of bourgeoisdom resembling the geese that were said to have saved Rome. They talked of the necessity of putting the lyrical muzhik through the "factory melting pot." At that time, too, the autocratic government, in deference to the "demands of the times," began to set up parish schools, in which the teachers were rural priests, in opposition to the zemstvo, or lay, schools. Together with all this, there came a sharp change in the attitude of literature toward the muzhik: the soft-hearted lyrical dreamer vanished, and there appeared the savage, drink-sodden and strange "Muzhiks" of Chekhov, Bunin and other writers.

I am not disposed to think that this change of type took place in reality; but it did take place in the literature of the early twentieth century. This literary metamorphosis does not speak very convincingly of the social independence of art, but it points very forcefully to the harmony between the voice of the "free-minded individual" and the voice of his class, and to the supplanting of the idea of persuading by the idea of humouring.

And so, in the twentieth century the bourgeoisie had a not very engaging literary portrait of the muzhik. In 1905-07, the original of this portrait, deciding to clear the land for his own use, began to burn and destroy the mansions of the landlords; but he looked upon the workers—the "strikers"—testily and with no great confidence. In 1917, however, he sensed the truth about the working class and, as we know, stuck his bayonet in the ground and refused to destroy the workers and peasants of Germany.

We also know that the German army, on the plea of the "right of conquest," thoroughly despoiled the Russian muzhik, while the European capitalists, affronted by his unusual action, sent their muzhiks and workers to subdue and exterminate the recalcitrant Russians. This villainy had the support and approval of the majority of the Russian liberal and radical intellectuals: they rose in defence of capitalism, sabotaged the Soviet regime, hatched conspiracies against it and resorted to terroristic acts against the leaders of the workers and peasants. The shot fired at Lenin showed the worker and peasant masses who was their true friend and leader; it revealed to them the utter iniquity of their enemies, and aroused their hostility toward this section of the intelligentsia, a hostility justified by the latter's treachery. The European intellectuals might draw a lesson from this for their own benefit.

* * *

Since then fifteen years have passed.

What has been accomplished in the Soviet Union in this period? I shall not speak of the gigantic work of industrially equipping a technically backward country, a country whose primitive economy was completely shattered by the European capitalist war, followed by the war of the working class against its native savages and the savages of Europe, a war in which the workers fought for the right to culture, and the intellectuals for the right of the bourgeoisie to rob.

I shall point instead to the extensive development in these fifteen years of universities and scientific research institutes, and to the multiplicity of mineral deposits discovered in this period, enough to ensure the economic and cultural growth of the land for many centuries to come. All this is known. Only those fail to observe these conquests of mind and will who are blinded by their bestial interests and inhuman class prejudices. Only those fail to see them who are unwilling to see, and the journalists, whose masters have forbidden them to see the truth.

In the Soviet Union there is one master. That is its basic achievement and what distinguishes it from bourgeois states. This master is the workers' and peasants' state, which is guided by the organization of the disciples of Lenin. The aim it sets itself is perfectly clear: it is to create for every one of the 160,000,000 individuals of its multinational population conditions for the free development of his talents and abilities—in other words, to transform the sum-total of potential and passive neuro-cerebral energy into active energy, to awaken its creative faculties. Is this possible?

It is being done. The masses, before whom all the roads to culture have been opened, are promoting from their midst tens of thousands of talented young people in all fields of application of energy: in science, technology, art and administration.

Of course, we are not free from mistakes in our life and work, but the proprietary instinct, the stupidity, laziness and other vices inherited from past ages cannot be eliminated in ten or fifteen years. Yet only a madman, or a man driven insane by fury, will venture to deny the indisputable fact that the distance which in Europe separates the young generation of workers from the incontestable achievements of universal human culture is, in the Soviet Union, being reduced at fantastic speed.

Basing themselves on all that is undeniably valuable in the old culture, the peoples of the Soviet Union are boldly developing their national, but universally human, values. Of this anyone can convince himself who is willing to turn his attention to the young literature and music of the national minorities of the Soviet Union.

Mention should be made of the emancipation of the women of the Turkic and Turko-Finnish tribes, their aspiration to new forms of life, and their activity.

Legislative activity in the Soviet Union originates and arises among the working masses, on the basis of their working experience and the changes that take place in their conditions of work. The Council of People's Commissars only frames this experience into laws, and can do so only in the interest of the working masses—for there is no other master in the country.

All over the world laws fall like a hail of stones from above, and they all have two purposes: to exploit the labour energy of the working masses, and to create obstacles to the conversion of physical energy into intellectual energy. If the resources that the bourgeoisie spends on armament for the purpose of mutual robbery were spent on public education, the terrible aspect of the bourgeois world would probably not be so revolting. The hatred of the bourgeoisie for the Soviet Union compels the latter, too, to waste its time and metal on armaments—and this must be regarded as one more crime of the European bourgeoisie against their workers and peasants.

No one can point to any decree issued by the Council of People's Commissars which was not designed to satisfy the cultural demands and requirements of the working people. Leningrad is being reconstructed, and in the conferences on the subject participate doctors, artists, nurses, architects, writers and, it goes without saying, workers, representatives from the factories. As far as I know, this is not the custom in Europe.

The press in the Soviet Union, with a captiousness which, in my opinion, is excessive and even harmful—as it arouses unrealizable hopes in the mind of the philistine—lays bare all mistakes in work, all the vices and follies of the old way of life. This is something the bourgeois press dare not do; it prefers to pervert the uneducated reader with detailed and sadistic descriptions of murders, or enticing stories of dexterous frauds.

In these fifteen years the worker and peasant masses have promoted, and are continuously promoting, from their midst thousands of inventors, who are helping the Soviet Union to economize tens of millions of money and are gradually relieving the population of the need for imports.

The worker, feeling himself the master of industry, is naturally developing a sense of responsibility to the country, and this induces him to strive to improve the quality of wares and to reduce their cost of production.

The peasant before the revolution worked in seventeenth-century conditions, entirely dependent on the elemental caprices of nature and on his exhausted land, which was broken up into tiny strips. Now he is swiftly equipping himself with tractors, seeders and combines, widely uses fertilizers, and has twenty-six agricultural research institutes working for him. Having had no idea of science before, he is now being graphically convinced of its strength, of the power of the human reason.

A village lad who comes to work in a factory built in accordance with the very latest and most up-to-date achievements of technology, finds himself in a world of phenomena which strike his imagination, awaken his mind and rid it of wild and ancient superstitions and prejudices. He sees the workings of reason incarnated in the most intricate machinery and machine tools. He may, of course, from inexperience, spoil one thing or another, but the material damage he causes is compensated by the growth of his intellect. He sees that the masters of the factory are workers like himself, that the young engineer is the son of a worker or peasant. He very soon arrives at the conviction that for him the factory is a school which offers him an opportunity for the free development of his abilities. If he possesses ability, the factory will send him to one of the higher educational establishments, but there are already factories which have started their own technical high schools. His neuro-cerebral energy, in which man's capacity to investigate and cognize the phenomena of the world lies latent, is powerfully stimulated by a sum-total of conditions which were entirely unknown to his father.

He visits theatres which are acknowledged to be the finest in Europe, he reads the classical literature of Europe and old Russia, attends concerts, goes to museums and studies his country as nobody has studied it before him.

Some time ago Comrade Kuibyshev * invited the Komsomols to take part in the work of prospecting deposits of metallic and non-metallic minerals all over the country. This means that tens of thousands of young people, working under the direction of the Soviet Union's most eminent geologists, are to enrich the economy of their country by the discovery of new deposits of raw material, and to enrich themselves with new knowledge and experience. The organization of such armies for such purposes is beyond the capacity of capitalist countries, and what is more, there is nothing to search for in these countries, which have been ransacked and plundered by the misrule of the capitalists. And if the European vampires do attempt another bandit raid on the Soviet Union, their armies will find themselves faced with soldiers everyone of whom knows what he is defending.

* * *

The capitalists bank in their cynical game on the stupidity of the masses; but in the Soviet Union the working masses are being educated, by a developing and organized process, in the knowledge of their right to rule. A new man is arising in the Soviet Union, and his qualities can already be unmistakably defined.

He possesses a faith in the organizing power of reason, a faith which the European intellectuals have lost,

---

* V. V. Kuibyshev (1888-1935) was an outstanding Party worker and distinguished Soviet statesman, member of the Politbureau of the C.C., C.P.S.U.(B.), and Chairman of the State Planning Commission.

they having been exhausted by the fruitless effort of reconciling class antagonisms. He feels that he is the maker
of a new world, and although his conditions of life are still
hard, he knows that the creation of different conditions is
his aim and that it depends upon his rational will, and he
therefore has no reason to be a pessimist. He is young
not only biologically, but historically. He is a force which
has only just realized its road and significance in history,
and he performs his work of cultural development with all
the boldness of a young force that has only just begun
to operate and is guided by a simple and clear doctrine.
It is funny to him to hear the groans and howls of the
Spenglers who are terrified by technology, because he
knows very well that technology has not yet worked for
the cultural development of the hundreds of millions of
slaves of physical labour. He sees that the bourgeoisie, in
banking on individualism, has ignominiously lost, that it
has actually done nothing to promote the growth of the
individual, but has selfishly restricted that growth with
ideas which covertly or overtly proclaimed its lawless
power over the majority of man to be an "eternal truth."
Rejecting the brutish individualism of the bourgeoisie,
the new man is fully aware how highly integral is the individual who is firmly united with a collective; for he
himself is such an individual, freely drawing his energy
and inspiration from the masses, from the process of their
labour. Capitalism has led mankind into anarchy, which
threatens him with prodigious catastrophes—that is clear
to every honest man.

The aim of the old world is to restore by methods of
physical and moral violence, by means of wars on the
battlefields and bloodshed in the streets of cities, the old,

thoroughly decayed and inhuman "order," without which capitalism cannot exist.

The aim of the new man is to emancipate the labouring masses from the ancient superstitions and prejudices of race, nation, class, religion, and to create a universal fraternal society, every member of which will work according to his abilities and receive according to his needs.

(1932)

TO THE DELEGATES
OF THE ANTIWAR CONGRESS

(A Speech That Was Not Delivered)

I CORDIALLY greet the men and women who have determined to raise their voice against international wars, which are organized by the capitalists for the sake of their own enrichment and which sow hatred among the peoples.

I greet you, and would be happy to believe that your protest might shake the evil will of the enemies of mankind, because they are again planning an international shambles.

But the past does not inspire the hope that the words of the pacifists have the power of triumphing over the destructive designs of a numerically insignificant caste of people who are utterly irresponsible and have already gone out of their minds, but who still dominate the life and will of nations.

You will all remember, of course, that after the defeat of Austria and France by Prussia, pacifism was continuously preached for forty-three years, and that Bertha von Suttner's celebrated book, *Down With Arms!* was, among others, received with approval and read by intellectuals all over the world. But neither this book, nor the preaching of Leo Tolstoy, nor anybody in general, could prevent the capitalists from destroying millions of people in their struggle for the seizure of colonies, or from engineering the march on Peking and the sacking of the capital of China, or prevent the Balkan Wars and that most shameful holocaust, the European war.

That war should not have caught the European pacifists unawares. But the humanitarians were easily caught by it; it set them one against the other, arms in hand, in the ranks of the millions of involuntary assassins; and the preachers of peace exterminated one another with the fury of savages. By involuntary assassins I mean the workers and peasants, who have no reason to destroy each other in order to strengthen the power of their class enemy, but who still lack the sense and will to put a stop to fratricidal massacres of nations. We know that in 1914 the crafty social-jesuits, the leaders of the Second International, villainously deluded the labouring folk of Europe and caused the workers to forget who the real enemy of the working class is, and why the enemy finds it necessary to provoke bloody conflicts between nations. The humanitarians likewise fail to see who is the real enemy of humanitarian culture. In 1914 they easily became infected with the madness of the people of their class.

For the people of this class there is nothing more precious in the world than gold, and everything—science, which investigates the phenomena of nature; technology, which was developed in order to lighten the physical labour of men; art, whose mission it is to ennoble them— is coined by the capitalists into gold, just as they do the blood of the labouring people. This affirmation is borne out by the fact that the biological sciences lag very considerably behind other branches of knowledge.

The bourgeoisie, of course, makes a business and profit out of medicine and hygiene, but these sciences, whose function it is to protect human health, are not such good money-makers as chemistry and physics, for instance, and especially mechanics, which is made to work for the armaments industry, that is, for the mass destruction of human beings.

Each of the national groups of capitalists, upholding its preferential right to plunder the earth and its inhabitants, frantically competes with other national groups of marauders, skilfully playing on the "national instinct," the primitive instinct which divides people into hostile camps. It is on this instinct that the capitalists rely at the needed moment to turn the pacifists into their obedient servants. It has long been quite obvious that the "interests of the nation" have come to imply the interests of a group of industrialists, of exploiters of the physical and mental energies of the nation. It is also known that each of these groups is capable of betraying its "nation." Are facts needed to prove this? Here they are.

"On February 14, 1912, a representative of the French Société de Carbures obtained an order from Krupp for ferro-silicate, which is required for the manufacture of gun steel. In his letter he wrote: 'Krupp insists that we keep a stock of 1,000 tons in close proximity to the plant. I don't think that it is transport difficulties as such that worry Krupp in this instance; his demand is actuated by the Germans' belief that a European war is inevitable *in the next two years,* and at the moment of general mobilization Krupp may experience great difficulty in securing all the supplies he needs. . . . It is for this reason that Krupp desires to have 1,000 tons of ferro-silicate close at hand.'"

It will be seen that the French Société de Carbures was fully aware that Krupp was buying ferro-silicate in the belief that war was inevitable. Nevertheless, the French "patriots" sold Krupp electrometal for the manufacture of guns, which were later to mow down French soldiers by the thousand. And not only before the war, but even during the war, the Société de Carbures supplied Krupp with war material, as the French investigatory authorities have established.

"At a time when Franco-German antagonisms are becoming increasingly strained, when a section of the French press is threatening Germany with sanctions should she refuse to bear the reparations burden, and when the French militarists are more and more frankly brandishing the mailed fist in Geneva, the 'patriots' of the I.G. Farbenindustrie are supplying the French war department with sodium nitrate and other materials for the manufacture of explosives! Obviously, the German 'patriots' have no guarantee that these means of destruction will be used only against the Chinese in the Far East, and not somewhere closer by. Today, as twenty years ago, the warmongers are carrying on their criminal activities with impunity, reckoning on amassing piles of gold in a welter of human blood."

You know that the capitalists' irresponsible and criminal game went unpunished everywhere, except in tsarist Russia.

What are the industrial barons out for in engineering another world shambles? They imagine that war will help them escape from the jaws of the economic crisis brought about by the anarchy of production and the idiocy of the profit-lust.

Figuratively speaking, they are anxious to bathe again in the blood of the working people, hoping that it will cure their senile decrepitude. I positively assert that capitalists are insane—nothing else can explain the enormity of their baneful lust for wealth. Gluttony is a disease. The glutton keeps on devouring food even when his stomach is overloaded. The capitalist is a profit-maniac, and one that also suffers from megalomania. Apart from these abnormalities, he is usually ignorant, his mentality being cramped by the instinct of the vulture. It is absolutely incorrect to bestow on him the title of "organizer of industry" —industry is organized by the scientists and engineers, operating through the physical energies of the working class. We don't say of a man who has learned to milk a cow that he is the inventor of milk. Yet when you read the biography or autobiography of a capitalist, Ford, for instance, it is evident that he imagines himself to be the inventor of milk, and not of methods of milking cows. It is the scientists, engineers, artists and the workers of the mills, factories, mines and railways that, by their incessant labour and creative work, have instilled, and instil, megalomaniac beliefs in the mind of the capitalist. It seems to him that everything they do is done by him, just because he pays them money, which has also been robbed from them, the real masters of culture. One feels rather awkward having to demonstrate something that is self-evident and obvious.

I am speaking of the genuine makers of universal human culture, who consider action the basis of knowledge and who are deeply sensitive to the poetry of labour, the people to whom mankind owes the indisputable treasures of science and art; I am speaking of the people who are not

335

tempted by the sordid paradise of the bourgeoisie, and who clearly see how feeble and beggarly is the creative energy of the modern bourgeoisie, how loathsome is the life it has created, and how it poisons and corrupts the masses—the reservoir of creative energy.

History has firmly posed before these masters of culture a plain and simple question: *What is needed?*—criminal wars of one national capitalist group against another, wars of which there will be no end; or a war of the proletarians of all countries against the capitalists of all countries, a war which will make bloody massacres, the destruction of millions of the most healthy individuals and of the products of their labour, forever impossible?

With whom must the masters of culture march toward the future?—with the men who exploit their creative energies, who are already oversated with it, being amply surrounded with objects of material culture, and who have long ceased to have any need for the development of intellectual culture and are even beginning to restrict its development?

Or must they march with the new class, which history is advancing to the forefront, and which, in a country with 163,000,000 inhabitants, has already taken the power into its hands?

The *social-jesuits*, as the Second International leaders should rightly be called, are opposed to the class war. For them, the sanguinary national wars of the proletarians provoked by the capitalists are far less dangerous. They are afraid of the class war, because it will inevitably place them in the despicable position of that fellow Noske, who has been rightly nicknamed the "bloody hound."

In 1914 the leaders of the Second International made it perfectly evident to the world that their internationalism in no way differs from the internationalism of the traders in the energy and blood of the working class. I personally would not be in the least surprised if these leaders were to acknowledge, together with *L'Osservatore Romano*, organ of the head of the Most Christian Church, "the necessity for the concentration of all the forces of Christian Europe against the spiritual anarchy emanating from Russia."

By anarchy, in this case, is meant the achievements of the working class in building a socialist economy and culture. Anarchy, forsooth, is the growth of intellectual energy in the Soviet Union, the rapidity of which may be illustrated by the following figures: as against 57,000 engineers and 55,000 technicians in the Soviet Union in 1929, there are 163,000 engineers and 138,500 technicians in 1932. In 1932 the working class—the sole master in the Soviet Union—has 400 universities and colleges and 1,609 vocational schools, with a total of two-and-a-half million students. But even with this number of students, it will not be soon before the need for scientific workers in the Soviet Union is fully satisfied. But take Germany; there the Reichsverband der angestellten Ärzte lodged a complaint with the government against the employment of foreign medical men in the hospitals, although it turns out that there are only 145 of them. This, of course, does not imply that the health service in Germany is ideal, but only that 145 German medical men are unable to earn their bread in their own country.

Of course, this is a small, an insignificant fact in the tragic chaos of European life. But behind it lurks another:

Germany's higher educational establishments annually turn out 40,000 graduates, but the government can provide employment only for 6,000. "Overproduction" of intellectual energy is a phenomenon common to all Europe, and to the United States as well. But you know, of course, that the labouring masses are not served by this energy and are unable to absorb it; "overproduction" only signifies that, under the capitalist structure of states, a proper distribution of the cultural forces of the world—which is absolutely essential for the further promotion of culture—is impossible.

This year, 1932, in the Soviet Union, which has 163,000,000 inhabitants, the entire able-bodied population is employed; not only are there no unemployed, the country is even experiencing a shortage of labour. The sole master of the country—the working class—has boldly tackled problems of vast economic and cultural importance: it is linking seas by canals, diverting the waters of rivers to irrigate arid steppes, enriching the whole country with electric power, laying miles and miles of road, and erecting scores of huge mills and factories. The magnitude of the work done in these fifteen years is truly fabulous. And this is anarchy, according to the Adlers, the priests and the jesuits of other professions, men who are determined to be blind because they fear a truth which is to their disadvantage, but which is quite obvious, namely, that the working class can be a more efficient manager than the capitalists.

Even some of the marauders are coming round to a recognition of this fact; but this, of course, does not convince the rest—it only tends to inflame their class hatred and brutal inhumanity.

Though the working class of the Soviet Union is managing economic affairs more rationally than the capitalists, it does not regard the development of material culture as its sole and ultimate end; it does not confine the aim of its efforts solely to the enrichment of its country, that is, to self-enrichment. It realizes and knows that it needs material culture as the soil and foundation for the development of spiritual, intellectual culture. Its creative energies are nourished and strengthened by the great idea of the world brotherhood of nations.

What idea does capitalism promote? It sows racial and national hatred all over the world. Now the capitalists have set up a talk-shop known as the League of Nations. For months the obedient servants of capital dilated in this establishment on the necessity for European disarmament, and meanwhile, as you know, the capitalists of Japan openly and with impunity plundered China, seized Manchuria, and massacred, and are continuing to massacre, tens of thousands of innocent people. Vast cultural treasures, of importance to all humanity, were destroyed in Shanghai.

This criminal act did not arouse the indignation of the pacifists, it did not move them to protest, it did not even seem to attract their attention. Yet capitalist crimes are being committed not only in Shanghai and Manchuria, but all over the world, in all the cities of Europe, and everywhere in the sight of the humanitarians and pacifists. They are not ignorant, they know that in the United States workers are dying of starvation at a time when the capitalists are turning wheat into brickets to fuel locomotive boilers with; yet this monstrous fact does not seem to discredit the capitalist system of economy in their eyes. In the streets of German cities every day bloody conflicts take place, workers are killed, and minor rehearsals are performed of the civil war which the bourgeoisie have provoked and are fanning with increasing cynicism. How do the pacifists react to this? What, except eloquence, can they oppose to capitalist anarchism and cynicism? The "armaments international" is constantly at work under their eyes. The *Washington Post* has published data on the military expenditures of America's European debtors.

Based on official figures, they show that in 1930 Great Britain spent $608,000,000 for military purposes; France—$547,000,000; Italy—$322,000,000; Poland—$123,000,000; Rumania—$67,000,000; Yugoslavia—$47,000,000; Czechoslovakia—$41,000,000; Belgium—$23,000,000. According to another source, in this same year Japan spent $240,000,000 on re-armament, while the military budget of the U.S.A. amounted to $709,000,000.

We know that in 1931 he military expenditures of all the bourgeois states showed no reduction, but on the contrary were still higher. The budgets for the current year provide for further increases of military expenditure.

The war industries are operating at top speed. It should be noted that the hope that the military operations in the Far East would mean a boom for the armament industry was not justified. The Berlin *Deutsche Allgemeine Zeitung* remarked in this connection: "It turns out that the Central countries can do good business only when really rich powers are locked in war."

With these billions, of course, a prodigious massacre of human beings may be arranged, and cities destroyed and the products of labour annihilated on a fantastic scale.

I ask: is this what capitalist "civilization" has come to? Is this inevitable? Can this be justified? I cannot imagine a devil who could palliate this crime. But I can imagine what would happen if these billions were spent to enrich the men of physical labour with intellectual energy. I can imagine it, because I am a citizen of the Soviet Union, a country where there are no capitalits, and where, in truly difficult conditions, the working class is displaying amazing talent in all spheres of application of energy to the work of building a new culture. The thoughts of the patriots are least of all occupied with the working people at a time when, in Europe and America, they go about unemployed and die of starvation, and in the capitalist colonies are mown down by machine guns, fighting for liberation from exploitation by the marauders.

Really, it is very difficult to understand what is worrying the pacifists and what they are out for. Perhaps the only explanation of their worry is that they, the pacifists and humanitarians, dwell in the rear of the armies, and that the generals are threatening that the next holocaust of nations will not spare even the meek denizens of the rear.

Generally, one gets the impression that the humanitarians have already for a long time been living in the rear of events, at the back of history, and that their principal urge is for self-preservation and tranquility. It is hard to imagine how the pacifists will behave when the inevitable and last war breaks out, the war which will destroy all possibility of national wars.

We know that all the fury of the nationalists' hate is directed against the Soviet Union. It is likewise clear that if the capitalists believed that all the working class of the Soviet Union is doing were nothing but an"unsuccessful experiment," they would have no cause to hate the people of the Soviet land so ferociously. They could live calmly and go about their usual business of mutual robbery and destruction at home, in their own countries, and wait until the "unsuccessful experiment" finally collapsed and then hurl themselves upon the Soviet Union. But the experiment is obviously a success, and they themselves are beginning to admit this aloud to one another. And so France is again dreaming of a march on Moscow.

The preaching of war against the Soviets is strongest of all in France. All the more gratifying is it to see here Frenchmen who are opposed to a war against a people which does not want to fight but is compelled to prepare for defence. This people has resolutely and without sparing its strength set about a cause which is incontestably of importance to all mankind. Only the enemies of working humanity, the exploiters of its energies, people whose actions are obviously and undeniably criminal, and whose designs are more criminal still, can hinder it in this.

As I understand it, the purpose of this congress is to find ways and means of counteracting these designs. An honourable purpose. On the subject of how to combat the organizers of another mass slaughter of human beings, I have already expressed my views definitely enough; I see no other way, and I do not think professional assassins can be re-educated by talk.

It is the accepted thing, when concluding a speech, to express some wish. Addressing myself to the proletarians of all countries (and among the "proletarians" I include honest-minded intellectual workers), my wish is that they realize as speedily as possible that every capitalist war is a war against the workers, against the labouring people, against culture, and that, having realized this, they devote all their efforts and all their might to organizing the last, decisive battle against the class enemy, who is destroying the culture created by centuries of effort of the workers by hand and brain.

(1932)

"SOLDIERLY IDEAS"

SOME time ago a Stahlhelm parade was held in Berlin, and the chief of the organization, Seldte, a liqueur manufacturer, said: "When the Stahlhelm marches it means that the soldierly spirit of Germany has been reborn. Soldierly ideas and so'dierly deeds are again meeting with understanding in Germany."

In a biography of the philosopher Fichte written some thirty years ago—I don't remember by whom—it was said: "Germany is a country of philosophers, and whereas in France the policy-makers are lawyers, in Germany it is the philosophers that govern the mind of the nation." But now, as we see, in Germany liqueur manufacturers have begun to be the policy-makers. This is not a new innovation, of course, and, bad though it is, in a capitalist state it is quite natural. Nevertheless, a liqueur manufacturer can scarcely be called a philosopher. We know that the bourgeois philosopher is a lover of wisdom, who exercises his brain to "explain the world" or to explain the technique of mental reasoning about the world. This is his profession, and from the point of view of men of living deed, men who transform the world, the bourgeois philosopher may—without offence to him—be called an "idler." The liqueur manufacturer is not a philosopher; he too is a man of deed—of "soldierly deeds."

What is meant by "soldierly deeds" may be easily imagined: the bloody horror of such "deeds" in 1914-18

344

is not quite forgotten, as may be clearly seen from the mood of the masses reflected at the antiwar congress in Amsterdam. Nor have the horrors of the villainous European intervention in the Soviet Union been forgotten. We recently had a reminder of "soldierly deeds" in the destruction of Cha-pei by the Japanese. Generally speaking, we are being almost continually reminded of "soldierly deeds."

But what are "soldierly ideas"? As far as I know, the history of philosophy makes no mention of such, and there is every ground for asserting that "soldierly ideas" are altogether an impossibility, because always and everywhere the soldier has been taught "not to think," and if he did think he was punished for it.

The system of training the soldier in the tsarist army was borrowed lock, stock and barrel from Germany. The soldier was forbidden to answer a question of his commander with a simple and honest, "I don't know"; he had to answer in the formula: "I cannot know." By this formula, *the soldier was forced to renounce his ability and right to know anything that* in the slightest degree went beyond the *Military Manual*—one of the most loathsome documents produced by bourgeois civilization.

Once a man was clapped into soldier's uniform, it was instilled into him that not only was he unworthy, and forbidden, to know, but by his very "nature as a soldier" he could not know, was bereft of the ability to know, anything that went beyond the laws and regulations of his service. The soldier in bourgeois armies is a man whom his class enemy stultifies in order to strengthen his power over him—the peasant or worker. The European soldier is a man who is a captive of his enemies, who is hypnotized by them and who works for them in return for beggarly pay and a wretched hunk of bread. Yet the soldiers are men whose fathers, mothers, brothers and sisters work and pay enormous taxes in order to clothe, arm and feed their sons or brothers while they are serving in the army. And when life becomes so hard for the fathers and brothers that they "revolt" against their age-old class enemies, the soldiers are obliged to fire on the "rebels." And they do fire—so utter are the depths of idiocy to which they have been reduced by the capitalists.

For over half a year the factotums of the capitalists prated about disarmament at Geneva. The soldiers of the European armies remained deaf to this chatter; yet they could have turned it into something real and serious. They might have said some very weighty things about the constantly increasing expenditure on armaments, the senseless squandering of metal on guns and tanks, and the new world carnage which the capitalists are planning, and which demands that millions of living, healthy men shall be converted into corpses, and millions of others into cripples. But the soldier is turned into a man who cannot know and does not think. The liqueur manufacturer is lying: the rank-and-file soldier has no "soldierly ideas." But inasmuch as there are no small numbers of proletarians in the imperialist armies, they are naturally doing their proletarian, historically necessary, work in the barracks, and the bourgeois soldiers are beginning to think.

There is only one army in the world whose soldiers have the right and the duty to think. It is the Red Army, our army. Its soldiers do not say, "I cannot know"; they have the right to know, and it is their duty to know everything, or as much as possible. And they know the chief thing—who the enemy is and where he is to be found;

they know that their enemy is the property owner, and that he wants to live on the labour of others, and only for himself; that he wants to live the predatory life of the spider. The soldier of the Red Army is a citizen of his country, its master, its guardian and the builder of its future.

* * *

When I once asked from what class the members of the Stahlhelm were chiefly recruited, I was told: "They are mostly the sons of men killed in the war of 1914-18; they are avengers of their fathers and of their desecrated Fatherland." There are, of course, many such young men in France too, and the governments of all the countries that fought in the European war are training "avengers" so as to set them at loggerheads with one another. In inciting war "orphans" against similar orphans, the myrmidons of capital, the corrupt souls, the press fakers and pen pirates conceal from the youth the plain and simple truth that in cases of manslaughter, it is not so much the hand of the physical manslayer that is guilty, as the villainous mind of the inciter to manslaughter. And no one will venture to deny the obvious, namely, that the inciter is the capitalist, the worshipper of the idol of private property, a being deformed by an insatiable greed and envy and an insane passion for the accumulation of money and things, a being in human shape, but who is more and more losing even physical resemblance to a normal human being.

The "war orphans" and "avengers of their fathers" are like tin soldiers in the hands of degenerate and wicked boys. When they get tired of the toys, they find pleasure in breaking off the heads and legs of their tin soldiers.

347

The only difference between the tin soldier and the "avenger" is that before the "avenger's" head is torn off, it is stuffed with poisonous nonsense. He is made to believe that there is something called a Fatherland, and that he must defend this Fatherland, which entirely belongs to irresponsible and inhuman vampires, manufacturers of guns, liqueurs and other "cultural" values. Anarchic exploitation of the physical energy of the working class has brought upon the European "fatherlands" the horrors of mass unemployment and starvation, which of course undermine the health of the working people, of the "nation." Unemployment leads to results like this: on one day, August 10, fire brigades in Berlin were called out fifteen times to render aid to suicides who had poisoned themselves with kitchen gas. This does not include the suicides who drowned themselves, hanged themselves, shot themselves or threw themselves out of windows. The common cause of all these suicides was unemployment.

"That is not so much for Berlin," said one of the intellectuals whose minds have been stultified by capitalism, one of those people who see and understand very well that their master is stupid, banal and inhuman, but is, nevertheless, a "man of means," and therefore must be worked for. To work against him, together with the advanced international party of the working class, is beyond the courage of the stultified intellectual, although he ought to see that *history is already sternly asking him whether he has the right to allow himself to be stultified.*

There is a provision in the laws of nearly every bourgeois country—I do not remember its exact wording, but the gist of it is that a man who witnesses a crime and does not come to the aid of the victim, is himself an accessory to the crime. I know that it is naïve to talk of justice in present-day capitalist society, although, I believe, when the victim of the crime happens to be a bourgeois, the bourgeoisie does apply this provision. But, it goes without saying, it has never been applied in the case of crimes against the working masses, against the toiling people. Today the working class—the object and victim of the criminal actions of the capitalists—is raising its head everywhere, all over the world, and beginning to apprehend that the right to legislate and to try belongs to it. It certainly has a lively recollection of many a staggering instance of criminal indifference on the part of the onlookers to cynical acts of capitalist lawlessness. The time will come when the working man will recall that when he was unemployed and dying of starvation, wheat and coffee were mixed with tar and turned into brickets for fuel. He will recall that British fascists volunteered for the armies of Bolivia and Paraguay, and that the Bolivian consul in London counted on purchasing ten thousand of these hired assassins. He, the supreme judge, will recall many things which are passed by with indifference by people who have been stultified by capitalism and who feel no loathing at living in a welter of incredible crimes.

Who are these people, and what opinion do they have of themselves? I think they are fairly accurately described by a character in one of the modern English novels, who says something to the following effect:

"Life, it seems to me, demands so much care, so much strain is needed to live decently, that all zest for life is lost. I am speaking, of course, of what is called civilized life, not life on the Fiji Islands or in Zululand. With us, everything is so measured, weighed and prescribed and demands such careful deliberation and circumspection, that we never live simply and easily, to say nothing of the joy of existence, which is beyond our ken. We seem to be all the time walking on a tight-rope, and are happy only when we can say: well, that bit is passed. If you decide not to think and to snatch whatever pleasure you can, you soon become surfeited and everything loses its interest. And if you try to avoid being surfeited, it requires so much effort that you get no pleasure out of life at all. If you swim with the current, you are bound to land on the rocks; and if you try to steer your bark, it is one continuous strain. The trouble is you can't trust life—you have to be watching it all the time and keep luffing and tacking. So that the only pleasure you can get out of it is like that which some people get from fiddling with a wireless set or a gramophone. It works as long as you keep changing the wave-length or record. You can't just sit back and listen to the music."

That's the aim of life: sit back and dispassionately observe the storms and tempests of life, without taking any part in it. Of course, not by any means all the European intellectuals have reached such a degree of realization of their impotence, such a state of stark despair. But it is very significant that such a dreary confession of spiritual poverty should have appeared in England, the England of Kipling, the poet of imperialism.

Having noted this fact, and also that this mood is spreading like a mould or fungus all over Europe and is even infecting low-brow America, let us return to the "soldierly ideas." I have already said that the soldier has no "soldierly ideas," and I believe the time is past when such ideas could be driven deeply, like nails into a tree, into the minds of the European armies. But soldierly ideas certainly do exist, and in our time they are being intensively preached in the form of fascism. They are not new ideas, their origins may be traced in the books of German writers—the celebrated historian Heinrich Treitschke, for instance—and Friedrich Nietzsche gave them philosophical and artistic shape in his "blond beast." One of the exponents of these ideas is Benito Mussolini. In an article he contributed to the *Italian Encyclopedia*, he takes his stand on the precepts of the psychopathic Nietzsche, with his preaching of *Liebe zum Fernsten*, and contemptuously rejects the idea of the brotherhood of nations and the social equality of human beings, and also, of course, rejects the right of the majority to rule.

Mussolini lauds imperialism, under whose tyranny people perish by the million, and extols war as the supreme manifestation of all man's faculties—this was preached before him by the "futurist" Marinetti, and it is the maniacal idea of all militaristic writers. War, in their opinion, "ennobles" man—with which the vanquished in war are scarcely likely to agree. No one has ever heard the vanquished saying to the vanquisher with admiration or astonishment: "Oh, how nobly you have mutilated and robbed me." In 1914-15, the Belgians and French did not speak of the "nobility" of the German victors; on the contrary, the vanquished cried out against "Teuton ferocity," and accused them of bloodthirsty savagery and other qualities which are the very opposite of "nobility." Neither did the defeated and plundered Germans speak, and still do not speak, of the nobility and generosity of the victors. It would be very odd, exceedingly odd to apply the epithet "noble" to such actions of the armies of intervention in Russia as the shooting of the twenty-six Baku commissars by the British, or the pilfering of the gold reserve in Kazan by the Czechs, or the action of the French and Greeks on the day they evacuated Kherson, when these noble warriors locked up two thousand peaceful civilians in the warehouses on the wharf and set fire to them, burning their victims alive. General Graves, who commanded the American forces of intervention in Siberia, has likewise positively nothing to say about the "nobility" of warriors and soldiers. One might also recall the depredations of the Germans in the Ukraine, and many other things which are a disgrace to "cultured" Europe.

Nor will the opinion of the militarists and fascists about the "nobility" of war be shared by those hundreds of thousands of "victors" whom the war crippled, and whom the morally crippled victors now have to beat up and disperse, as was the case with the "bonus army" in Washington.

Nor will the opinion of the fascists be shared by the millions of vanquished and victors who are now deprived of the right to work and are dying of hunger. The Italian fascists are dreaming of the time when Rome will rule the world; Hitler preaches that fascism will "elevate the German people above all mankind"; there is an individual in Japan who asserts that very soon the whole white race will be under the power of the yellow bourgeoisie; the French imperialists would like to pocket the whole of Europe—and one cannot find words to express how wretched and vile, how senseless and disgusting this all is. Mussolini holds that never before have the "peoples" yearned so passionately for strong rule.

It is very likely that the bourgeoisie will still manage here and there to enthrone idiots with crowns stuck jauntily on the side of their heads and with brains of lead under their scalps. But not for long, of course. These are but the convulsions of a degenerate and dying class, the raving and agony of a deathbed patient. Literary artists, when describing dying people, often make them recall the past, scenes of their childhood and youth. It is the past that is now haunting the sick bourgeoisie of the world, while the European bourgeoisie recalls the close of the eighteenth century, when it fought under the slogan of liberty, fraternity and equality—and recalls the struggle, apparently, as a deplorable error of its youth. Oh, if everything could only be reconstructed on the feudal pattern! That is what the "soldierly ideas" of fascism chiefly boil down to.

The present-day sentiments of the bourgeoisie were recently expressed in quite naked form and with the naïve cynicism of a savage in Hitler's *Völkischer Beobachter* by a certain Alfred Rosenberg, in connection with the sentence passed on five fascists who had tortured and killed a Communist in Beuthen. The murder was committed with such sadistic ferocity that even the bourgeois court condemned the murderers to death. Says Rosenberg:

"The verdict reveals the profound abyss that divides our way of thinking from liberalism. The prevailing liberal principles of law assert that all men are equal. This is also recognized in America. But there an impassable barrier exists between white and coloured people. Not only must a Negro not marry a white woman; he must not even ride in the same streetcar as whites. A Negro who rapes a white woman is lynched. This, of course, is 'bad,' but it is necessary for the protection of the white race. On the outbreak of the world war the French pacifist Jaurès was killed and the court acquitted the killer, but the man who made an attempt on the life of Clemenceau was executed—and in both cases France acted in accordance with her vital interests. In the case of the five men sentenced to death for killing a Pole, who was a Bolshevik into the bargain, the sentence runs counter to the elementary instinct of national self-protection. We are waging an offensive against the liberal outlook as much as against the Marxist outlook. To us, every soul is not the equal of every other soul, every man is not the equal of every other man. We want to see the Germans a strong people. Only the doctrine of inequality can bring Germany political freedom."

Under the influence of such raving, the sentence was commuted to a milder one, and there is reason to believe that the murderers will be reprieved altogether. And this raving is the underlying substance of fascism. It is quite clear that Europe and her labouring folk are ruled by madmen, that there is no crime of which they are incapable, no amount of blood they would shrink from shedding. To reach such a state of raving madness, it was necessary to outlive or eradicate Goethe and Kant, Schiller and Fichte and a good hundred other great thinkers, poets, composers and painters. Bourgeois culture remains untouched—or rather untouchable—in the libraries and museums, while bourgeois life becomes ever more sordid and savage, and its policies ever more sadistic and inhuman. The world outside the Soviet Union is governed by madmen.

(1932)

PROLETARIAN HUMANISM

"THE world is sick"—this is asserted not only by the Bolsheviks; it is also asserted by lyrical-minded humanitarians who have at last understood that "love, mercy, magnanimity" and the other sentiments with which the biped beasts of prey endeavoured to conceal their wolfish "nature" cannot be put to practical use, cannot be turned into a commodity and do not find purchasers, and have a baneful effect on the growth of commercial and industrial profits.

"The world has gone mad"—cry ever more loudly the people who have made it their trade to defend and justify the irresponsible and inhuman rule of capital over the world of labour, and the unrestricted, and already senseless, exploitation of the energy of the workers by the masters.

Capitalism's "sickness" began almost immediately after the bourgeoisie wrested power from the enfeebled hands of the feudals. It may be taken that the first to notice this sickness and to raise a desperate outcry over it was Friedrich Nietzsche, a contemporary of Karl Marx. There is no such thing as chance, every phenomenon in life has its reason; and it is no chance that, at a time when Marx was scientifically and incontrovertibly demonstrating the inevitability of the downfall of capitalism and the inevitability of the rule of the proletariat, Nietzsche was preaching with the frenzy of a morbid and frightened fanatic the legitimacy of the unrestricted rule of the "blond beast." Before Nietzsche, the bourgeois state, religion and morals were impugned by Max Stirner, who asserted the right of the individual to unrestricted egotism. This anarchist denunciation is essentially a denunciation of the "humanism" which the bourgeoisie had already begun to evolve in the Middle Ages, in the beginning of its struggle against feudalism and the Church, the ideological leader of the feudals. The bourgeoisie realized the inconvenience and self-contradictoriness of this "humanism" in its own practical life very early, which is borne out by the church reform of Luther, Calvin, etc. What this reform actually amounted to was the supplanting of the "humanitarian" Gospels by the Bible, which not only regards tribal enmity, slaughter, robbery, deceit and all the rest without which the bourgeois state cannot exist, as quite natural, but even as praiseworthy. Prior to Luther, the Church adjured the handiworkers of culture to suffer in patience for Christ's sake. Luther, with a fortrightness alien to the priests, taught in the sixteenth century, at the time of the revolutionary uprising of the peasants and artisans: "Live and work in such manner as to make it easy and pleasant for the kings and barons to govern you. Be patient, yield, surrender body and property, do not rise up against your superiors and tyrants!"

There is no need to demonstrate the falsity and hypocrisy of bourgeois "humanism" in our day, when the bourgeois are promoting fascism and discarding their humanism like an outworn mask which can no longer conceal the fangs of the beast of prey—are discarding it because they have come to understand that humanism is one of the reasons for their divided personality and decay. The facts mentioned above show that whenever sensitive people, disturbed by the spectacle of the villainies of the world, preached human love in a naïve effort to abate these villainies or to conceal them with a veil of eloquence, the masters of life, the shopkeepers, would permit such preaching only as an endeavour to appease people who were irritated by poverty, tyranny, oppression and the other inevitable consequences of the world-wide "cultural" activities of the shopkeepers. But no sooner did this irritation of the working masses assume social-revolutionary forms, than the bourgeoisie retaliated to "action" with "reaction."

Our liberal bourgeoisie willingly submitted to this law. After the events of 1905-06, they publicly declared in that book of repentance, *Vekhi*: "We should be grateful to the government for having protected us with its bayonets from the fury of the people." The government was at that time in the hands of Minister Stolypin, who dictatorially hanged more than five thousand workers and peasants.

In our day government is formidably confronted with the historic and scientifically-founded, genuinely universally human, proletarian humanism of Marx-Lenin-Stalin, a humanism whose aim is the complete liberation of the working people of all races and nations from the iron talons of capital. This genuine doctrine of human love has irrefutably proved that the capital's iron talons are made by the workers, and that it is the proletarians who create the "fine life" for capitalism, while they themselves remain downtrodden paupers.

This revolutionary humanism gives the proletariat the historically justified right to wage relentless war on capitalism, the right to destroy and annihilate all the atrocious foundations of the bourgeois world. For the first

357

time in the history of mankind, genuine human love is being organized as a creative force; it sets itself the aim of emancipating the hundreds of millions of toilers from the inhuman and senseless power of an insignificant minority; it tells the hundreds of millions of physical labourers that it is precisely their labour that created all the treasures of culture, and that, utilizing these treasures, the proletariat must create a new, universally human, socialist culture, which will firmly establish fraternity and equality among the working people of the world.

This proletarian humanism is not a fantasy, nor is it a theory; it is being militantly, boldly and heroically practised by the proletariat of the Socialist Soviet Union, and has already demonstrated that in formerly bourgeois, muzhik, "barbarous" Russia, with its multitudinous national and racial elements, brotherhood and equality of nations has been really achieved, and the process of converting vast quantities of physical energy into intellectual energy is really and indisputably developing.

What are the capitalists of all countries doing to counter the growth of the revolutionary consciousness of the working class?

Straining every ounce of their energy to perpetuate their power over the billions of working people and to protect their liberty to go on senselessly exploiting labour, the capitalists are organizing fascism. Fascism is the mobilization and organization by capital of the physically and morally unhealthy strata of debilitated bourgeois society, the mobilization of the young progeny of alcoholics and syphilitics, of hysterical children suffering from the impressions of the war of 1914-18, the children of the petty bourgeoisie, "avengers" of defeat, and of victories

358

which proved to be no less disastrous to the bourgeoisie than defeat. The mentality of these youths is characterized by facts like the following: in the early part of May of this year, in the city of Essen, Germany, "Heinz Christen, a lad of fourteen, killed his friend, Fritz Walkenhorst, a boy of thirteen. The murderer calmly related that he had dug a grave for his friend beforehand, had then thrown him into it alive and kept his face pressed to the sand until he suffocated. He said that he was moved to commit the murder because he wanted to get hold of a Hitler stormtrooper uniform belonging to Walkenhorst."

Anyone who has seen fascist parades will know that they are parades of rachitic, scurvy, consumptive youths who want to live with all the passion of sick people, and who are capable of accepting anything that allows them liberty to give vent to the putrid ferment of their envenomed blood. Among thousands of grey and anaemic faces, the healthy and blooming faces stand out very distinctly, because they are so few. They are the faces, of course, of conscious class enemies of the proletariat, or of petty-bourgeois adventurers, yesterday's Social-Democrats, or petty tradesmen who want to be big tradesmen, and whose suffrages the German fascist leaders purchase by presenting a little fuel or potatoes to the tradesmen free, that is, at the expense of the workers and peasants. Head-waiters want to have their small restaurants, petty thieves would like to engage in the thievery permitted by the powers that be to big thieves—and it is from these that fascism draws its "cadres." A fascist parade is simultaneously a parade of both the strength and the weakness of capitalism.

Let us not close our eyes: among the fascists there are not a few workers—of the category that do not yet realize the decisive strength of the revolutionary proletariat. Let us not hide from ourselves that the world parasite—capitalism—is still fairly strong, because the workers and peasants continue to leave the weapons and the food in its hands and continue to nourish it with their flesh and blood. This is the most deplorable and shameful feature of these stormy times. How disgusting is this meekness with which the working class feeds its enemy, a meekness instilled into it by its Social-Democratic leaders, whose names are now and for all time surrounded by the yellow and oily fulgour of shame. How amazing is the patience with which unemployed and hungry people tolerate such facts as, for instance, the destruction of foodstuffs in order to maintain market prices at a definite level, at a time when unemployment is spreading, wages falling, and the purchasing power even of the petty bourgeoisie is declining.

One would think that the human dignity of the British proletariat should be stirred to deep and active resentment by such cynical insults to their unemployed brothers as the following:

"A pastryshop for dogs, the first of its kind, has been opened in a town in Surrey, England. This shop sells pastry for all dogs, and provides food and shelter for homeless and hungry dogs. The shop has been opened with funds bequeathed by Mr. James Patterson, who died a few weeks ago in Brockhurst."

Disgraceful and cynical extravagances of this type are becoming more and more frequent in England, the land of the "aristocratic race." It is very possible that they are a manifestation of the inner presentiment of the Pattersons that their downfall is inevitable, and are indicative of the aristocratic urge of the Pattersons, on departing from life, to vent their vengeance by doing as much dirt as possible.

Arming adolescents and youths with, in addition to revolvers, obsolete nationalist and racist ideas, and inculcating into the youth social cynicism and a sadistic lust for murder and destruction, the capitalists are not only organizing them into aides of the police in the fight against the revolutionary proletariat, but are also turning them into a poison which will be injected into the blood of the army of workers and peasants equipped with modern mechanical weapons of human slaughter. The capitalists well remember that in 1918-20 the workers and peasants who had been disciplined by brutish barrack training showed that there is a limit to which they will senselessly, suicidedly and automatically serve their class enemy, and that beyond this limit—after millions of workers and peasants have slaughtered and mutilated one another—the bayonets and guns cease to serve the interests of capital. "Better late than never," of course, but in this case it is well to learn from the class enemy: the capitalist destroys the worker before the worker has time lawfully to raise his honest hand against him.

Not scores, but hundreds of facts speak of the destructive and corruptive influence of fascism on the youth of Europe. It makes one's stomach rise to enumerate these facts, and, what is more, one's memory refuses to be loaded with the filth which the bourgeoisie keeps fabricating with growing zeal and in increasing abundance. But I would mention that, whereas in the country where the proletariat is boldly and successfully ruling, the youth-corrupting vice of homosexualism is regarded as a social crime punishable by law, in the "cultured" country of

great philosophers, scientists and musicians, it is practised freely and with impunity. The sarcastic saying has
already been coined: "destroy homosexualism and fascism
will disappear." It should be pointed out that Semites,
people of a race that might, if need be, boast of its purity,
a people that gave humanity so many truly great masters of
culture—and the greatest of them, that genuine Messiah of
the proletariat, Karl Marx—are driven out by the fascist
bourgeoisie of Germany, while the fascists of Britain—where
not a few Semites have stood at the helm of state and have
been accepted into the aristocracy of the land—are also
beginning to preach the disgraceful doctrine of antisemitism.

In the land where power belongs to the working class,
on the other hand, an independent Jewish republic has
been formed—the Jewish Autonomous Region.

The capitalists of the various nations are feverish-
ly preparing for another world war, anxious to redivide
the world in order more extensively and conveniently to
exploit the labour of the workers and peasants. Small
countries are again in danger of finding themselves in the
iron clutches of big countries, and are again menaced with
the loss of the right freely to develop their culture.

Among the proletariat of diverse tongues and races,
imperialism and fascism are sowing the evil seeds of national strife and racial arrogance and contempt, which may
develop into racial hatred and impede the development in
the world of the toilers of the consciousness of the oneness
of its class interests—that saving consciousness which is
alone capable of emancipating the workers and peasants
of the world from the status of defenceless and downtrodden slaves of the demented shopkeepers. Their national
commercial and industrial enmity may easily lead—and

is already leading—to the preaching of racial enmity and racial wars. Today they are preaching antisemitism—and are already despicably practising it; tomorrow they will return to the preaching of anti-Slavism, recalling the shameful opinions of the Slavs held by Mommsen, Treitschke and others, and forgetting how many talented men were contributed to German culture by the Poles, Pomors and Czechs. Since all the factory owners and shopkeepers of Europe produce and trade in the same kinds of goods, enmity and wars of the German race against the Romance, as well as the Anglo-Saxon race, are quite natural. There are alliances, of course; but if you must sell, why not betray? For example: Britain has an alliance with Japan, but the Japanese sell silk stockings in London at threepence a pair; this is a little matter, of course, but Japanese "dumping" is quite sufficient reason for the growth of enmity and hatred towards the yellow race. What the Japanese imperialists are doing with impunity in Manchuria, China, is very enticing to the imperialists of Europe.

Race theory is the last ideological reserve of moribund capitalism, but its putrid breath is capable of poisoning even sound-minded people, because people in general have been corrupted by seeing for so long the heavily armed European whites enslaving with impunity the unarmed Hindus, Chinese and Negroes.

Only the revolutionary proletariat, joined in a united front, is capable of resisting the insiduous poison of seeing its class brothers atrociously robbed with impunity.

This proletariat, educated in the Marxist-Leninist ideology, which its leader, Stalin, is wisely putting into real practice, has shown the world that in its multinational land all tribes and races are completely equal in the right to life, labour and the development of their culture. The Russian worker has opened the wide road to knowledge to illiterate, semisavage peoples who formerly did not have their own alphabet.

The rapidity of the cultural growth of the inhabitants of the Soviet Union is acknowledged by honest men and women in all countries. One would think that, having acknowledged this fact, honest men and women should draw the very simple, morally hygienic conclusion from it, namely, that, subjectively and objectively, it is far more useful, far more honest, to live in a healthy medium than in a medium that is mortally infected with social diseases and doomed to perish. Having acknowledged that the proletariat is capable of social creativeness, it is far more useful to give every encouragement to the development of its thirst for knowledge and its talents, and of the consciousness among the mass of the proletariat of its historical mission, which it has already begun to perform in a country with 170,000,000 inhabitants. One would think that the sense of dignity of the masters of culture, of the humanists, should be profoundly outraged by the shopkeepers' denial of culture, by their crusade against the promotion of all technology except the technology of war, designed for the annihilation of human beings. But it is not observable that the masters of bourgeois culture are outraged by the burning of books disapproved of by fascism, by the preaching of hate, which is implicit in nationalist and racist theories, by the preparations for a new and ferocious war—for the senseless extermination of the most healthy individuals, for another destruction by fire of century-old cultural treasures, for the razing of cities and annihilation of the products of the arduous labour of the masses, who erected the mills and factories, tilled the fields, built the bridges and roads. The frenzy of the marauders cannot be cured by eloquence; tigers and hyenas do not eat pastry.

It is not observable that the "humanists" are capable of genuine love for humanity, nor that they are sensitive to the supreme and heroic drama of our epoch, or are aware who precisely are its heroes. The time is coming when the revolutionary proletariat will step like an elephant on the insane and feverish anthill of the shopkeepers and trample it to dust. This is inevitable. Mankind cannot allow itself to perish because a certain insignificant minority have become creatively decrepit and are stricken with corruption and decay owing to their terror of life and a morbid and incurable lust for wealth. The destruction of this minority would be a supreme act of justice, and this act history is commanding the proletariat to perform. After this great act, the peoples of the world will set to work in universal harmony and brotherhood on the free and splendid building of a new life.

Is this just faith? For the proletariat, the time has passed when faith and knowledge were as inimical as falsehood and truth. Where the proletariat rules and everything is created by its mighty hand, there is no room for dissension between knowledge and faith; there faith is the product of man's knowledge of the power of his reason, and this faith, while it creates heroes, does not create, and will not create, gods.

(1934)

THE FOG

THE city is wrapped in a yellowish-grey humidity; it might be likened to wet smoke, if such a thing were possible. Five paces in front of you the moisture seems so dense, even solid, you would think there can be no air there, that it must have been swallowed up by this grimy vapour. But you walk into it as into any other mist, except that you find it hard to breathe and your eyes are helpless. The sounds of the vast city are all strangely merged into a muffled, colourless, opaque roar; only rarely do you hear the blare of automobile horns, still more rarely human voices, and that perhaps only because you are expecting them. The peal of bronze bells loses its fluid resonance; it does not die away slowly but breaks off abruptly, as if after every stroke a hat had been clapped over the belfry. The sirens on the river carry a note of dejection, as if the steamers were tired or afraid to navigate in the fog.

Dripping taxis, carts and horses glide out of the mist and slip back into it as if greased with oil; people, damp and strangely silent, their coat collars turned up, their hands thrust in their pockets, their necks craned forward, move toward one another at a gait indicative of a desire to avoid accidents. The fog envelops them in a semiopaque film, and in it a man looks like a yolk within the white of an egg.

Two old ladies crouch against a damp wall, struggling with a large black umbrella; in trying to open it they jab its end into the side of a little fat fellow; he lets out a roar and the two old ladies, like mechanical toys, throw up their hands simultaneously and in a similar manner, trembling and emitting phrases consisting of nothing but interjections.

The walls of the houses and the windows of the shops are covered with beads of moisture. Everything is softened, as if made of dirty ice which is melting. Your imagination takes fantastic turns: perhaps, unforeseen by the astronomers, the sun has suddenly exploded and melted the dead moon, and its fluid mass, cooled to the temperature of new milk, has dripped down and enveloped the earth in a gaseous stifling humidity, infecting it with a mysterious damp rot; this vast city, with its millions of inhabitants, has begun to melt too, and soon its brick, glass, metal and wood will all silently begin to flow in thick turbid streams, and will also begin to evaporate and turn into greyish-yellow fog. . . .

But the people of this city lightly dispel the grim play of your excited fancy. The first to sober you are the policemen, monumental beings all cast of one material, who act mechanically, calmly and confidently. On all the streets the policemen are the same, and you are filled with respectful surprise at the power with which the culture of the "aristocratic race"—the most energetic plunderers of the world—dehumanizes people and achieves "uniformity in multiplicity."

That mighty lever of order, the hand of the policeman, summons carriages, automobiles and loaded carts out of the fog and sends them back again, inspiring confidence that the doom of this city has not yet come. Motor cars glide smoothly up to the doors of houses and shops filled with light and dry warmth, and out of them step too rigid or too rounded gentlemen wearing top hats or other diverse-shaped headgear; they politely and imperiously offer their arms to exquisite ladies, who, with laughter and exclamations which cannot be denied musicality and with squeamish grimaces on their porcelain faces, set their dainty feet on the damp asphalt or stone of the pavement, and the shops swallow them up, like a gourmand swallows oysters.

What an abundance there is in this city of footwear, clothing, linen, hats, furs, leather goods, portmanteaux, cigars, pipes, walking sticks, crockery, fishing tackle, sports guns, toys for children and adults, watches, gold ware, jewels! A dazzling abundance. And they all glitter so powerfully that the question of the right of the ladies and gentlemen to the use of them pales in their enticing glow.

Particularly multifarious and plentiful are the comestibles. Their diversity sets one pondering on the progress of gastronomy, on the development of the culinary art, on the refined wisdom of the stomachs of highly-cultured people. In the windows of the provision shops are proudly displayed the tribute of all the lands, seas, lakes, forests and rivers of the world. Fresh, smoked, salted and canned meat, fish, crab, game, vegetables, fruits, spices, sauces, cheeses, sausages, pastry, confectionery, biscuits, cake, chocolate, cocoa—all these are gathered probably in thousands of tons, and all this the ladies and gentlemen will have to masticate, digest and turn into manure for the soil. . . .

Along a deserted street lined with uniform houses, each of three storeys with three or four windows to a storey, swiftly strides through the fog a. long-legged individual in the costume of a Scotchman: a cap with two ribbons at the back of it, a rusty much-worn jacket with a patch coming away on the right elbow, a short skirt reaching to the knees, the legs bare from knee to ankle, and the feet clad in huge down-at-heel shoes. Under his arm is tucked a bagpipe which he presses against his side with his left elbow, and as his red hands noiselessly finger the keys the treble reed emits a gay, piercing, high-pitched melody, which the base reed seconds in a monotonous muffled drone. The face of the musician is ashy and gaunt, the cheek-bones sharply protrude, drawing the skin so tight as to form red patches, the boney nose droops into red angrily-bristling moustaches, and the chin is also covered with coppery bristles. The deep-set eyes peer forth with unusual sharpness from their sockets, and the bluish pupils seem to be swimming on the surface of the inflamed whites, swimming and glittering—one would almost say that the eyes were red-hot. The musician makes eighty-three swift strides beneath the windows of four houses, then turns at the corner of a wealthy street and, with the persistence of a madman, returns swaying on his beat, the torn patch on his elbow fluttering as if it were trying to break loose. He inflates his cheeks, twitches his moustaches, and fills the bag with wind, then, removing the reed from his lips, he coughs hackingly and expectorates, never for a moment stopping in his stride. He must keep on walking because the police forbid him to stand under the windows of happier people and disturb their repose with his music. But he may play as long as he keeps on the move: for the subjects of the King of Britain, that classic land of compromise, are free men. The musician coughs and expectorates clots of dark · blood, and, as though unwilling to trample on the blood with his dirty shoes, he spits not on the pavement, but on the greasy walls of the houses. One does not think he does this deliberately, but one has a presentiment that, having made another dozen strides, he will collapse from hunger and fatigue.

A SPLENDID BOOK

WITH a plain and relentless truthfulness, this book*
tells how men of different nations, but all equally rational, exterminated one another and destroyed the secular
fruits of their arduous and magnificent labour, reducing
temples, palaces and homes to piles of rubbish, and annihi-
lating cities, villages and vineyards; how they ravaged
hundreds of thousands of acres of land which had been
splendidly tilled by their forefathers and which will now
for long years to come be cluttered with splinters of iron
and poisoned by the putrifying flesh of slaughtered innocent people.

While engaged in this insensate work of self-extermi-
nation and destruction of culture, these men are capable
of considering rationally everything that irritates their
skin and nerves or agitates their hearts and minds. They
pray to God, pray sincerely and, as one of the characters
in the book puts it, "with idiotic uniformity," after
which they again set about the wild work of self-slaughter,
and with similar "idiotic uniformity." On pp. 437-38
the reader will find a description of these prayers of
Germans and Frenchmen, who alike sincerely believe

* Henri Barbusse's *Under Fire.—Ed.*

that in their vile and bloody work of war "God is with us."

Yet they themselves afterwards say: "God doesn't give two straws for us!" And they themselves, these heroes, martyrs, fratricides, ask one another:

"What is this God thinking of to let everybody believe alike that He's with them?"

These men think with the simple and touching naïvete of children—but in general with "idiotic uniformity."—While shedding each other's blood, they say:

"If there was a God of goodness, there wouldn't be any cold."

But having reasoned so clearly, these great martyrs again set to work to slaughter each other.

Why?

What for?

They know that too. They say of themselves:

"Ah! We're all of us not bad sorts, and we're unlucky, and we're poor devils as well. But we're too stupid, we're too stupid!"

Yet, realizing this, they continue their shameful and criminal work of destruction.

Corporal Bertrand knows more than the others. He speaks with the tongue of a sage.

" 'The future!' he cried all at once as a prophet might. 'How will they regard this slaughter, they who'll live after us, to whom progress—which comes as sure as fate—will at last restore the poise of their conscience? How will they regard these exploits which even we who perform them don't know whether one should compare them with those of Plutarch's and Corneille's heroes or with those of hooligans and apaches? . . . And for all that, mind you, there is one figure that has risen above the war and will blaze with the beauty and strength of his courage. . . .'

"I listened, leaning on a stick and towards him, drinking in the voice that came in the twilight silence from the lips that so rarely spoke. He cried with clear voice:

"'Liebknecht!'

"He stood up with his arms still crossed. His face, as profoundly serious as a statue's, drooped upon his chest. But he emerged once again from his marble muteness to repeat:

" 'The future, the future! The work of the future will be to wipe out the present, to wipe it out more than we can imagine, to wipe it out like something abominable and shameful. And yet—this present—it had to be, it had to be! Shame on military glory, shame on armies, shame on the soldier's calling, that changes men by turns into stupid victims or ignoble brutes. Yes, shame. That's the true word, but it's too true; it's true in eternity, but it's not yet true for us. It will be true when there is a Bible that is entirely true, when it is found written among the other truths that a purified mind will at the same time let us understand. We are still lost, still exiled far from that time. In our time of today, in these moments, this truth is hardly more than a fallacy, this sacred saying is only blasphemy!'

"A kind of laugh came from him, full of echoing dreams—'To think I once told them I believed in prophecies, just to kid them!' "

But while expressing thoughts like these, this calm and courageous man, who was respected by his whole platoon, leads them into senseless carnage and dies in a field of mud, among rotting corpses.

All this is suffused with the bright and mocking flame of a devastating contradiction which degrades men into docile instruments, into disgusting machines created by an evil and sinister force to serve its diabolical ends.

These unhappy heroes appeal to our heart and sympathy; but, truly, they seem like lepers, carrying within them a never-to-be reconciled contradiction between reason and will. It seems that their reason is already so strong and firm as to be capable of ending this revolting carnage, of stopping this world-wide crime, but . . . they have no will, and, although they understand all the villainy of manslaughter, and loathe it in their hearts, they yet go on slaying and destroying and dying in blood and mud.

" 'It's with us only that they make battles,' they say. 'It is we who are the material of war. War is made up of the flesh and the souls of common soldiers only. It is we who make the plains of dead and the rivers of blood, all of us, and each of us is invisible and silent because of the immensity of our numbers. The emptied towns and the villages destroyed, they are a wilderness of *our* making. Yes, war is all of us, and all of us together.'

" 'Yes, that's true. It's the people who are war; without them, there would be nothing, nothing but some wrangling, a long way off. But it isn't they who decide on it; it's the masters who steer them.'

" 'The people are struggling today to have no more masters that steer them. This war, it's like the French Revolution continuing.'

" 'Well then, if that's so, we're working for the Prussians too?'

" 'It's to be hoped so,' said one of the wretches.

" 'The people—they're nothing, though they ought to be everything,' then said the man who had questioned me, recalling, though he did not know it, an historic sentence of more than a century ago, but investing it at last with its great universal significance.

"Escaped from torment, on all fours in the deep grease of the ground, he lifted his leperlike face and looked hungrily before him into infinity."

What will he see there?

We believe he will see his descendants free, wise and firm-willed.

*　*　*

This terrible, yet gladdening book was written by Henri Barbusse, a man who had himself lived through the horrors and madness of war. It is not the stately book of Leo Tolstoy, whose genius contemplated war in the distant past; nor is it the plaintive work of Bertha von Suttner, *Down With War!*—a work written with the best intentions, but incapable of persuading or dissuading anyone.

This book is as simple as the Gospel. It is infused with prophetic wrath; it is the first book to speak of war simply, austerely, calmly and with invincible truthfulness. It does not romanticize war, it does not paint its blood and filth and horror in all the colours of the rainbow.

Barbusse writes of the commonplace everyday life of war, he depicts it as a job, the hard and sordid job of mutual destruction of innocent people, innocent of everything except stupidity. There are no poetic and heroic battle pictures in the book, no descriptions of the valour of individual soldiers. Barbusse's book is full of the stern poetry of truth, it depicts the courage of the people, the courage of hundreds of thousands and millions of men doomed to death and destruction by that supreme provoker of strife among nations—capital. It is this Devil, this absolutely real devil indefatigably operating in our midst, that is the chief personage in Barbusse's book. Having blinded millions of simpletons with the false glitter of ideas and doctrines which stifle their will and poison them with the venom of greed, envy and covetousness, he herded them into the fertile fields of France, where for four years they destroyed and annihilated everything created by the labour of many generations, thereby once more proving to themselves that man's worst enemy is lack of will and reason.

Barbusse has peered deeper than anyone before him into the nature of war and revealed to men the immensity of their delusions.

Every page of his book is a sledgehammer blow of truth at the mass of lies, hypocrisy, cruelty, dirt and blood which in their aggregate are called war. It is a sad book, and terrible in its ruthless truth; but always through the gloom of its depictions gleam the flamelets of a new consciousness—and we have faith that it will not be long before these flamelets will grow into a world-wide conflagration, which will purify the earth of the dirt, the blood, the lies and hypocrisies created by Devil Capital. The people of whom Barbusse writes are already beginning boldly to deny the power of God over man, and this is a sure sign that soon they will come to realize, with shame and anger, how criminal and disgusting is the power of man over his fellow men.

We live in tragic times, life is intolerably hard, but we are on the eve of the day when all the good forces in man will awaken for free creation and free labour. This is the truth, and it should console us and infuse into us new strength and courage.

M. Gorky

The above was written fifteen years ago, in that tragic hungry year which saw the victorious end of the war of the starving proletarians, workers and peasants, against the armies of the Russian manufacturers and landlords abundantly armed by the European capitalists, and against the troops sent by the European shopkeepers to aid their fellows in fat and spirit. Among these troops there was even a cavalry brigade mounted on asses.

In this decade and a half the proletariat of tsarist Russia and its colonies have, by assiduous and miracle-working labour, turned a boundless and illiterate land of semipauper peasants and semisavage and greedy petty bourgeois into a mighty socialist brotherhood of nations

Today the European capitalists are again plotting a war, with the basic aim of attacking the Socialist Soviet Union. Before they can start this war, the capitalists have to be united. The most brazen and insensate group among them expects to achieve unity by following Napoleon's example: by beating its neighbours and then seizing the vanquished by the collar and hurling them against the Socialist State. It is a clear and simple plan and it is this plan that reminded me of the asses.

The disgraceful role of asses, as we know, was played in the war of 1914-18 by the leaders of the German Social-Democrats, the Russian Mensheviks and S. R.'s and many other leaders of the petty bourgeoisie, whom the capitalists in these fifteen years have been moulding into fascists.

It seems to me that the socialist-revolutionary value of the work of Barbusse and other writers akin to him in spirit is particularly clear and evident when regarded from this aspect. His book was one of the first which in these fifteen years sobered many thousands of blood-intoxicated minds, and the antifascist movement, which is spreading wider and wider these days, should recognize Barbusse as one of its first founders.

M. Gorky

September 11, 1935

ON CULTURES

THE keynote sounded for the Writer's Congress in Paris was the protection of culture from the destructive encroachments of fascism. It was presumably taken for granted that the real and actual content of the concept modern bourgeois "culture" would be understood by all the delegates in one and the same way and could not give rise to any differences of opinion. But is this so?

Fascism is a product of, a cancerous growth on, bourgeois culture, which is already in a state of decay and disintegration. The theoreticians and practitioners of fascism are adventurers advanced by the bourgeoisie from its own midst. In Italy and Germany, the bourgeoisie has turned over political and physical power to the fascists, commanding them with almost the same Machiavellian craftiness as the medieval bourgeoisie of the Italian cities commanded the condottieri. It not only looks on the nefarious extermination of proletarians by fascists with satisfaction, and encourages it, but permits the fascists to persecute and eject from the country writers and scientists— that is, representatives of its own intellectual power, which until very recently was its pride and boast.

In deference to the desire of its master, the imperialists, for a new "redivision of the world" with the help of another world war, fascism advanced the theory that it is the right of the German race to rule over the whole world, over all other races. This is the long-forgotten idea of the superiority of the "blond beast" evolved by the morbid mind of Friedrich Nietzsche. It proceeds from the fact that the Hindus, Indo-Chinese, Melanesians, Polynesians, Negroes, etc., have been subjugated by the red-headed and fair-headed. This idea flourished at the time when the German bourgeoisie, having vanquished the Austrian and French bourgeoisie, conceived the desire to share in colonial rapine with the British, Dutch and French bourgeoisie. This theory of the right of the white race to exercise sole sway over the world permits every national bourgeoisie group to regard not only all coloured peoples, but even its white European neighbours, as barbarians who have to be subjugated or destroyed. This theory, which the Italian and Japanese bourgeoisie are already putting into practice, constitutes one of the real elements of the modern conception of "culture."

We hear the cry raised ever louder by eminent representatives of the European bourgeoisie that there is an overproduction of intellectuals, that education must be restricted and "barriers" put in the way of the development of culture, that there is even a superfluity of machinery and there must be a return to hand labour. The Archbishop of York declared at the opening of a school in Bournemouth: *"I should like to see all invention cease. If I could abolish the internal combustion engine, I would certainly do so."* His confrère in his discredited profession, the Archbishop of Canterbury, evidently recognizes the necessity for machinery, because he preaches a "crusade" against the Soviet Union, and the next war, we are told by the experts, will be a "war of machines." If the speeches

380

of the London and Rome vicars of Christ on earth, as well as of the other bourgeois advocates of the restriction of cultural development, who have clearly been driven insane by their hatred of the proletariat or by their fear of the inevitable social catastrophe—if these speeches had been delivered in the 1880's, say, they would have been regarded by the bourgeoisie as a sign of idiocy, as a call for a reversion to barbarism.

In these days, when the bourgeoisie has lost all sense of the difference between courage and shamelessness, the appeal for a return to medievalism is called a "courageous idea."

We thus see that European bourgeois culture does not represent that "monolithic entity" which bourgeois historians make it out to be. Its "man power" has disintegrated into shopkeepers and bankers, who regard all other people as a cheap and abundant commodity and desire at all costs to retain their high and socially-comfortable positions; into people who insist on their right to work for the advancement of culture; and into fascists, who perhaps may still be called humans, but who, as a result of a prolonged beery intoxication spread over several generations, have grown wild and need to be strictly isolated or subjected to even more vigorous measures in order to put a stop to their loathsome and bloody crimes.

* * *

A certain Maurice Bourdet believes it necessary, and possible, to "define and restrict the limits of culture." Its basic creative energies are labour, or physical energy, and technological, or intellectual energy. The writer of these lines is inclined to think that every ideology is—fundamentally and in the broad meaning of the concept—technology, that is, a system of labour and logical methods with the help of which man widens his world outlook in order gradually to change the world. We see that the modern bourgeoisie, being quite content with what it already has, is really and quite effectively "restricting the normal development of culture" by creating a huge army of unemployed, agitating for the restriction of technology, and curtailing funds for the maintenance of institutions of higher learning, museums and the like. We know that the only industry that operates uninterruptedly and that is continually expanding is the war industry, whose aim and purpose is the annihilation of millions of workers and peasants in the future battlefields, where the West-European bourgeoisie intends to settle its international dispute as to which of its national groups shall dominate the rest. The military commanders of the future war which the bourgeoisie is organizing in order that it may batten on the blood of its subjugated neighbours, are publicly and coolly declaring that this war will be even more bloody and destructive than the war of 1914-18. It is appropriate here to recall certain facts about the last war, the losses and destruction of which have already been made good by the labour of the proletariat and peasantry, that is, by the classes that suffered most from the insanity of the bourgeoisie.

The facts are these. In 1915 the Germans were already suffering from a shortage of lubricants, so much so in fact, that they paid 1,800 marks in Copenhagen for a barrel of lubricating oil which at that time cost not more than 200 marks. The American ambassador in Berlin wrote his government in December of that year that the shortage of lubricants would soon lead to Germany's defeat. Yet at this same time British ships were carrying barrels of this much-needed oil to Copenhagen. This is borne out by the statistics of the British Board of Trade. In the early months of 1915 Germany would have been experiencing a shortage of coal, if she had not been receiving British coal through Scandinavian countries. For example, in September 1914 Sweden received 33,000 tons of coal, which were almost entirely turned over to the Central Powers.

Only because of this outrageous generosity on the part of Britain, did Ludendorff refuse in June 1917 to assign 50,000 men from the army for work in the Ruhr mines.

Coal exports to Sweden soon rose to the enormous figure of 100,000 and even 150,000 tons a month, which was double the amount of coal annually consumed by these countries before the war. Sir Ralph Paget, British ambassador to Copenhagen, reported that this coal was helping the slaughter of British soldiers, but his voice went unheeded.

It has been established that during the war the French shopkeepers supplied their enemies, the German shopkeepers, with nickel and zinc, and that a British gun manufacturer exchanged destructive inventions with a German manufacturer. Many no less vile and criminal facts have not yet been disclosed, that is, have not yet been made public. We see from this that war is no hindrance to trade, and that "lovers' quarrels are lovers' delights"—for which millions of proletarians have to pay with their blood and their lives. Unfortunately, the proletarians have not yet realized that it is foolish of them to slaughter and maim their class brothers, that after the war it is they that have to work, for a wretched pittance, to repair all the damage and to cover all the losses of the shopkeepers.

Simple, plain and genuinely humanitarian justice tells us that the products of labour should belong to those who made them, and not to those who ordered them to be made. Weapons—all weapons—are the product of the labour of the workers.

And so, we have already learned something about the real and actual meaning of the concept: the West-European "culture of the modern bourgeoisie founded upon Graeco-Roman cultural values." To this should be added something from the realm of "international ethics," something perpetrated only the other day by the British bourgeoisie. This insular bourgeoisie long ago earned the reputation among its neighbours of being "perfidious," that is, shameless, hypocritical, jesuitical. As we know, it gave certain solemn promises to the French bourgeoisie, the sum and substance of which was that it would defend the French hucksters should they be involved in war with the German. It was even said that "Britain's frontiers are on the Rhine," that is, on the Franco-German frontier. This phrase has proved to be ambiguous, since the British bourgeoisie has come to terms with the German, in complete violation of its promises. It may be that Britain's frontiers will yet prove to be on the Rhine, but it will not be for the defence of the French, but only after they have been defeated by the British and Germans. Everything is possible among people who know "neither honour nor conscience."

* * *

French journalists ask:

"Is our culture, which is so many centuries old and has inherited the cultural values of the Greeks and Romans, to carry on its mission in spite of all obstacles, or is it to go down before the new form of culture that is preparing to proclaim the primacy of economics over intellect?"

In speaking of the "primacy of economics over intellect," Messrs. the journalists are unthinkingly and mechanically allowing themselves to be swayed by their ignorance, or—which is more probable—by their shamelessness. However, it is possible that some of them have not yet disburdened themselves of the naïve illusion of "intellectual" independence, although they are completely dependent on their editors, who are entirely dependent on the newspaper owners—the bankers, lords and gun manufacturers. Naïve journalists—if there are such—would do well to look around them attentively and open-mindedly; they would then see that the "economics" of the biped spiders, expressed in the crudest materialistic forms, predominates precisely in the bourgeois states, and that the aim of the "new form of culture" is to liberate labouring humanity from the tyranny of that already meaningless economics which has been created by the "mentality" of Sir Basil Zakharov, Deterding, Vickers, Creusot, Hearst, Schneider, Ivar Kreuger, Stavisky and the other real headmen of modern bourgeois culture. It is ridiculous to dream, and still more ridiculous to speak, of individual independence in a society in which men—including journalists—are easily and "freely" bought and sold, like so many sheep or cucumbers.

How poisonous is the putrid spirit of modern bourgeois culture is very convincingly shown by the enormous prevalence of swindling and by the paltriness of the swindlers—a paltriness that clearly testifies to the exhaustion of the specific talent of the European bourgeoisie, to a "degeneration of type." John Law is a genius compared with Stavisky or Ivar Kreuger the "match king."

The "spiritual" corruption and disintegration of the modern bourgeoisie is vividly manifested in the growing quantity, and the increasingly villainous "quality," of traitors: before the 1920's the world scarcely knew such traitors as Noske—the "bloody hound," as he was not ashamed to call himself—and his confrères: Ebert, Haase and the Second International leaders generally.

The life of the bourgeoisie, its manners and habits, as the European journalists imperturbably depict it day after day, presents an awful and disgusting spectacle. It is quite conceivable that the professional habits of the journalists, accustomed as they are to working day in and day out amid blood and filth, blunten their perceptions and kill all desire to draw conclusions from their observations. Impassively "registering the facts," they paint their bloodiness and filth even still more crudely in order to divert the bourgeois reader, and the latter, feeding on descriptions of crime, becomes still more brazen and stupid. We know that the form of literature most popular with the middle and petty bourgeois is the crime novel.

One may well ask, where among this filth and decay, and in what forms, are the "cultural values of the Greeks and Romans" preserved? As "material" values, they are preserved in museums, in the collections of millionaires, beyond the reach of the labouring masses and the petty bourgeois. As "intellectual" values—the works of Aeschylus, Sophocles, Euripides, for instance—they ought to be shown in theatres; but that is not the practice in Europe. In the bourgeois universities, professors lecture on Roman law, ancient Greek philosophy and other values, including international law and even medieval humanism. We shall leave it to the European journalists to discover in the chaos of modern life where these values are located, and to explain their practical, educational value. It seems to us that if modern Europe is reminiscent of Ancient Rome at all, it is the Rome of the era of its decline and fall.

*   *   *

In the process of decay and disintegration of the dominating class of modern Europe, the bourgeois intelligentsia plays a strange and sad role. "Like clings to like," of course, and in defending an obsolescent "culture," the intelligentsia is defending the power of its class. Technologically, as well as ideologically, this power has always been served, and is still served today, by more or less highly qualified intellectuals. In 1914 the European bourgeoisie sent thousands of such intellectuals to the battlefronts as common soldiers and compelled them to destroy one another. Before they were maimed, gassed or killed, the "masters of culture" helped to the best of their ability in destroying cities, spoiling fertile land, and doing other destructive damage to culture.

The majority of these intellectuals were proletarians, yet they suicidedly destroyed themselves for the sake of strengthening the power of the property owners. After this, scores of intellectuals wrote books describing the madness of war, and execrating it. Now the bourgeois are preparing for another international shambles, and on an even larger scale. Since in the recent past the iron hand of war did not spare specimens and depositories of cultural treasures, it is quite possible that in the coming war the British Museum, the Louvre, the Capitole and the innumerable museums of the ancient capitals will be reduced to rubble and ashes. And it goes without saying that, together with millions of the sturdiest workers and peasants, thousands of receptacles of intellectual energy—"masters of culture"—will be annihilated. For what reason? Because of the urge of every big group of shopkeepers and bankers to subjugate and rob its neighbour. After all, it has been repeatedly and irrefutably demonstrated that the periodical bourgeois wars are nothing but armed robbery, that is, a crime punishable by the laws of all bourgeois countries.

The idiotic criminality of bourgeois conflicts is all the more revolting when one considers the enormous amount of intelligent and most valuable labour, metal, and invention the shopkeepers destroyed yesterday, and will destroy tomorrow. How many cities, mills, factories will be reduced to dust and ashes, how many splendid ships will be sunk, and how much land spoiled! Multitudes of children will be exterminated. In the final analysis, the criminal madness of the fat-man class consists in the fact that it compels the workers, peasants and intellectuals to work for the annihilation of the work of their own hands and for their own mutual annihilation.

The fullest and completest expression of the "primacy of economics" is the crude, zoological materialism of the property owners. No attempt is made today to conceal the poisonous "mentality" of this predatory materialism of the bloated biped spiders with the tattered rags of religion and philosophy. Fascism and racist theory are the preaching of armed rapine in cynically naked form. There you have the "spirit," the loathsome and shameful spirit, of modern bourgeois "culture." And we see that honest intellectuals, fearing to be stifled in it, are fleeing from the country where it is today expressed most brazenly and crassly; and tomorrow it will just as cynically and brazenly announce itself in the countries to which they are fleeing—that is, if the proletariat permits it. It is quite natural to ask: what right to power has the modern bourgeoisie, which has already rejected the fundamentals of its culture, which has lost the faculty of economic management, which is creating unemployment on an ever more terrible scale, and which is shamelessly plundering the peasants, workers and colonies for the purposes of war—what right to exist and rule has a class which is senselessly exhausting the labour and creative energy of the whole world, a class, moreover, which is quantitatively paltry, and qualitatively vicious and criminal? Yet this class holds in its bloody grasp nearly two billion European, Chinese, Indian and African peasants and workers. The incredible atrociousness of this fact is brought out still more clearly when we consider it side by side with another fact.

*　*　*

There is a country where the will and reason of the entire mass of the workers and peasants are stimulated and educated by work that is necessary to the state and also beneficial to every working individual, and where the entire labour energy is enlisted in the multiform work of creating new conditions of life, that is, a new, socialist culture.

A country, where the proletariat, following the teachings of Marx and Lenin, and led by Joseph Stalin, has liberated the peasantry from the idiotic "tyranny of the land," from meek submission to the caprices of nature, from the stultifying influence of private ownership—where the proletariat has made the property-owner a collectivist.

A country, where the proletarian, the drudge in bourgeois society, is proving that when he is armed with knowledge he is quite capable of being a consummate master of culture and maker of culture.

A country, where the cultural work of the individual is appreciated by the entire mass of the labouring population more highly than it has ever been appreciated anywhere, and where this appreciation is constantly stimulating the growth of the individual and the heroism of his labour.

A country, where women, who constitute half the population, enjoy equal rights with men and heroically work side by side with them in all fields of application of rational energy for the remaking of the world; where the talent, boldness and labour enthusiasm of women are developing at fantastic speed.

A country, where children are brought up free from the crippling influence of the church, whose aim it is to inculcate patience, meekness and submission to the "powers that be."

A country, where a number of diverse, even numerically small and semisavage tribes formerly did not have their own alphabet, but are armed with an alphabet today, have received the right to develop freely, and are displaying to the world the primitive freshness of their perceptions, their creative talent, and the splendid simplicity of their poetry.

A country, where ancient tribes whose culture was repressed by the colonial policy of the shopkeepers and the tsar, are now revealing their magnificent talents and the precious treasures of their liberated spirit.

In this country the artist and scientist is restricted only by the will of the labouring people, the will to acquire all the genuine cultural values of mankind.

But this country is surrounded by enemies, who envy its wealth, are terrified of its beneficent influence on the labouring people of the world, and are dreaming of launching a piratical attack upon it. Consequently, the ardent desire to know the past, inasmuch as a knowledge of the past is necessary for the building of the future, is restricted in this country by the necessity of having to work for defence against its enemies, and this is somewhat retarding the development of its material culture and the growth of its wealth. The desire for knowledge of the past is also to some extent restricted by the fact that, in the heritage of bourgeois culture, honey and venom are closely mingled, and that the "truths" of bourgeois science regarding man's historical past have the same propensity as old and experienced coquettes to pass themselves off as innocent virgins.

To the proletariat the human individual is precious. Even if an individual has displayed socially pernicious proclivities and has for some time acted in a socially dangerous manner, he is not kept in corrupting idleness in jail, but is re-educated to become a skilled worker, a useful member of society. This firmly established attitude toward the "criminal" is a manifestation of active proletarian humanism, a humanism which has never existed, and cannot exist, in a society where man is a wolf to man.

The wise workers' and peasants' government of the Union of Socialist Soviet Republics gives care and thought to the mental health of the working population, and especially of its children and adolescents. With equal zeal and ability, it gives care and thought to physical upbringing, to the protection of physical health, for which purpose the All-Union Institute of Experimental Medicine has been founded—the first institution in the world for the all-round study of the human organism. One might point to a whole number of innovations which are effectively and rapidly enriching the country and changing its physical geography: industry is constantly expanding, agriculture is being reorganized, new food crops and fruit plants are being introduced into cultivation, and the cultivation of root crops and grain crops is being advanced farther and farther northward; marshes are being drained, arid regions irrigated, rivers canalized, more power stations are built from year to year, more and more deposits of coal, oil, metallic ores and mineral fertilizers are being discovered, the Arctic is being conquered—and all this, of course, is not a full enumeration of what is being done in a country where a shortage of labour is felt, at a time when the shopkeepers of Europe and the U.S.A. have created an army of tens of millions of unemployed. All that has been done in the Union of Socialist Soviet Republics has been done in less than two decades, and this speaks most eloquently of the talentedness of its peoples and their labour heroism. It shows that labour in our country is becoming an art, that the proletariat of the Soviet Socialist Republics, guided by Lenin's teachings and his Party, and by the inexhaustible and ever-growing energy of Joseph Stalin, is creating a new culture, a new history of labouring humanity. As against this, what is the real and actual meaning of the "culture" of the modern bourgeoisie?

The underlying foundation and motive force of all that has been briefly and incompletely enumerated here is the mighty creative power of proletarian humanism, the humanism of Marx and Lenin. This is not the humanism of which the bourgeoisie was until very recently boasting as the basis of its civilization and culture.

Between these two humanisms there is nothing in common except the name. Both are called humanism, but in actual content they radically differ. The humanism which originated five hundred years ago was a method of self-defence of the bourgeoisie against the feudalists and against the Church, which was the spiritual leader of the bourgeoisie, and which was also headed by feudalists. When speaking of the equality of men, the rich bourgeois—the manufacturer or merchant—only meant his own equality with the feudalist, the parasite in knightly armour or in bishop's surplice. Bourgeois humanism lived harmoniously side by side with slavery and slave trading, with *jus primae noctis*, with the Church Inquisition, with the wholesale massacre of the Toulouse Albigenses, and the burning at the stake of Giordano Bruno, Jan Huss and tens of thousands of nameless "heretics," "witches," craftsmen and peasants who were captivated by the re-echoings of primitive communism in the Bible and the Gospels.

Did the bourgeoisie ever resist the brutality of the Church and the feudalists? As a class—never. Individual bourgeois did resist, and the bourgeoisie exterminated them. In the past, the bourgeois humanists also assiduously helped the feudalists to exterminate the peasants of

Wat Tyler's army, the French "Jacques" and the Taborites just as cold-bloodedly and cruelly as in the twentieth
century the cultivated shopkeepers exterminate workers in
the streets of Vienna, Antwerp and Berlin, in Spain, in
the Philippines, in the cities of India, in China, everywhere. Need we speak of these abominable crimes, which
are known to all, and which testify that "humanism as the
basis of bourgeois culture" has in our day been expunged
from existence? It is no longer mentioned, presumably because it is realized that it would be too shameless to speak
of humanism and at the same time shoot down hungry
workers almost daily in the streets of cities, fill the jails
with them, and cut off the heads of the most active, or
send them by the thousand to penal servitude.

Generally, the bourgeoisie never has endeavoured to
lighten the lot of the working masses—except by charity,
which is an insult to the dignity of men of labour. In
practice, the humanism of the bourgeoisie took the form
of "philanthropy," that is, the granting of alms to the
robbed and disinherited. The idiotic and fraudulent "commandment"—"let not thy right hand know what thy left
hand doeth"—was invented and received general acceptance;
and so the "masters of life," having appropriated millions and billions, donated a few wretched pence to schools,
hospitals and asylums. The literature of the philistines
preached "mercy for the fallen," but the fallen were those
whom the shopkeepers had robbed, cast down and trampled
in the mud.

If the humanism of the bourgeois had been honest, if
it had sincerely desired to awaken and foster in the people they had enslaved a sense of human dignity, consciousness of their collective strength and of man's grandeur

as the organizer of the world and the forces of Nature, it would not have inculcated the vile idea that suffering was inevitable, nor a passive compassion, but would have fostered an active loathing for all suffering, especially the suffering caused by social and economic factors.

Physiological pain is nothing but a signal given by the human organism that something pernicious has invaded it and is interfering with its normal functioning. Pain is the voice of the organism crying: "Man, protect yourself!" In preaching the doctrine of suffering, bourgeois humanism bids us reconcile ourselves to that insulting pain which is due to the given, supposedly insuperable and eternally ordained class relations, the humiliating division of human beings into superior and inferior races and tribes, into white aristocrats and "coloured" slaves. This division retards the wakening of the labouring people to the knowledge of the unity of their interests, which is why it was instituted.

The humanism of the revolutionary proletariat is forthright. It does not speak loud and honeyed words about loving one's neighbour. Its aim is to liberate the proletariat of the whole world from the shameful, bloodthirsty and insane oppression of the capitalists, to teach people not to regard themselves as a commodity which is bought and sold, as raw material for the manufacture of gold and luxury for the bourgeois. Capitalism violates the world as a decrepit old man violates a young and healthy woman, being unable to impregnate her with anything but his senile diseases. Proletarian humanism does not demand lyrical professions of love; it demands that every worker should realize his historical mission, his right to power, his revolutionary activity, which is especially essential

on the eve of the new war which the capitalists are plotting—in the final analysis, against him.

Proletarian humanism demands an inextinguishable
hatred for the bourgeoisie, for the power of the capitalists
and their lackeys, for the parasites, fascists, butchers and
betrayers of the working class, a hatred for everything that
causes suffering, for all who live on the sufferings of hundreds of millions of people. I think that from this rough
enumeration of real facts, the value of bourgeois and proletarian culture will be fairly clear to all right-minded men
and women.

(1935)

A THOUSAND LETTERS

ONE of the Moscow broadcasting stations recently addressed a number of questions in several languages to listeners all over the world. Several thousand replies have been received, bearing stamps of all colours and shapes and the post marks of big cities and small, of world capitals and of out-of-the-way villages.

The letters are from young folk and old, from doctors, mechanics, shopkeepers and housewives, from Englishmen, Spaniards, Czechs, Danes and Frenchmen; some are handwritten, others are typed. But their authors all write voluntarily and disinterestedly, actuated by the sole motive of expressing their thoughts and feelings in response to that voice that came to them over the air from afar and put to them these simple and burning questions.

"How can war be prevented?"—asked the voice of the broadcasting station.

"Perhaps taking a plebiscite at the moment of danger might avert the threat of war, because the broad masses of the working people are always peaceable and are mostly drawn into war only by their ambitious leaders." This was written by a doctor in Switzerland. But he is contradicted by a Strasbourg worker:

"I consider that treaties and pacts can only postpone war, not prevent it. Only the working class can do this, by seizing power at the moment of mobilization, when the bourgeoisie places weapons in its hands. But for this preliminary explanatory work among the masses is necessary."

A proletarian who writes from Basle examines the question from all sides:

"The capitalists call wars 'conflicts.' Nowadays they do not consider it necessary to declare war. But we know that so long as capitalism exists wars are inevitable, because they are a consequence of capitalism. And we now have powerful means of combatting war: 1) Soviet Russia, with its Red Army and heavy industry, is a powerful instrument of peace. 2) The League of Nations and the peace work of Litvinov, who is coping with his job so splendidly. 3) The Chinese Red Army. 4) The united front of the working people is, under revolutionary leadership, making great headway, and if the bourgeois start a war they will pay dear for it. The workers, when they are called up for military service, are kept under tight discipline, but they will know against whom to turn their weapons."

The broadcasting station asked:

"What is the Soviet Union's biggest achievement?"

A diversified chorus answers:

"The conquest of bread." (A worker, South England.)

"Dnieprostroy." (A worker, Scotland.)

"The broad participation of the working people in government administration." (A peasant, Seville, Spain.)

"Maintenance of peace." (A small tradesman, British Africa.)

"The most amazing thing is the conversion into collective farmers of tens of millions of illiterate individual peasants scattered over such a vast territory." (A gardener, France.)

"The Soviet Union's foreign policy." (A worker, London.)

"Public education and the Communist Party's victory over religion." (An office worker, Norway.)

"The emancipation of women.". . .

"The union of so large a people, consisting of so many different nationalities." . . .

"Abolition of unemployment." . . .

"Abolition of rationing, which was a slap in the face to the disseminators of anti-Soviet lies." . . .

"The Soviet Union's entry into the League of Nations and establishment of diplomatic relations with the Great Powers." . . .

"Industrialization." . . .

"The abolition of classes." . . .

Another question: "What should be the Soviet Union's next task?"

And again animated replies and friendly voices, considerate and admonitory:

"The most important task for the U.S.S.R. is to carry on its good work until it eclipses all other countries in the wealth, happiness and prosperity of its people." (A metalworker, Leeds, England.)

"Whatever you do, keep out of war, at least until you are quite strong, and then come to the aid of the workers of our island." (A worker, member of the Labour Party, Burnley, England.)

"Build a powerful air force and a strong army to defend the land of the workers against all invaders."

"Build up light industry."

"Get rid of bureaucracy."

"Ruthlessly and unceasingly combat all whiteguards

and counterrevolutionaries still surviving in the Soviet Union."

"Go on as you have begun, so that all workers in the U.S.S.R. become shock workers, all plans are fulfilled 100 per cent, and everybody studies."

Through the lurid mist of coming wars and revolutions, people peer into the future. What will things be like twenty years hence?

A reply comes from two peasants in Spain:

"It is not given us to know what mankind will be like then, but we believe that capitalism will already have been abolished."

A fellow countryman of theirs, another Spaniard, is more cautious in his predictions:

"In the U.S.S.R. there will be a classless society, but Europe will still be only on the way to building Socialism. The bourgeoisie of some countries will be seeking a way out in war against the U.S.S.R., but the proletariat will already be capable of putting a stop to it. In my opinion, victory will come most painfully to the proletariat of China, because of the war the imperialists are organizing against her."

And fifty years hence? One hundred years hence?

To this question, the replies are more circumstantial and more uniform, and written in a solemn and positive style. An Austrian worker speaks in detail of a World Planning Commission, a World Cultural Soviet, and a World Executive Committee. . . . "The boundaries of states will coincide with language boundaries, every nationality will have its own government, the colonial peoples will be liberated." "Socialism will be victorious, people will be happy, war, poverty and want will be abolished.

Technology, science and art will have attained unsurpassed heights."

However, here too some of the prophets are very cautious. An Essex shopkeeper believes that "the next hundred years will witness broad government planning of industry and social advancement. The world will become more and more humane. I think we shall take the path of evolution."

A fellow countryman of his chimes in from Birmingham:

"The age of machines will not necessarily be happier than the present."

A Prague student has quite a gloomy view of the coming age:

"People will have huge arms and tiny bodies. Everyone will be able to see the whole world by radio, there will be no secrets, and women will have a pretty dull time."

But a Klagenfurt bricklayer has a different idea o the personal life of the future:

"Thanks to equality of the sexes, love and marriage under Socialism will no longer bear the features of slavery. Marriage will no longer be regarded as a practical device for the production of cannon fodder. The family will be a source not of suffering but of joy, because Socialism makes it easy to raise a family."

He is seconded by a Zurich motor mechanic:

"In classless society there won't be women who sell their bodies, nor women whose only aim in life is to bear children. Lovers will not be threatened with a gloomy future. Physical intercourse will be the consummation of mutual love. And all this will be stamped with the consciousness of collective responsibility for all."

It is in this way that common people of the world crowd, people who live in congested capitals and in quiet out-of-the-way villages, speak of their present and of the future of their descendants. Some suffer and fight, others suffer in patience, but in all of them there has awakened a deep discontent with the way people are living on our planet, and this discontent will never again subside. How can the protest be stilled, how can the yearning for the remaking of the world be quenched, when on one-sixth of the surface of the world the remaking has already been accomplished, and life has taken a different course, a just course, which debars the exploitation of man by man? Drawn, as in a magnetic field, by all the finest, honest and boldest fibres of their souls to the far-off happy land of Soviets, the motes in the world crowd no longer feel solitary. They sense that on that side of the border lies their defence, their home, their family, a warm hearth, and the realization of their most fabulous desires. This sense of having acquired a protector is best of all revealed in their choice of great men.

Of course, to many millions of people the real or imaginary founder of Christianity still remains the greatest man in history. But among the enslaved part of humanity that has awakened to class consciousness, the power and influence of the dreary Christian legend is steadily waning. Of the thousands of letter-writers, only a score or so are admirers of Christ. Positivist and semimaterialist intellectuals mention other names. Among them we find James Watt ("the man who started the age of machinery"), Humphrey Davy ("the inventor of pain-killers for the amelioration of human suffering"), Michael Faraday ("the great physicist"), Plato and Socrates. Others name

402

Alexander the Great, Julius Caesar ("because he came, saw and conquered"), Keir Hardie, Marconi, Mahommet. . . . And a girl from Southampton is convinced that the greatest man is none other than the present reigning King George of England ("because he looks on the people as his family and is very kind"). Among the list we also find Abraham Lincoln, Columbus, Lord Kitchener, Edison.

But the vast, the absolutely overwhelming majority of the replies name two other men as the greatest in history. Of course, the interesting and significant thing is not the predominance of these replies, because the convictions and sympathies of the writers of the letters are indicated by the very fact that they listen to the Moscow radio; the interesting and significant thing is the contents of the replies, their maturity and deliberation, their austere conviction, born of suffering.

"The greatest man in history was the worker who first had the courage to stand up and suffer for his fellow workers. I do not know who he was. There were many such."

This was written by a Chicago factory mechanic. And, as though in echo, comes the reply of a Belgian hotel clerk:

"Lenin. He did more good in seven years than all the great men of the world in twenty centuries. Compare them, and judge for yourselves. Long live Lenin! A hundred years hence there will not be a city or village on the surface of the globe which has not erected a splendid monument to him. And wherever there is a place of honour, it will belong to Lenin."

An Arab student in Algiers adds:

"Karl Marx. If Lenin had not had Marx's teachings, instead of building on the Marxian plan he would have had to lose a lot of time working it out. I find it very hard to choose between Marx and Lenin, because there is Marxism and there is Leninism. One was an architect, and the other an architect and builder simultaneously."

A London worker: "History has known many great men, but I call only those really great who dedicated their talents to the emancipation of mankind from slavery and ignorance. I therefore regard Lenin as the greatest man in history."

Besides the history of the past, there is the history of the present, the living history of our epoch. Here, too, people in different parts of the planet, of different nationalities, cultures and upbringings, write in scores of languages and in thousands of hands one and the same thought, and all with equally passionate conviction.

"Stalin, who has amazed the whole world." (An electrician, Karlstadt, Sweden.)

"The great genius, Stalin." (A coal miner, Seraing, Belgium.)

"Stalin. He proved to the workers and all the rest of the world the truth of the teaching of Marx and Lenin that the emancipation of the working class must be the work of the workers themselves." (An office worker, Trondheim, Norway.)

"Stalin—he has more followers and supporters than any other leader of our time." (A seaman, Deepfields, England.)

"To us young people, whose hands and hearts ache from idleness, and who are dying before we have begun to live, the five-year plan sounds like music. It is our dream." (A railwayman, Nemecky Brod, Czechoslovakia.)

"Stalin, a man who sat in prison for so many long years, became the most active force in the greatest era in world history, the name of which is—the Russian Revolution." (A worker, Västeras, Sweden.)

"He stands at the head of the first people in history to have thrown off its chains, a people which is already entering classless society." (A doctor, Sydney, Australia.)

"Stalin is the only head of state who promotes and protects the interests of all the working people, regardless of nationality." (A worker, Poschiave, Switzerland.)

"This honour belongs to Stalin. He has shown that a people of 170,000,000 and consisting of more than a hundred nationalities can build Socialism." (A peasant, Neustadt, Czechoslovakia.)

"All working people unanimously regard the present leader of the U.S.S.R. as the greatest man of our time. He symbolizes the conscientious type whose bravery, strength and daring facilitate the magnificent struggle on all fronts, marching from victory to victory, and surpassing anything we could ever dream of. His name, like the name of Lenin, is great and immortal." (A plumber, Salet-Puy Inferieur, Belgium.)

Swift and jostling are the lines of these thousands of letters from common people, individuals of the world crowd. And this pile of letters is only a drop taken as a sample from the ocean. The peoples of the world are fettered hand and foot, but they are mustering their strength for the leap into freedom, for the decisive assault of the capitalist Bastille. Their gaze is bent in meditation, yearning and wrath. And only when they turn to the Land of Soviets do the eyes of men become warm and gleam with hope, joy and admiration.

TO THE CONGRESS IN DEFENCE
OF CULTURE

I DEEPLY regret that my health prevents me from being physically present at the International Writers' Congress, among people who keenly feel what an insult the rise of fascism is to them, who see how the baleful and poisonous effects of its ideas are spreading, and how it is committing its crimes with impunity.

Fascism is not a new cry of bourgeois wisdom; but it is the last—the cry of the wisdom of despair. It is more and more brazenly revealing itself to be the denial of everything that passes under the name of European culture.

Why has war been declared on this "humanitarian" culture, whose achievements until so recently were the pride and boast of the bourgeoisie? We know that Luther would not have renounced Catholicism, the religion of the feudalists, if this had not been necessary for the usurers and shopkeepers of his time. In our day, the national groups of bankers, gun manufacturers and other parasites are planning a new war for the right to dominate Europe, for the liberty to ravage colonies and to rob the working people generally. It will be a war for the extermination of this or that nation. It will not only demand the comple. renunciation of the "foundation of culture," bourge. humanism, which has always in bourgeois practice play the role of a "camouflage" and "a means by which the big bourgeoisie selected for its ranks the best among the petty bourgeoisie"; in organizing the new massacre of peoples, fascism regards humanism as an idea inimical to its basic aims.

On the initiative of the writers of France, the honest writers of the world are rising up against fascism and all its villainies.

This splendid aim is quite natural for "masters of culture," and it may be confidently expected that the scientists will follow the example of the artists.

And it should also be borne in mind that history has made it abundantly clear that the logic of humanism is beyond the comprehension of the biped wolves and boars, and that there is only one class in the world that is capable of understanding and sympathizing with the universal significance of humanism. That class is the proletariat.

Our efforts, therefore, should be directed not to reconciling irreconcilables, not to reforming bourgeois society, which, by its very structure, cannot live, is incapable of living, without enmity, without oppressing the majority of mankind—our efforts should be dedicated to the work of releasing the inexhaustible reserves of intellectual energy latent in the hundreds of millions of working people.

The only genuine humanism is the humanism of the proletariat, which is setting itself the lofty aim of changing the very foundations of the social and economic life of our world. In the country where the proletariat has taken the power into its hands, we are able to see how immense is the energy latent in its mass, what great talents are awakening in it, and how swiftly it is changing the forms of life by imparting to them a new content.

Dear comrades, the only ones capable of understanding the honest words of right-minded people are the proletarians, the handiworkers of culture, the working intellectuals and the labouring peasants, who want to be, and deserve to be, masters of culture.

Maxim Gorky

Printed in the Union of Soviet Socialist Republics